AUTHOR

CLASS E02

TITLE
HOW it was.

HOW IT WAS

A North Lancashire Parish
in the Seventeenth Century

MOURHOLME LOCAL HISTORY SOCIETY
1998

This book is dedicated to

John Lucas
Born Carnforth 1685, died Leeds 1750

John Lucas left Warton parish when he was still in his twenties and spent the rest of his life as a school master in Leeds. It is our good fortune that he did not forget his birth-place, but between 1710 and 1745 compiled a *History of Warton Parish*. It is further our good fortune that what he wrote was not so much a history of the parish, but rather an account of it as he remembered it from his childhood and youth.

It is still further our good fortune that the manuscript, after being apparently lost for two hundred years was re-discovered in 1931 by two amateur historians resident in the parish, J.Rawlinson Ford and J.A.Fuller-Maitland, who also brought out a printed version, skilfully editing out many, many pages of the tedious (to modern readers) antiquarian lore for which Lucas had such a fondness, but retaining all his invaluable insights into Warton parish as he knew it at the end of the seventeenth century. Without John Lucas this present book could scarcely have been written.

Supported by

rural action
FOR THE ENVIROMENT

CONTENTS

ILLUSTRATIONS. Most of the line drawings which embellish this book have been supplied by Leslie Rockey. They are all based on the most accurate information available; photographs of surviving buildings, objects from museums etc. but by using the imagination of an artist he has recreated the scenes as they might have been seen by seventeenth century eyes. Sources are acknowledged in the captions.

ACKNOWLEDGEMENTS

The following is a list of those people known to have helped in transcribing wills, inventories and other seventeenth century documents which have formed the basis of this book, and/or to have worked on the text itself. Great efforts have been made to make the list complete, but people did not always sign their work, and so some names may have been left off the list despite our best intentions.

W. M. Atkinson	J. Findlater	F. R. Macrae
E. Aynge	K. Greaves	J. D. Marshall
R. L. Bassenden	Robin Greaves	K. Millen
P. H. W. Booth	Harry Gregson	Anne Morley
C. R. Brierley	Trixie Hardman	J. Peacock
C. E. A. Burnham	Win Hayhurst	Arthur Penn
K. M. Burnham	Kate Hodgson	David Peter
E. M. Castle	Desmond Holmes	Gwen Phillips
Mary Chalmers	J. E. Housley	P. A. M. Riley
B. Clarke	Sue Ireland	S. Seddon
Joan Clarke	J. Jenkinson	Barbara Simpson
Margaret Clarke	Joyce Jenkinson	Muriel Smalley
L. M. Clarkson	Jenny Johnstone	Neil Stobbs
Emily Dixon	N. Kaye	Nancy Thomas
M. Dodgson	E. M. Kidd	M. White
		Michael Wright

To help us meet the cost of publishing this book we
were grateful to receive grants and donations from:-

Lancashire Rural Action for the Environment, The Marc Fitch Fund,
Mr.K. Broadhurst, Mr and Mrs Harris, Geraldine Smith M.P., Sir Mark Lennox-Boyd,
Dr W.Rollinson, Brigadier Tryon-Wilson, Silverdale Parish Council, Warton Parish Council,
AXA Insurance, Barclay's Bank, Lancaster and Jobling and Knape Solicitors.

Reproductions of documents from the Lancashire Record Office, from Lancaster Public Library local history collection and from the Museum of Rural Life, University of Reading are acknowledged on the relevant pages. Cambridge University Press gave permission for the use of the drawing of agrarian regions of England, and R.Speake for the reproduction of his drawing of the vital statistics of the parish. The Vicar of Warton agreed to the inclusion of a page of Archbishop Matthew Hutton's Bible. The Lancashire Record Office, Preston, Cumbria Record Office, Kendal and Lancaster Reference Library have been unfailingly helpful in assisting us to examine the source material in their collections.

PREFACE

This book, which has been subtitled as 'A North Lancashire Parish', might have been more lengthily called the story of Borwick, Carnforth, Priest Hutton, Silverdale, Warton, Yealand Redmayne and Yealand Conyers, for it is about all these places. They all lie within some seven miles of each other in the extreme north-west of Lancashire, just where it abuts (to-day) on Cumbria. They have, historically, a closer connection with each other than mere geographical proximity. Until the nineteenth century they were all included in a single parish, a parish which took its name from what was then the largest settlement, Warton. They were 'townships' of the parish, a township being, the Oxford English Dictionary says, 'a local division...in a large original parish...containing a village or small town.' They were the smallest unit of local government. They were also, rather like present day villages, the unit to which men and women felt their primary loyalty. One belonged to one's township, before one thought of oneself as belonging to the parish.

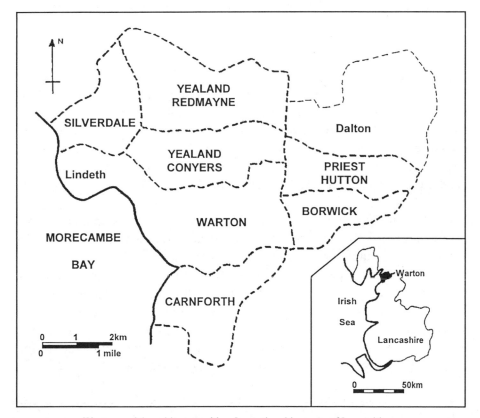

Warton parish and its townships. Inset: the old county of Lancashire.

The story of these townships in the seventeenth century, told in this book is the outcome of many years of work by the members of the Mourholme Local History Society.* Indeed the work for this book goes back beyond the foundation of the Society in 1980. It was begun by members of a Liverpool University Extension Studies course under the leadership of P.H.W. Booth in the 1970's, who then formed themselves into the Warton History Group to carry on with research and publication. The group was also instrumental in founding the Mourholme Local History Society. Nancy Thomas, a member of the group and of the Society, took over the direction of the transcription of the seventeenth century probate material and members of her group spent many hours working on accurate transcripts of wills and inventories. The names, not only of those currently working on the book, but of all those involved over the years are listed on p.iv as a small token of how indebted this book is to them.

Thanks are also due to the University of Liverpool which most generously paid the cost of having photocopies made of original source material in the Lancashire Record Office. These photocopies are now housed with the Society's archives and have been of immense help in compiling the present book.

In 1990 Dr.J.D.Marshall agreed to take over the direction of a new group which was set up to work specifically on putting together a history of the townships in the seventeenth century. Dr Marshall has been tireless in supporting and encouraging the group in their work, and though he consistently refused to write a word of the book himself he did, to the group's great joy, agree to contribute an introduction, setting out more clearly than we could do the aims of the book.

Lastly, but most importantly, we in the group owe an apology to the people of Dalton for we have left their township out. To be honest we did not know, till quite late in our studies, that it once formed the eighth township of Warton parish. Now it does not even lie in the same county as the others, having been ceded to Westmorland in the nineteenth century. The omission is perhaps the more excusable because even in the seventeenth century its few inhabitants (and though it was large in area it was very thinly populated) seem to have only half belonged to Warton, for they and their township seldom appear in Warton records.

---

* *Mourholme was the name of a one-time castle in the area and was chosen to represent all the townships equally.*

Warton village and the Crag

Introduction

Dr. J.D. Marshall
Honorary President, Mourholme Local History Society

This is a survey of the lives of the people of the old parish of Warton - as far as the available documents have allowed us to study them - during a century of slow economic development and considerable religious upheaval. It is a study of day-to-day life as it was experienced by local people in contrasting social situations, so that the world of a lord of the manor is seen in conflict, as well as in harmony with, the world of yeomen and husbandmen and their wives and children. The respective authors have carefully sifted a mass of small details, aimed at throwing light on the human condition as it then appeared. It will be understood that the details have not been collected in an antiquarian spirit, that is for their own sake, but in pursuit of themes and, where possible, the answers to relevant questions. We have tried to adhere to this, the historian's approach, throughout.

This is not a community history in any meaningful sense, although, if one is to employ that portmanteau word, the old parish of Warton comprised not one 'community' but many. As was common in that period, Warton was a multi-township parish typical of many parishes in the north of England, with a mother church in the central township of Warton-with-Lindeth, and with the additional townships of Borwick, Carnforth, Priest Hutton, Yealand Conyers and Yealand Redmayne and Silverdale (later a chapelry). The total parish area of 11,100 statute acres is of course a fairly large one, with a boundary of roughly twenty-two miles in circumference, and it can be seen that its seventeenth century population of about 1200 has been widely spread into at least seven scattered 'centres' of settlement. Now, we can reasonably assume that each of these centres represented a community for workaday purposes, while the respectable inhabitants of each could expect to meet each other at the mother church on Sundays. But, as this story unfolds, it becomes clear that religious aspirations and challenges, imposed and locally created, were beginning to define distinct sects and interests; and the Yealands became a stronghold of

1

Quakerism, whilst, as was not uncommon in Lancashire, the Lord of the Manor of the Yealands and Silverdale displayed not only a Catholic commitment, but had a group of followers of a small and varying size which received the attention of visiting priests (see the insights in Chapters 15,16). The point is that there were religious 'communities' as well as geographical ones, although it is not disputed that the Anglican congregation, with its connections with the local government of the parish, was the most significant. There were probably puritan groups at different times within the church, however, and it may be that there was a somewhat ill-defined group of irreligious people. The parish registers suggest the existence of family groups, bearing one common surname, in given townships or settlements; so that the names of Waithman, Ward and Jackson were common in Warton itself; Hadwen, Nicholson and Waithman in Carnforth; Gibson, Waller and Cockeram in Priest Hutton; Burrow, Hadwen, Jackson and Clarke in Silverdale; Hubbersty, Hopkin or Hobkin in the Yealands and Manser, Williamson and Whormby in Borwick. These family 'clans' might strengthen the feeling of community in the places concerned, but could also, of course, be responsible for feuds.

Our survey, then, ranges over miles of countryside and many lives and several generations. Its subject is a microcosm of seventeenth century rural life, with many of the features that one would find in almost any northern parish. But closer examination shows that Warton and its townships have had a special character, and that the whole territory is not even simply a Lancashire parish, but one on the extreme northern edge of the County Palatine, in contact with Westmorland and Kendal. But the Warton geographical and economic framework occupies a more distinctive place than even this would imply, and it is thanks to the topographical research in Chapter One that our main generalisation is made possible. Warton is a parish resting on a foundation of grey-white carboniferous limestone, which in turn had deeply influenced its hydrology and distribution of water supplies, and therefore the siting of its farms and settlements. This geology has also given it some highly characteristic scenery and building material. It is in fact one of a group of parishes, all of this character, stretching round Morecambe Bay in a horseshoe, and traced anti-clockwise from Bolton-le-Sands through the Warton area to the old parish of Heversham, round to another great parish, that of Cartmel, and thence to much of Plain Furness.[1] All of these localities face Morecambe Bay and have a substantial stretch of coastline or flattish ground near the sea, usually embracing both salt marsh and former peat moss; usually, too, a length of valley (as at Arnside or Carnforth and Warton) runs up from the lower territory, and limestone scars and pavements make for a memorable topography. Nor is this a matter of impressive scenery only; the marshes and mosses have been important to the economies of the parishes concerned, in that they have provided winter grazing and fuel, and the nearness of the sea

2

has been instrumental in providing fish and (often) salt from brine. The occupational analysis provided in Chapter 14 refers to sailor, 'salt weller', fisherman and ship's carpenter. It is worth remembering that a trading vessel used by William Stout, the *Content*, was built at Warton,[2] although it should be stressed that present-day Wartonians are scarcely conscious of the sea as a factor in their lives, unless they live facing it.

The limestone parishes here mentioned are either in Westmorland or in the old Lancashire, and although they were not then (or at other times), a proven economic unity, the sea and Morecambe Bay sands exerted a powerful influence which brought them into contact. First of all, the sands provided an easily accessible highway from the eastern side (Hest Bank and Silverdale), to the Cartmel side at Kents Bank and Allithwaite, and John Lucas, the Warton chronicler, had no doubt as to its significance; he described the Warton Sands as 'remarkable for the great Road leading over them into *Cartmel, Furness &c.*, which is much frequented every Day, but especially at *Whitsontide*, when there is a fair at *Cartmel*, particularly noted for the hireing of Servants, who stand in the Market there for that purpose'.[3] This strongly suggests that Warton parish was part of a sub-regional agricultural labour market, held together by the movements of farm servants and by the road across the upper Bay; such labourers are known to have sought work each year within areas of this size, changing their masters or mistresses as required. It remains only to add that land transport in the region was at that time poor, even though the main highway between Kendal and Lancaster passed through Warton parish. Meanwhile, traders and travellers from both ends have long used the over-sands route, and the Cartmel parish registers contain numbers of references to persons tragically drowned on the journey in the seventeenth century.

The old parish of Warton was certainly not a closed economy. Marriage data in the Warton parish registers show that some thirty per cent of recorded marriages involved a partner from outside the parish, mostly from not more than twenty miles away (see Chapter 8). More than this, however, the coastal shipping trade of the north-west was slowly developing, and supplies of haematite iron ore were obtained in Furness in order to make iron at a bloomery forge in Milnthorpe owned by Sir George Middleton of Leighton after the middle of the seventeenth century.[4] Our point here is that the iron ore could be easily brought by boat provided that the Bay waters were passable, but that its carriage by land would have been disastrously uneconomic. The Bay and its sands really did give the area an advantage, and the reader can be forgiven for wondering why material and industrial advances did not rest in the parish more securely. In fact, most of our Wartonians were peasants living in a world that was always likely to be touched by catastrophe - the bubonic plague, a series of bad seasons, or starvation followed by an epidemic of several diseases after resistance had gone.

3

Most of the families in Warton district were dependent on a largely subsistence agriculture which might leave them with small surpluses for sale at local markets, and, as was afterwards shown by the case of Cumberland and Westmorland,[5] any more ambitious trading was achieved through the purchase and sale of livestock. The cattle droves from Scotland were beginning to play a large part in the creation of a truly British economy, and cattle could be fattened on the sweet pastures provided by the limestone foundation of the area, as well as by glacial deposits which left the basis for a richer soil.[6] To be sure, there were few really rich peasants, but the instances of Cartmel and Hawkshead do in fact show a marked and even steady growth of peasant wealth between 1660 and 1750,[7] and it is at least reasonable to suspect the commencement of such a process in Warton area by the end of the seventeenth century. As is shown here, there were distinct signs of affluence on the part of the better-off families in the second half of the century, and some indications of such material gain before that (see Chapter 7).

Culturally, the Warton area was evidently in touch with the countrysides to the north and west of its Westmorland boundary, and some interesting minor pieces of evidence are still to be seen in the local building styles; in particular in the use of cylindrical chimney stacks on farmhouses or major buildings; examples are to be seen in Warton area itself, as well as in Bolton Holmes, and the feature is a common one in Furness and South Westmorland. This type of embellishment, sometimes accompanied by rain-deflecting slates set in an inverted 'V', was valued by Wordsworth in his appraisal of Lakeland peasant houses.[8] There is only one rather doubtful reference to slate in the local probate inventories in the seventeenth century, but Lakeland slate was clearly used after that in the area, as the thatch or other roof coverings of the older buildings were replaced. Cargoes of slate certainly travelled coastwise in the north-west region in the early eighteenth century,[9] and seem to have been shipped to and from Piel harbour in Furness. We have already seen that the Warton area shared an iron-making culture, through the Middleton family, with Low and High Furness (see Chapter 14), just as it shared a shipbuilding one with Lancaster.

We must also never lose sight of the fact that this early modern world still carried some medieval features as part of its inheritance, including an element of the collective sense of the medieval manor or village. The Warton area still had its common or town fields, which were administered in each case by a manorial jury, but it has to be remembered that individualism had been growing since the end of the middle ages, and that Lancashire had become a county with a multitude of private enclosures, so much so that John Leland in early Tudor times saw it as an enclosed area - that is to say, as containing a patchwork of hedged or walled fields.

The typical small landholder occupied, or otherwise had a right to, at least a few of these fields, however thin the soil or however tiny the enclosures. But here we must develop our argument that Warton area was only typical of its own small group of neighbouring parishes, and was to that extent also atypical of Lancashire as a whole, certainly in soils and topography. We must ask, too, if ancient small enclosures were encountered in the border territory on which Warton stood, and it can be said here that the maps and papers for the Cartmel enclosures in 1796-1809 differentiate very sharply between the parliamentary enclosures of the open common, and the older enclosures, which appear in valley bottoms near farmsteads, and which are irregular and still to this day easily visible. As our text suggests (see Chapter 2), these small enclosures could easily have been made over long periods, and bit by bit, and it is clear that the Warton area still has the evidence for many of them in its landscape.

We have pointed out that Warton was under manorial administration and, as is stressed in Chapter 2, there was, in the seventeenth century, 'still extant a medieval view of land, as not fully any one man's possession, but as belonging, in some sense, to all those who lived on it and worked on it'. As is made clear in our survey, the arable field systems that were common in the Lancashire and Cumbrian lowlands did indeed involve common administration, through the manor court. These arable fields were not great in extent, as compared with those of the Midlands (which literally stretched as far as the eye could see, as in Laxton in Nottinghamshire), and they were known as Town Fields, containing widely scattered pieces of ploughland in which oats or barley, or sometimes peas and beans, were sown in spring. As the growing period lasted only through the spring and summer months, these ploughlands have been called 'half-year lands', and after the harvest had been lifted, livestock could be turned on them to dung the ground conveniently.

Oats are by their nature a spring-sown crop, and they provided the staple food of the area, oatmeal or haverbread. Whether much barley bread was eaten can be seen as a disputed point, for it is an unappetising food, and perhaps the barley was fed to livestock as well as malted and used for small beer. As for the working of the town fields, it seems at least likely that the main work of ploughing was done collectively, with ox teams. The invaluable Lucas (as cited in Chapter 2 of our text), shows that in Carnforth there were at least four town fields, one of which was 'never pastured', that is, it would be regularly ploughed and heavily dunged. The other three were each allowed to lie fallow in turn. Although Lucas does not say so, crops probably followed a rotation in these fields, so that ideally there should have been a different main crop each year in each field and, if this was the case, such an arrangement is similar to the Midland systems of crop rotation in the great open fields.

However, this is not the whole story, for our north-western forms of open field operation seem to have originated in the so-called Celtic system, or *run-rig*, and the influence of this latter system can be detected through the use of the significant name Infield, which occurs in Yealand in 1746, and also at Roose, Cocken, Newbarns and Hindpool in Low Furness.[10] Historically the infield was the one to be established first, near the hamlet in which the cultivators lived, and would get the main supplies of dung. Other fields would be ploughed out of virgin land, would be brought into use as required and then simply left fallow as the soil became exhausted. Some of these fields were used for strips of hay meadow in this region.[11] Variegated and irregular strips, and unequal ownership, were ultimately features of the town fields, placing a limit on rotation of main crops.

These fields were in any case comparatively small, in Furness accommodating from four to sixteen tenants (or manorial copyholders). We may note that our Warton parish examples were scattered round the townships, and they betoken the existence of a 'community' in each, in this case an agrarian one of the primitive type imagined by the pioneer sociologist Ferdinand Tönnies.[12] The manorial records make clear that the cultivators shared important goals in common, the prerequisite of an operative community. However, as our conclusions indicate, individualism had long begun to creep into township life. The old system of town fields was a means of assuring subsistence, of a sharing out of resources and of oxen for ploughing. A community of peasants, accustomed to occupation 'in severalty' (i.e. to private occupation of fields) would wish to experiment in the course of attempts to obtain a saleable surplus of cereal or meat. In fact, it is possible to exaggerate what could be achieved in this direction; there are few signs in Warton parish of new crops in the century, save increased appearance of wheat and rye, and this in smallish quantities, and there is only one recorded case of potato growing (Chapter 3) - which nevertheless spread immensely in the West Lancashire plain in the next century.[13]

There is one other connection of Warton with territories farther north, a connection of great significance. In an account of the tenant right struggle on the part of the Warton yeomen and husbandmen against, firstly, the Crown and, secondly, the Middletons of Leighton, our research traces events which followed roughly the same path as a conflict which had raged in the Barony of Kendal and across much of north-west England. Briefly, Warton 'tenants' (i.e. of the manor) had once been sworn to bear arms in case of invasions by the Scots, and this service, it was held, gave them especially strong and certain tenure of their land. The accident of the accession of James I, creating a union of the crowns of Scotland and England, removed the need for what was called border service - or so James held. Immediately thousands of Cumbrian and other peasants felt their positions to be threatened, in that their special tenure was questioned.

It is fascinating to learn that border tenure had reached into Lancashire manors, where it does not seem to have been general - perhaps because the Scots did not usually penetrate beyond the Ribble. However, as regards the Warton area, the pele towers of Arnside and Beetham were stark reminders of a troubled past, and local folk-memory was evidently strong. Here was yet another factor that united the Morecambe Bay parishes with the Cumbrian mainland and its attitudes or general culture. The Warton tenants found themselves repeating manorial disputes, which had been widespread in the Barony of Kendal, in fighting their own landlords, in the end fairly successfully. Our conclusion says that 'it is not easy to clothe these legal and financial details with a feeling of day to day life in these manors, but we can, by virtue of this account and others in the region, gain a sense of the soul-sapping insecurity of peasant life in the seventeenth century, especially when one's life was conducted under an oppressive landlord'.

Existence on a manorial holding, then, suffered from two forms of insecurity; that created by landlord's exactions, and that engendered by the struggle to provide for family subsistence. But there were other directions in which the enterprising yeoman or husbandman might travel in the search for a source of income, and the best-attested one was that of developing a secondary occupation, e.g. a skilled craft or one involving personal service. Probate inventories and wills throughout the region show that manorial tenants, while keeping their landholdings in full use, became weavers, blacksmiths, carpenters, wallers, masons, quarry men, saltboilers, fishermen, tanners, maltsters, innkeepers, sailors, shoemakers, tailors, butchers, small merchants or chapmen, coopers, ironworkers, charcoal burners, woodsmen and, in some appropriate cases, money-lenders. As is shown in Chapter 14, the Warton area provided examples of most of these trades.

All of this seems to be solid economic history. But it also tells us something of the aspirations of humble men, who were educating themselves in a very basic sense in the skills concerned. It points also to those activities which were later to fill out the worlds of an increased population. Our brief picture of parish demography, as set out in Chapter 8, shows, not altogether surprisingly, that the numbers of people in the locality were apparently maintained only by the level of subsistence available, and that any kind of crisis influencing that level might easily threaten the old, the weak and the very young, almost any of whom might be very poor also, and these crises, or checks, were later seen by the Rev. T.R. Malthus as effective controls on the growth of population - like war, disease and famine. The numbers of Wartonians clearly did not increase for any length of time, and seem to have fallen by 1700, this despite the increased economic activity that has been mentioned. However, this operation of Malthusian checks did not take effect in a number of Lancashire centres, even though it worked visibly in places as various as Cartmel, Hawkshead and Rochdale.[14] It is quite clear, therefore, that Warton parish was not alone in that it struggled against what would now be recognised as Third World demographic and social conditions. Did the frequently close proximity of death influence people's religious views in the seventeenth century? Did Wartonians ever become accustomed to losing children in infancy? Did they live in fear of the future?

Mention of the Third World will remind us that widespread poverty is no new condition. The world of Stuart North Lancashire and Cumbria was without doubt one of grinding poverty for as much as forty per cent of the population. There is considerable evidence for the truth of this assertion. First of all, people are known to have died of starvation or the side effects of famine, in 1623 and at other times in the century, notably in the 1630s and 1640s. Next, at least forty per cent of the adult male population were too poor to leave goods for entry in probate inventories, a fact indicating that the persons concerned had nothing of substance to leave to heirs. Thirdly the extreme north-western counties, Lancashire, Cumberland and Westmorland, were regarded by the central government as too poor to yield much by way of taxation,[15] whether through sparse population, the absence of a notably wealthy class or through the lack of visible signs of wealth in towns and villages. The imposition of Ship Money or the Hearth Tax alike produced poor results in these counties. There is reason to believe that Lancastrians knew they were generally under-assessed, and that they wished to remain in that happy state. Remoteness from central government had its advantages, and the far north was regarded by government as strange, probably Papist and unrewarding. However, we should remember that government officials probably lacked the time to analyse probate inventories as is done in this book, and we find that the 'middling' sort of North Lancashire countryman sometimes had more and varied possessions than those who would have taxed him in fact realised or understood.

We now come to the influence of religious belief on Warton and its area. Here we have a confession to make; we do not know how far religion affected substantial sections of the population, and Wrightson has argued that absenteeism from church was general in early Stuart Lancashire, and that churchgoing was seen more as 'a gathering of neighbours than...a religious exercise', whilst the alehouse provided formidable opposition to Sunday service.[16] On the other hand we shall remember that ignorance was widespread as was illiteracy, and how could a large section of the population, which could not read the Bible, do other than repeat garbled versions of religious exhortations, ideas and principles? Superstition reigned alongside ignorance and we must remember that this age was also the age of witch-hunting. This does not mean that dedicated and passionate men did not stand out from the multitude, or that many did not conform peaceably to the church and its changing prescriptions.

Certainly, the Tudor and Stuart religious history of the old parish reveals turbulence as well as faith and devotion. We have to assume that many Warton people gained strength and consolation from their faith, a strength which would at times be sorely tried. Margaret Spufford gently reproved the late W.G.Hoskins for ignoring the religious sides of villagers in his classic *The Midland Peasant* (1957),[17] and the contributions of our colleagues who have concentrated on religious themes (Chapter 15, 16) in the present volume, should certainly deflect any criticism of this kind. However, it will also be borne in mind that religious organisations had a profoundly political tinge and significance in the seventeenth century, whatever the depth of dedication and piety that marked individuals, and that political divisions often had religious causes. Political parties as such did not exist in that age, and it was the Bible itself that provided material for manifestos. But the small sects of the middle years of the century also produced reverberating political ideas, like those of the Diggers and Levellers, or social and sectarian notions like those of the Muggletonians, which represented a whirlpool of influences and included statements of sexual libertarianism. Ludowic Muggleton and his followers, with the so-called Ranters, had some limited effect on Quaker ideas in the 1650s, and since parts of the Warton area and south Westmorland received George Fox and the Quakers with joy and passion, and equally with violent repudiation, it would be improper not to consider the locally relevant histories of Fox and his followers.

The Warton religious story, then, commences with a world shaken by the Reformation, the English side of which was a largely political movement. Bishops replaced the Pope, and the churches were stripped of images and 'idolatry'. The Catholic faith had had deep roots in parts of the north-west, and those who refused to be separated from it became 'recusants', just as a reforming zeal allied to Calvin's ideas produced what became known as 'puritanism'. Anglicanism, of whatever ultimate flavour, was in effect imposed from the top downwards as a perceived political necessity. Warton provides examples of each system of belief or policy; the parish congregation did what was required, but one of the early seventeenth century vicars, Anthony Bugg, had Calvinistic and puritan leanings if we may deduce his ideas from his books (see Appendix 3), while Archbishop Hutton, Bugg's mentor and the founder of Warton's Grammar School, also leaned in this direction (see Appendix 4). The prescriptions of Archbishop Laud in the country at large in the 1630s, which seemed to swing the Anglican church towards Rome, must have grated on parishioners with strongly puritan leanings. The victory of the parliamentarians in the Civil War led to the firm establishment of a puritan and Presbyterian order which lasted until 1660 - and Warton's church found itself to be one of ten in a Presbyterian *classis* (the equivalent of a diocese but smaller). There were nine ministers in the *classis*, and one of these was Richard Walker of Warton. The *classis* was, however, partly run by a group of elders, though none came from the townships of Warton.

The main dissent to such arrangements had been, of course, Catholic, but protestant dissenters, Quaker and other, had emerged before the Restoration in 1660. It is important to bear in mind that George Fox treated Presbyterian ministers as misguided deviants from his idea of truth. After the Restoration the established church met even more resistance from the Quakers, who were a vital and determined sect, and the parishioners of Warton undoubtedly felt a sense of disturbance to values which had already been challenged before the Civil War and during the Commonwealth. Unhappily we do not know much about the deeper responses of the parishioners themselves, although the campaign of church attenders for their own licensed minister at the small chapel in Silverdale does seem to tell us something about the needs and feelings of a given flock. It is in the way of things that we know much more about the ministers than we do about the congregations. However our researcher's point (Chapter 16) about the continued centrality of Warton church should be well taken. The church and its building stood for permanence and godliness, and also for festivals (Chapter 18), including those within the regular church calendar, and of course including not only the highly personal ceremonies like baptisms, marriages and burials, but those resting on a distant popular tradition, and possibly even a pagan one. The celebration of harvest, as described by Lucas, seems to have been of that character at the time (Chapter 18). The parish church and its vestry or parish meeting had deep connections with local government, but in Warton's case the functioning manorial courts dealt with much business that might actually have been carried out by parish officials, there was such administrative overlap generally between such bodies.

By this point, we seem to have covered most of the recognised subject matter of Tudor and Stuart local history, given that many topics can stand further development, and that many questions remain unanswered. Education (Chapter 19), seen in an account of Archbishop Hutton's Grammar School, is properly sited near our discussion of religious movements, and we regret that an account of the volume of education, or even its quality, could not be given. The basic matter of likely degrees of literacy in the parish are taken seriously by the research team, and while we were certainly of the view that literacy could have developed in the seventeenth century, over half the jurors named in the Warton Manor Court records between 1608 and 1613 could not sign their names, but had to make a mark. The situation had considerably improved in 1668-1677, when fewer than half the jurors were unable to sign.

Our point here is that any local social movement of the time, educational or religious, rested on a mass of non-literate culture. It is not surprising that relatively few books appear in Warton probate inventories.

Our survey does not stop there. Chapters 9 to 11 deal with social levels (a tabulated analysis of social structure remains to be done in the future) and the nature of status and gentility. It examines the middling sort of people, the yeomanry, whose wills and probate inventories have survived in quantity. In Chapter 11 we look at the Great Neglected, the poor, not wholly from the near-obligatory standpoint of the Elizabethan Poor Law of 1601, or that of the Act of Settlement of 1662, or that of the overseers' accounts (for, like hundreds of other parishes, Warton does not possess any), but through a discussion of the questions that need to be asked on this subject. Gregory King's now somewhat discredited table[18] of the social structure of England in 1696, gives 'Cottagers and Paupers' as making up one quarter of the then population of the country, and it is this section of the poor and propertyless that must cause uneasiness to any local historian, in that he or she cannot keep such a large group in view for very long. However their names do appear in the parish registers where some are described as 'paupers'.

The survey also does something else that is becoming a little more fashionable in the local historical world; it examines the situation of women and children in a local society of the seventeenth century kind. What was the experience of women in relation to husbands, household, work and outer society? Was the childhood of many children a nightmare containing devils that had to be exorcised by beating? Our report here is careful to explain what is not known by way of answer to these and many associated questions. Such discussions are important, and it is not an index to the worth of a survey of this kind that it has to be judged in terms of 'facts per page'. The discussants are trying to evaluate what may be facts, and what may not. For the rest Margaret Spufford suggested that attempts to reconstruct a parish 'community' might in any case be doomed to failure, and added that 'in part the task is impossible, because the source material simply does not exist'.[19]

From a necessarily limited amount of straw, our research team has produced some impressive building material, and has even built an edifice with it. We have assumed throughout that fellow historians will add to the structure, and at the end we suggest some tasks that may in the future be profitably done. One final word; the present writer wrote nothing that is in the book's text, which is the work of the Mourholme Society over a period of seven years - and, to be fair to staunch members, over the longer period since the Society's formation, when its very admirable collection of copied local documents was made. We have tried to show what can be done with such material.

CHAPTER ONE

HOW IT WAS

The Setting

History is the study of people, how they lived and how they organised themselves. Focusing that study on a single parish makes it possible to identify many of the local factors which influenced people's way of life and varying prosperity. Much flowed from the qualities and characters of the people, but these elements had to operate against the background of the resources provided by nature and by the work of previous generations of parishioners - the cultivated land, the woodlands, the fish and game, the houses and trackways, the building-stone and minerals, the fuel resources in wood and peat. All this constrained by the topography, the difficulty of movement about the land in winter, and the climate. This opening chapter sets out, briefly, the natural stage on which the parishioners acted out their lives.

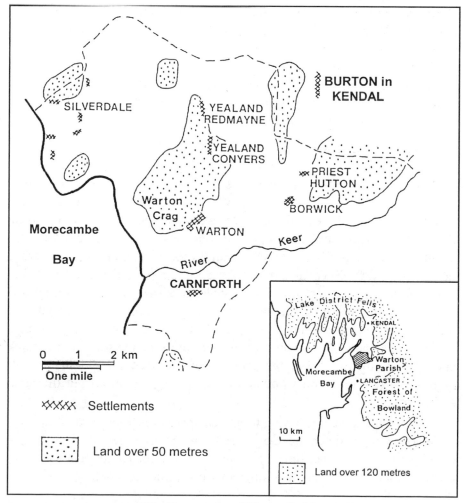

The Topography of Warton Parish

A Lowland Parish

Most of the old parish of Warton, consisting of Warton village and six surrounding villages (see Preface), lies less than fifty metres above sea-level. The parish's fertile lands contrast sharply with the wilder upland areas of the Forest of Bowland to the south and the Cumbrian fells to the north. This would have been a matter of importance in the seventeenth century when England was going through a period of climatic cooling, and upland areas were particularly badly affected.

Much of the lowland ground of the parish is formed by the Keer valley, and the two settlements of Warton and Carnforth stand opposite one another on each side of the lower reaches of the river, close to the sea. Behind Warton rises Warton Crag, with its continuation north into Cringlebarrow Wood sheltering it from the strong westerly winds blowing in from Morecambe Bay. Warton Crag overlooks the main coastal routes northward from Lancaster: the inland routes passing east of the crag, one through the Yealands and Beetham, and the other through Burton-in-Kendal; and the cross-sands route west of the crag, over Morecambe Bay to Furness. Yealand Conyers and Yealand Redmayne lie tucked beneath the craggy top of Cringlebarrow Wood, looking east across the fertile lowland corridor that lies north of this low ground, while Silverdale's scattered collection of hamlets and farms is on the undulating ground northwest of Warton Crag, overlooking the bay. The eastern part of Priest Hutton includes a spur of high ground that extends south from Dalton Crags.

The Rock Foundation

The rock underlying most of the parish is hard grey-white Carboniferous Limestone. It can be seen in crags and rocky outcrops, screes and limestone pavements in much of Warton, the Yealands and Silverdale, and it is also present beneath the Keer valley and the lowland to the north, though here thickly covered with glacial deposits. It is visible at the surface again near Borwick. On the limestone the soils are thin or absent. There is no surface water except in limited areas where the limestone has a thin cover of glacial or later deposits. Elsewhere rainwater soaks through the soil and into the cracks in the underlying rock. The thin soil dries out very quickly after rain, so that limestone areas have always been favoured routes for cart tracks and paths. Over most of the limestone the soils are not thick enough for cultivation but the ground can be used for grazing. If left ungrazed a dense natural woodland cover will grow on all but the most rocky areas.

Small mineral veins carrying iron and copper ores occur in the limestone on Warton Crag and near the Cove and elsewhere in Silverdale. These were exploited before Roman times, and again in the nineteenth century[1], but there are no records of any workings in the seventeenth century.

Ancient wall on the Lots, Silverdale, incorporating large blocks cleared from fields

Originally the limestone areas would have been littered with blocks and fragments of weathered limestone, but by the seventeenth century much of this material would already have been cleared from the fields and built into field-walls. Occasionally the line of a wall has been determined by the position of a particularly large block that could not be moved. The limestone has been used to construct houses, farms and barns. However, it is not the best stone to use for building. Some parts of the limestone weather into large blocks that are difficult to handle and cannot be readily split into more conveniently shaped pieces, and other parts weather into irregularly-shaped fragments that are difficult to use when constructing walls. In a few localities the rock is kinder to the builder, breaking into useful flaggy pieces, or in limestone pavement areas yielding long slabs suitable for lintels and gateposts.

The high ground in the eastern part of Priest Hutton and Borwick townships is formed by alternating beds of shale and sandstone that rest on the slightly older limestone. The sandstones are hard and form ridges of high ground with thin, acid soils, suitable mainly for grazing-land. The sandstones form excellent building-stone, since they are jointed into blocks of convenient shape and size. They have been used to build houses, farms and field walls. The intervening beds of shale are much more easily weathered and form hollows with acid soils in which the shale has weathered to a soft grey clay. Areas where the shales occur are frequently damp or marshy, and sometimes have peat deposits and small surface streams. This damp boggy ground would have been difficult to cultivate in the days before the development of efficient land-drains. Some of the weathered clay would have been suitable for use in building, or for baking into earthenware.

Glacial Deposits

The periods of intense cold and repeated glaciations that have occurred during the last two million years have greatly modified the topography of the area.

15

Thick layers of glacial ice forging down from the Lake District mountains scraped away any existing soils and loose rock, and eroded the underlying limestones, sandstones and shales. Billions of tons of debris were frozen into the ice, pushed beneath the ice, or carried on the glacier surface south and southwest into the Irish Sea basin. During this process the boulders and fragments of rock were ground together and rounded to cobbles and pebbles, while the weaker materials were ground into rock-flour. Each successive glaciation eroded the deposits left by the preceding one, and at the end of each glacial episode vast quantities of loose debris were further moved and sorted by meltwater.

The last glaciation to affect the Warton area came to an end about 13,000 years ago when climatic warming halted the process of snow accumulation and glacier movement. As the ice slowly melted it revealed the mounds of debris that had been moulded beneath the glaciers. Clay, sand and gravel that had been held within the ice or had rested on top of the ice were released, and much of this loose material was rapidly redistributed by glacial meltwaters and streams. The glaciations have left Warton parish with large areas of potentially fertile arable ground. The bulk of the glacial deposits lie in the low ground between Carnforth and Milnthorpe. Not only are there large elongated mounds (drumlins) of clayey, sandy gravel, but there are also quantities of gravelly and sandy sediments draped over these mounds. Mounds of glacial sand, clay and gravel also lie spread over the higher ground east of Borwick and Priest Hutton, and there are thinner spreads of glacial deposits on much of the lower-lying areas of limestone around Warton, the Yealands and Silverdale.

Ground for Cultivation

The Keer valley and the low ground east of Warton are covered with sands, silts and gravels that were washed out of the glacial deposits as the ice was melting, before the ground became stabilised by a cover of vegetation. Other outwash deposits floor the many hollows and depressions left in the surface of the glacial deposits after the underlying ice melted away. The natural forest cover that spread into the area as the climate improved stabilised the ground and formed a fertile soil. By the seventeenth century much of the area covered by glacial deposits would have been cultivated for many centuries. Each of the villages within the parish is close to large tracts of arable land formed by glacial deposits. Best placed were Warton and the Yealands, with the broad easterly slope of good ground sheltered by the limestone hill of Warton Crag and Cringlebarrow Wood. Priest Hutton and Borwick had good shares of reasonable ground on the lower slopes, and Carnforth is surrounded by glacial deposits. Even Silverdale had areas of reasonably thick glacial deposits spread over the intractable limestone.

The earliest stages of cultivation of the glacial deposits were greatly hindered by the presence of innumerable pebbles and boulders, some lying on the surface and some just below, but shallow enough to be hit by a plough. The clearance of these took considerable time and effort. The most difficult to break up and clear were the hard erratics of igneous rocks that had been brought by the ice from the Lake District. Several different varieties were recognised, and in the neighbouring parish of Beetham they were given colourful names such as Dog-flint and Thunderstone. These rocks remained 'unconquered by man's hammer or his chizel [but] Agriculture has driven Them into the bottoms of Fences, into the foundations of old houses'.[2]

The stones that were cleared away can still be seen at the field-edges, where they have been built into walls or into low soil-covered banks planted with hedges. Large quantities of pebbles and cobbles were used to construct and pave the cart-tracks that intersected the fields, and these show through the unimproved road-surfaces of side-roads. John Lucas (see Bibliography) comments that some large boulders were not moved to the edges of the fields, but were buried in pits dug alongside the boulders, 'not without great Hazzard to the diligent Husbandmen'[3]. Where the glacial deposits are particularly gravelly, as for example round Carnforth, they have long been dug as a source of material for roadworks and other construction.

Alluvium and Peat

Since the glaciers melted there have been many smaller-scale climatic changes and minor changes to the local topography. Alluvium formed by deposition of silts and gravels from floodwaters during high stages of rivers and streams occupies much of the Keer valley, and overlies glacial outwash gravels. There are smaller patches of stream deposits along Leighton Beck and other streams. This ground could be cultivated, but was more likely to have been used for grazing in the seventeenth century owing to the danger of periodic flooding. It is not known whether there were any flood-control mechanisms on the River Keer to prevent incursions of saline water during high tides, but Lucas mentions the use of barriers and flood-control doors on a stream just to the south of Carnforth to prevent peat diggings from becoming flooded by sea-water[4].

Warton parish contains several peat-mosses, some of which it shares with neighbouring parishes. They arose from shallow lakes or inlets of the sea, which underwent a complex history of sediment accumulation and vegetational changes. White Moss and Hawes Water, in the northwest of the parish, were partially filled with fine sediment and a shell marl. As the water shallowed reed-beds became established and later, moisture-loving trees such as alder. At Hawes Water much of the lake remains today as open water with shell-marl on its floor. On its northwest shore there are clay deposits which used to be dug, probably for building work and for the manufacture of earthenware at Silverdale Pottery. But at White Moss the lake became completely filled and a raised bog grew on top of the other vegetation. At both sites successive layers of vegetation decayed to form distinctive layers of peat.

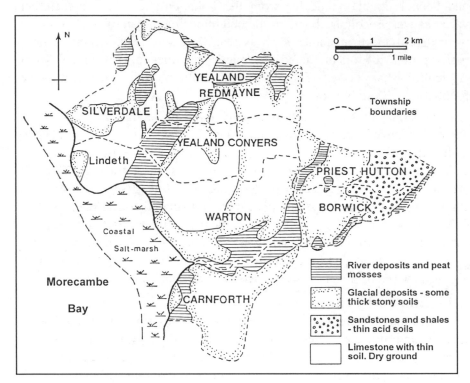

Warton parish: geology and land-use

Two other basins in the limestone, Silverdale Moss and Storrs Moss, are at a lower elevation and were inundated by salt water when sea-level rose about 6,000 years before the present day. Later changes led to the re-establishment of freshwater conditions. Reed beds spread into the shallow fresh water and the succession of peat-forming vegetation followed, as at White Moss and Hawes Water. There were many other low lying areas where drainage was poor and peat deposits formed in the ponded water. Among the more important were Hilderstone Moss in Yealand Redmayne and Longhaws Moss in Carnforth.

The accumulation of peat, which had taken thousands of years, was interrupted when the local population started to use the peat deposits for fuel. Peat had been an important fuel in Medieval times, and by the seventeenth century the local peat-mosses were the most important source of fuel in the parish.

Coastal Salt Marsh

The glacial and post-glacial deposits in Morecambe Bay are constantly being eroded and re-deposited by strong tidal currents. Sediment carried up the channels and creeks by the incoming tide is deposited at slack water along the coast, forming sandbanks and mudbanks that may eventually become covered with grass and other vegetation. The resulting salt-marsh is covered by only the highest tides, and it forms a very valuable addition to the grazing-land of the villages bordering the bay. But the whole system of estuary channels is very unstable. Tidal channels can, for no obvious reason, move close to the shore, causing rapid erosion of the salt-marsh. Over two-thirds of the marsh at Silverdale was washed away between 1967 and 1996, after a long period of accretion from 1910, when the marsh grew from 40 hectares to 244 hectares in 57 years. Fluctuations in the area of the salt-marsh on a similar scale have probably occurred ever since the bay became flooded in post-glacial times. Comments in William Stout's diary suggest that soon after the middle of the seventeenth century the marsh in Warton parish was very extensive, but a cycle of erosion appears to have begun at the end of the 1670s.[5] For much of the seventeenth century the marsh must have been extensive enough to be an important asset to those farms that lay next to the estuary.

Water Supply

The limestone that is present over most of the parish plays a crucial role in the movement of underground water. The areas where the limestone is at the surface are dry, because the rain and surface water sink into the joints (cracks) in the rock. Once in the joint system most of the groundwater flows down to the main water-table, but a small proportion is intercepted by thin bands of shale. These small accumulations of underground water, ponded on shale bands high within the limestone can form springs on the higher limestone slopes.

Where the lower slopes of the limestone hillsides are covered with glacial deposits the limestone water seeps into them, saturating them and sometimes bursting through to form springs. On the higher slopes where there is a high proportion of limestone pebbles in the glacial deposits the percolating rainwater dissolves some of them and renders the upper few metres of the deposit permeable. Consequently shallow wells in the glacial deposits can produce reasonable quantities of water for household use.

The pattern of water-supply in the parish is thus dominated by the presence of large areas of dry limestone uplands. Surface water is found only on the very lowest ground, where the main limestone water-table is close to ground level. The upper part of the Keer may have been usable, but the lower reaches, near Carnforth, would be polluted with sea-water and silt.

Springs and Wells

The scattered distribution of surface water meant that most of the population was dependent on groundwater in the form of springs and wells. All these were hard-water sources. The lack of soft water could present problems for such tasks as fleece-washing. The roofwater collecting systems that became so widely used in the nineteenth century were not feasible in the seventeenth century since very few buildings had slate roofs.

Of the three types of groundwater sources in the parish the most useful and the largest are the many large springs around the foot of the limestone hills from the main limestone water-table. To have lived close to one of these would have ensured a reliable year-round water-supply for personal use and for livestock. The large springs at Warton(the Weir and Senset Well) may have been a factor in the original settlement of that village. At Silverdale similar springs arise around the edge of the village, close to the sea and the peat-mosses.

The second type of groundwater source was provided by perched water-tables in the upper part of the limestone. These small springs and wells were much less reliable. They usually provided enough for the modest personal needs of the seventeenth century, but may not always have been adequate for watering cattle and horses. The upland parts of Silverdale were dependent on such sources, and this was no doubt the reason why the village developed as a series of small hamlets, each with a public well or wells close by. Large storage tanks were built at places such as Woodwell and Burton Well to collect water for livestock. Wells in the higher parts of Yealand Conyers and Yealand Redmayne may have tapped similar perched water-tables in the limestone.

The third source of groundwater, the glacial deposits, had to be exploited mainly by means of wells. At Carnforth these were in fairly gravelly and sandy glacial deposits, and at Borwick and Priest Hutton in saturated low-lying glacial sands, clays and gravels. On the higher slopes, however, as in the higher parts of Warton, and along the same hillside in Yealand Redmayne and Yealand Conyers the glacial deposits are well above the main limestone water-table, and shallow wells tapped water from the weathered top of the glacial deposits. Such sources would have been unreliable in droughts and may have been barely adequate for watering livestock year-round.

Pattern of Settlement

While water-supply may have been a factor in the location of some of the settlements in the parish it was clearly not always the most important one. Warton village has historically dominated the parish, with its church, its former market and its large population - in the seventeenth century about double that of Carnforth, the next largest settlement in the parish. Warton occupies a climatically well-favoured site, facing southeast, close to large areas of arable land, near to a good mill-site and with copious water-supplies from large springs. In the seventeenth century it lay at a focal point for local

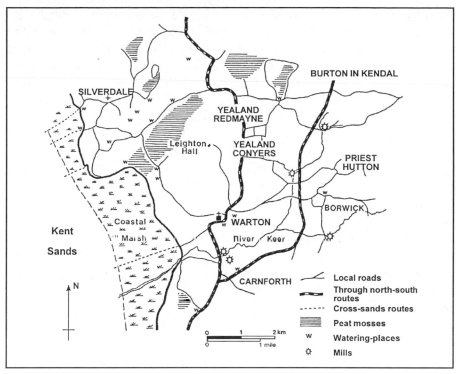

The seventeenth century network of roads in Warton Parish

transport, close to a bridge over the Keer by which parish traffic passes on the way to Lancaster.

The other large settlements are scattered around the parish, each close to the arable lands which the inhabitants were farming. Though dating from medieval times or earlier, the settlement sites still met the needs of their inhabitants in the seventeenth century. Almost the entire population was engaged in farming, and most lived together in villages that were close to their often scattered landholdings, and to their supplies of fuel in the peat-mosses. The layout of the old townships can still be traced in the villages shown on the earliest Ordnance Survey maps of the area, which were surveyed sometime in the 1850s and 1860s. This is not so surprising since the townships, apart from Carnforth, never underwent industrialisation. In the two hundred years between the mid-seventeenth century and the mid- nineteenth the population of the parish increased only from an estimated 1,200 (see Chapter 8) to 2,099 according to the 1851 census. That is to say the population did not even double itself. By contrast the population of Lancashire trebled itself between 1690 and 1801 [6] and nearly trebled itself again in the fifty years between then and 1851[7].

Warton and the Yealands

The houses in Warton and the Yealands were still, and indeed are to-day, strung in linear fashion, along an old route to the north from Warton which continued beyond the parish boundary to Slackhead and Beetham and which still exists as a modern road. It kept close to the lower edge of the limestone, probably because the ground was firm and comparatively dry along this line. Warton had a character of its own since it had once, in the thirteenth century, been a chartered borough with a market. The market never developed, among other reasons because of the devastation caused by Scottish raids in the early fourteenth century.[8] In the late sixteenth century the holdings were still being called 'burgages,'[9] but the name implied no special status the claim to be a borough having lapsed long before. The town planning of a borough remained, however. The uniform plots created on either side of the main street for the 44 burgesses can still be traced on the Warton Tithe plan of 1846. Indeed, basically, they define the shape of the centre of the village to-day, though their outline is blurred by later building. There are some infill houses on the Main Street of more modern times, but they apparently have been built on the original plots. The plots are narrow on to the street, but run a long way back, though rather less on the upslope side because of the encroachment of the crag. On the downslope side they run down to 'Back Lane', which once gave access not only to the fields, but also to Senset Well, one of the major watering places for the township. The original centre is still obvious from the style of the houses, though it is now embedded in peripheral pre- and post-war building.

Carnforth, Priest Hutton and Borwick

Carnforth was another linear village, lying largely along the main route north from Lancaster to Burton and Kendal at the point where it crossed the track that led down to the Keer bridge and on to Warton. This main road was not on the line of the present road north, the A6, but an older route still called to-day North Road, i.e the road to the north. It is only a minor route now and runs south of the town centre, since, with the coming of industrialisation in the mid-nineteenth century, the whole working centre of the town shifted north towards the then newly established railway station and ironworks.

Priest Hutton and Borwick both lie on low ground with plentiful water-supplies, and close to the main route from Carnforth to Burton. The houses in each cluster round a central village green, but villagers were within walking distance of their arable lands, and they could also collect peat from the higher ground within the townships.

Silverdale

Silverdale is different from the other settlements since it was divided into several small hamlets. This is probably a reflection of the scattered nature of the village arable land, and of the limited water-supplies in the higher parts of the village. Some building was also related to access to the estuary and the cross-sands traffic. The present centre, with hotel, post office and shops, was a creation of the nineteenth century, when a more sophisticated system of collection of roof-water made it possible for houses to move further from the scattered wells.

The comments set out in this chapter touch only on a few aspects of the complex story of the evolution of the local settlements. It is a topic which deserves to be fully researched, especially to determine whether the settlement pattern is essentially medieval or whether it is of earlier origin.

FARMING: *Town Fields and Enclosures*

Given the particular resources, described in the previous chapter, of the land in which Warton parish lay, how did the farming of the period exploit these resources? The matter is of crucial importance to any understanding of Warton parish in the seventeenth century. The whole of England at the time was a predominantly rural society. Such beginnings of industry as there were could only offer a living to a fraction of the population. Warton parish was a rural parish within this rural society. All but the merest scattering of people there drew their living from the land. They might have to eke out that living in other ways, particularly by weaving, spinning and fishing, but these crafts were only secondary to work on the land, a point which is discussed more fully in Chapter 14.

There are so many ways in which farming in the seventeenth century differed from farming in Warton parish to-day that it is hard to know where to begin. There are the enormous changes in farming practice, brought about not only by the change to the use of mechanical power, but also by increased scientific knowledge. The seventeenth century saw the beginning of these changes. It was a time when books of husbandry were the fashion and were recommending new crops, improved breeding of animals, more knowledgeable use of fertilisers and so on. Farmers, especially the better to-do who could afford to experiment, were beginning to put the advice into practice. The new practices first found a footing in southern England, and almost no evidence has been found that the new ideas were influencing farming in the northern parish of Warton even by the end of the century.

There have been two other major changes, not so much in the practice of farming, as in the basic concepts underlying land utilisation. Firstly, in the seventeenth century the inhabitants, since they were forced to wrest almost their entire living from the land, expected to gain from it more than just arable crops and pasturage for their beasts. It had to provide much else besides. Wood, stones, clay and lime for building and the making of husbandry gear, peat for fuel - these are only the beginning of what the land was expected to yield. Less visible, but just as basic has been the second change, the altered concept of land ownership.

Open Fields

At the beginning of the seventeenth century there was still extant, though no longer accepted without question, a medieval view of land as not fully any one man's possession, but as belonging, in some sense, to all those who lived on it and worked on it. It was a view which had found its expression in the medieval manor, and the system of 'Ancient Custom' which ruled it. An important part of this system was the 'Open Field' where the manor tenants grew their crops. An Open Field belonged not to one individual, but to a settlement, whether town, village or manor, which was collectively responsible for its husbandry. Within the Open Fields each tenant had his own holding, usually in the form of scattered strips of land, but the ploughing, sowing and management of the holdings was a communal matter. The tenure on which the strips were held no longer exists in England, except as an odd, preserved survival in Laxton in Nottinghamshire[1]. Although the strips in an Open Field were held individually yet, when the field was not under a crop, the whole field was open for all tenants to pasture their animals on. In more legal terms it became 'subject to common rights of pasture'.[2] In farming terms this right to pasture meant that the tenants' grazing animals helped put back into the land fertility lost by cropping.

Barn at Boon Town

Various subsidiary features arose from this basic right of pasturage. Strips were not fenced, but were divided one from the other at most by lines of 'merestones', or boundary stones. Temporary fencing might be used, but permanent fencing would have interfered with the common rights of pasture. The Open Field was so much the property of all that strips were sometimes re-allocated each year, though this was not a necessary feature of the system. It was usual for those who held strips in the Open Field also to have proportionate holdings in the communal meadows. Again once the hay had been cut the meadows became common to all tenants. A holding in an Open Field also usually carried with it the right to graze animals on the manorial commons and wastes, an important right which will be discussed in the next chapter.

By the seventeenth century this medieval system was on its way out and was being replaced by a more modern view of land as something which an individual owned and could do with as he chose. The change came at different times and in different ways in different parts of the country, and in considering Warton parish it must be remembered that it was never in what might be called classical Open Field territory. Open Fields were a particular feature of the Midlands. There the usual pattern was for the arable land of a settlement to lie in two or three large Open Fields. Every other year in the two-field system, and every third year in the three-field system, one field would be left to lie fallow and open to grazing animals to recover its fertility and, almost as importantly, to rid it of weeds by repeated ploughing.

There were, however, large regions where the two and three field systems never developed. This was true of much of the north and west. There, in upland pastoral regions, there might be no Open Fields at all. Farmers might grow the little grain they needed for domestic consumption in their own small fields, and graze their animals freely on the ample rough pasture. In Scotland and in much of Cumberland a different form of Open Field developed. Instead of two or three fields fallowed in rotation there was an Infield near the settlement and a larger Outfield. The Infield was permanently tilled and was kept in as much heart as possible by receiving any dung available. The Outfield was used as rough pasture but part would be ploughed up and crops grown on the ploughed area until the land there was exhausted. Then it would be allowed to go back to pasture to recuperate and another portion would be ploughed up[3]. Infield and Outfield were a type of open fields in the sense that any holding in them was subdivided into strips or 'ridges' which were intermixed with those of all the other tenants' holdings; a system that came to be called 'runrig'.[4]

The Manor Court

Plainly there must always have been some organisation, however rough and ready, to co-ordinate what was done on the Open Fields. Often enough it was the Manor Court. Indeed it seems to have been the case that where the fully fledged two- and three-field systems flourished manorial control was particularly strong. Manor Courts, representing as they did both the Lord of the Manor, the titular holder of all land in his manor, and the tenants who worked the land, were a natural place for the settlement of problems connected with the husbandry of the land. Many of the orders made by a court were simply the enforcement of what would still be considered good farming practice to-day; hedges were to be kept stock-proof, 'sufficient' as it was called; ditches were to be kept clear; tracks and bridges were to be maintained and so on. Other orders concerned matters which would now have to go to a civil court; arguments over rights of way, failure to shut other people's gates, interference with public water supplies etc.

The Courts also had powers, for which there is no local equivalent to-day, over the management of the Open Fields and the commons and wastes belonging to the Manor. The Manor Court could lay down, in detail, what might be grown and when, how much stock might be grazed and how it was to be managed. It appointed officials to help it in the task, primarily a constable, by-law-men (or barley-men as they tended to be called in the manors around Warton) and a pinder to impound and look after stray animals. The controls over agricultural practices to-day are not analogous. They are not primarily local, but spring from central and even international government.

In Lancashire, Open Fields seem to have been rare in the eastern uplands, but they were a usual feature in the lowland plain. They differed in certain ways from the Midland Open Fields, with their annual rotation of winter-sown crops, spring-sown crops followed by fallowing in the third year. A township in Lancashire would often have a number of fairly small Open Fields all of which were cultivated as what has been called 'half year lands'.[5] Crops were sown in the spring and, after they were safely gathered in, the tenants' animals were allowed on the fields to graze during the winter and fertilise the ground for the next spring's sowing, a matter more fully discussed in the next chapter. There has been a suggestion that, since this system occurs in the west, beyond the main Anglo-Saxon settlements, it was a Celtic inheritance. It seems as likely that it was a natural response to terrain and climate. Since winter-sown crops were relatively chancy in the wetter, colder north-west the concentration was on spring-sown crops. There was hence no need for a system which had to compensate for taking both winter and spring crops out of the land by allowing one-third of it to lie fallow each year.[6]

Tudor House Warton

Enclosure

Even by the sixteenth century Open Field agriculture was coming under strain. It had been adequate for the mainly subsistence farming of the Middle Ages but, with the opening up of urban markets, farmers began to want more land on which to produce a surplus and more freedom to farm their land as seemed to them most profitable. They wanted to 'enclose' their personal land and have undisputed possession of it, they wanted to keep their animals under their own eye, protected by walls and hedges from interbreeding with inferior animals and mixing with the diseased, they wanted to be sure that the dung from their animals was used on their fields. Enclosure normally involved the physical surrounding of land by fences or hedges. More basically it meant taking away land, over which farmers had once had common rights, and parcelling it out to individuals. Enclosing communal land could be an inequitable affair and socially divisive. Legally all tenants could take up enclosed land in proportion to the holdings they had lost in the Open Field, but not all could afford to do so as the legal costs and the expense of hedging or fencing were not small.

The Open Field system might have been cumbersome and inimical to agricultural progress, but it was well tried. Under it tenants had rights based on 'Ancient Custom.' In particular they had rights to free pasturage for their stock on the fallowed Town Fields and on the manorial commons and waste lands, rights which could make all the difference to the viability of smaller holdings. All these manorial rights are discussed in the next two chapters, but the point needs to be made here that when communal control of the Open Field was done away with, in the interest of increased profitability, a whole social system went with it.

In the south and east, where land for arable farming was most eagerly sought and enclosure tended to be on a large scale, opposition was fierce. In the more pastoral north-west enclosures tended to be small scale and 'silent'; that is they took place by agreement, without documentation or legal battles. Warton parish, though in the north-west, did not lie in purely pastoral country and a system of Open Field farming had developed there as it had in many of its neighbours such as Whittington, Melling, Arkholme, Hornby, and Bolton-le-Sands[7]. In contemporary documents the word 'Town Field' tended to be used in the north-west for the Open Field, and since Town Fields in the north-west did, as has been said, differ somewhat from the Midland Open Field this is the term that will be used from now on.

Town Fields in Warton Parish

The evidence for the existence of Town Fields in Warton parish in the seventeenth century is unequivocal. The problem is rather to estimate how much their place in the economy of the townships had been eroded by enclosure. Manor Court records survive in some numbers for two of the townships of Warton parish, Silverdale and Warton, though neither covers the whole of the century. The first impression from reading them is that the Town Fields remained of central importance. Throughout the century the Manor Courts met regularly, made orders controlling the Town Fields and recorded them carefully. A more detailed study suggests that the Town Fields were fading in importance and that enclosed, individually owned land was becoming predominant.

Because the loss of Town Fields could carry with it so many implications of a changing way of life it would be interesting to know details of the loss in Warton parish. There is, or was, a general feeling among historians that enclosures were initiated from above, and led to big landowners ousting the small. This was perhaps not always so. It has been suggested that the enclosure of commons in Cumberland, for instance, was less the result of a few big landowners seeking profit, than of many small holders responding to growing opportunities for live-stock marketing, though admittedly at the cost of dispossession of still smaller holders.[8]

Until more detailed work of this sort is done for Warton it is not possible to give a final account of the social impact of enclosure there. It is possible however, as a preliminary, to make some estimate of how fast the Town Fields were disappearing.

Silverdale

The amount of information found for the separate townships of the parish varies. In Silverdale the persistence of the place name 'Townfield', for an area to the west of the present church, suggests where one field was and it has been possible to come to a fairly exact estimate of how much of it remained by the end of the seventeenth century. The Townfield, and Silverdale Manor Court records always refer to 'the Townfield' or 'our Townfield' implying there was only one, was probably bounded on the north and south by roads, as it is to-day. On the west, from the evidence of the Silverdale Manor Court in 1697 concerning rights of access, it appears that the arable land was enclosed as far as the field known as 'Mary Butts' identifiable on the Tithe Plan of 1846. This would give the Silverdale Town Field an area of 14 statute acres in 1697, only about five percent of the estimated total of arable land in the township.

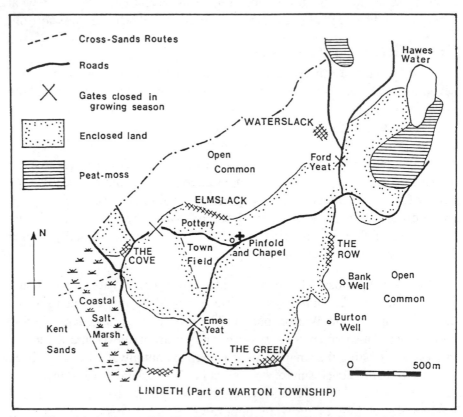

Silverdale in about 1690. The Town Field had shrunk to only about 14 acres.

Warton

Warton township seems to have had at least three Town Fields. There was one for the settlement in Lindeth, which was then part of Warton, not of Silverdale as it is to-day. A rental of 1511 made for King Henry VIII (as Lord of this Crown manor) mentions an 'Estfield' and a 'Westfeld'.[9] The site of the fields is not given, but an ingenious way of conjecturing where they lay was used by Paul Booth in 1967. In connection with the Tithe Commutation Act of 1836 very detailed and large scale maps were produced of parishes. The map for the Warton township was produced in 1846. The schedule which accompanied it gave information on which fields were counted as arable and which as pasture or meadow. If the arable fields are shaded in on the map it can be seen that such land lies in two main blocks, one to the north-east of the village and one to the south-west.[10] As Booth points out farming practice may have changed over the centuries, but not the nature of the land, so that the 1846 lay-out of arable land can be held to give a good lead to the position of 'Estfield' and 'Westfeld'.

Two further pieces of information can be added. The 1846 tithe map includes the names of fields and in particular it names Little and Great Threagill, Adcock Hinelands, Hindlands and West Hindlands, White Flatts, High Borwick Gate, Little Borwick Gate and Borwick Gate. These all lie to the east of Warton village on the south facing slope that leads down over Borwick Lane to the River Keer. In the Warton Manor Court records there are seventeenth century entries confirming that fields named Threaregill, Long Hindlands, White Flatt and Borwick Gate all lay 'within the Towne-fields of Warton'.

H.L. Gray, who in 1915 wrote a classic account of Open Fields, made an attempt to estimate the size of Warton's Town Fields compared with the enclosed arable land.[11] He based his work on a survey of Warton made in 1609 for King James I.[12] The survey, according to Gray, distinguished between enclosed land and land lying *in communibus campis* or 'in le Townefield'. Gray estimates that the Open Field arable accounted for only a fourth of the cultivated land of the township. Unfortunately his calculation is suspect for he appears to have thought there were only forty four customary tenants in Warton. A rental for the same year [13] certainly gives a list of forty-three tenants paying rent. These it decribes as 'burgage' rents (see Chapter 5), but it also lists forty-six further tenants paying 'customary' rents. The matter needs further research.

Carnforth

There is less information for the other townships of the parish. For Carnforth we have the evidence of Lucas's *History of Warton Parish*. He says 'In the western Part of this Township...are five large common Fields; one of which goes by the single Name of Thwaite; the other four which are contiguous to each other are called Huthwaits.'[14] He gives no real indication of the size of them.

He calls them 'large', suggesting perhaps that at the beginning of the eighteenth century Carnforth's remaining Town Fields were bigger than its neighbour's, but one cannot be sure for elsewhere he says 'I have heard some good Oeconomists say that this large Township has too much inclosed Land, and that if one half of it was lied common it would be better for the Inhabitants...'[15] There was a Townfield in the Yealands. In 1682 Thomas Hobkin was fined for 'grobing and ploughing' in a place called Rose Green 'belonging to the tenants of Yealand Redmayne'.[16] In 1746 a piece of arable land was described as 'Sometime since Enclosed out of the Open lands...'[17]

The Loss of Town Fields

Not enough evidence has yet been found to give any numerical estimate of how much of the parish land was still communally held in the seventeenth century. Comparison with other areas in Lancashire, including such near-by ones as Whittington, Melling and Arkholme, suggests that even at the beginning of the century it would have been less than the acreage held individually, or 'in severalty' as the contemporary phrase was.[18]

Enclosure pamphlet of 1692 (Rural History Centre,University of Reading)

Common-Good:
OR, THE
IMPROVEMENT
OF
Commons, Forrests, and Chases,
BY
INCLOSURE.
WHEREIN
The Advantage of the Poor,
THE
Common Plenty of All,
AND
The Increase and Preservation of
TIMBER,
With other things of common concernment, Are Considered.

By *S. T.*

LONDON,
Printed for *Francis Tyton,* and are to be sold at his shop at the sign of the three Daggers neer the *Middle-Temple* gate, 1652.

By the end of the next century the Town Fields of the parish were gone. Warton and Silverdale applied for Parliamentary Enclosure Acts at the beginning of the nineteenth century. They were concerned only with enclosure of the commons; arable and meadow land had apparently been already 'silently' enclosed. Only in the Yealands was there still some seventeen acres of common field mentioned in the Enclosure Act of 1778.[19]

As to how the Town Fields had been lost there is almost no information. 'Incroachments', both legal and illegal, are recorded in the earliest remaining Warton Manor Court record, that for 1593, but these seem to be small encroachments on the commons not on Town Fields. Encroachments by the big family at Leighton Hall were on a different scale, though again it seems to have been the commons and wastes that suffered. The tenants of Yealand complained in 1642 that Thomas Middleton of Leighton Hall had enclosed with a wall a 'large proportion' of these 'being the most fertile part thereof'.[20] In 1673, after the death of Thomas Middleton's son Sir George, the Warton Manor Court jury disputed the claim of Dame Anne Middleton, the widow, to 99 acres, which she claimed were demesne land. The jury pointed out that 'the custom of Warton' did not recognise any demesne land in Warton.[21] The outcome of the dispute is not known. 'Ancient persons' who knew the land averred that some of the land Dame Anne claimed was taken from 'Warton Common' but some was 'Copy hold Land'. The information is slight, but interesting as throwing some light on the change from communal to private possession of land in the parish of Warton.

The Field Pattern

Enclosure was often preceded by consolidation of holdings. It was plainly cheaper and easier to enclose holdings held in a block rather than holdings scattered throughout an Open Field. Exchanges between tenants to bring their holdings together have been found in other Lancashire Manors, sometimes as early as the thirteenth century[22]. There are no overt references to such a practice in either the Silverdale or the Warton Manor Court records. It is clear, at any rate, that scattered holdings were still common throughout the seventeenth century. Warton Manor Court records in particular are full of arrangements that had to be made to allow people to reach their scattered holdings, on the lines of the arrangements made in 1673 for Bryan Bland. He was to '...have weay through Elizabeth Dawson Stubings...that is to say after haij be mawne or corne be shorne untill the 27th day of meay...'[23] The idea of consolidation was there, however. Lucas praises a neighbour from another parish 'for perswading some of his Neighbours to exchange Lands with each other in the common Fields, and by that Means lay them so conveniently together, that, by Consent, they might be inclosed.' He then adds that his 'dear and honoured father' had been among the first that 'put that Method in Practice'[24], which would put it back well into the seventeenth century.

There are two accounts from the end of the seventeenth century which suggest that by then the landscape in the neighbourhood of Warton struck visitors as consisting of many small enclosures rather than of great Open Fields. In 1697 Celia Fiennes described the landscape just north of the Yealands as she travelled from there to Kendal:-

...very rich good land enclosed, little round green hills flourishing with corn and grass as green and fresh being in the prime season in July; there is not much woods but only the hedge rows round the grounds which looks very fine....[25]

Storrs Farmhouse, Yealand Redmayne

There was also a Scottish farmer, Andrew Blackie, who is said to have travelled down to these parts and to have left an account of his journey. His description of the landscape just north of Warton parish has been quoted as follows:-

The fences and shape of the enclosures are disgusting. The hedges are a medley of hawthorn, slowthorn, hazel and ivy. The enclosures are very small, and without any regular form.[26]

The quotation is tantalising. It is given in a series of newspaper articles on the Yealands written in 1911 by Mrs Ford, the wife of the noted local historian, Rawlinson Ford, the same who produced the invaluable edition of Lucas's *History of Warton Parish*. One would very much like to know more of this observant farmer who visited the neighbourhood 'more than two hundred years' before 1911, but all attempts to find the book from which the quotation was taken have so far failed.

Lucas, too, approved of boundaries. He praises provident nature which had plentifully supplied the Parish:-

...with Stones for the Building of Walls...but also with several Sorts of Trees & Shrubs, armed with Prickles and Thornes, not only to secure them from the browsing of Beasts, and to shelter Plants and Grass that grow under them, but also to render them very useful to Man...to make both quick and dead Hedges or Fences...[27].

32

FARMING: *What was grown*

What was grown on this jumble of land? And by what methods? That stock rearing formed part of the farming economy will come as no surprise to those who know the area to-day. The only surprise would be that there was once arable farming in the area. Ploughed land and grain crops are simply not seen to-day, only grassland. Yet there is much land capable of growing arable crops. When the Victoria County History of Lancashire was published just before the first world war it included a table of land utilisation taken from the statistics of the Board of Agriculture of 1905 [1] (see Table 3.1). Of the 8,341 acres of agricultural land in the seven townships 22½ percent was rated as arable. In Yealand Conyers and Redmayne as much as 32 percent. The maps and documentation produced in connection with the Tithe Commutation Act of 1836 show that at that period also the parish contained much arable land. It seems that, when market conditions are right, the land of Warton parish can be used for arable farming.

Table 3.1 Agricultural land in Warton parish 1905.*			
Township	Acreage		
	Arable land	permanent grass	woods and plantations
Warton with Lindeth	363	1,171	148½
Carnforth	255	1,009	2
Silverdale	153	516	155
Yealand Conyers	326	673½	230
Yealand Redmayne	532	734½	230
Priest Hutton	152	792	18½
Borwick	100½	825	15½
	1,881½	5,685	774½

* From the VCH, p.152

In the seventeenth century, even more than to-day, farmers had to work within the limitations imposed by natural resources. Those farming in the north and west of England, for reasons of climate and terrain, have inevitably tended to rely more on pastoral farming than did those in the south and east. England, in fact, fell into two main agricultural regions, but the pattern was not uniform in either region. In the pastoral north-west there were islands of mixed husbandry, especially in sheltered valleys and on coastal plains.[2] Map 3.1 shows that the land around Morecambe Bay lay in a

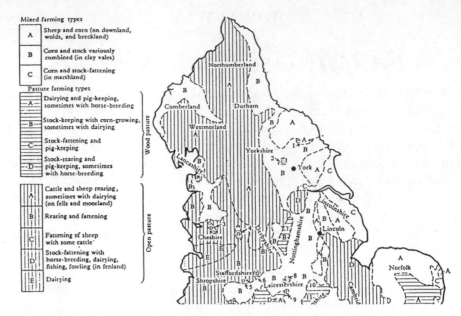

Fig 3.1 Farming regions in Northern England (From J. Thirsk, Ed. 'The Agrarian History of England and Wales' 1967, by permission of Cambridge University Press)

somewhat confused area, partly pastoral, partly mixed farming. It should be remembered, moreover, that the question is not straightforward. In the days before easy transport made it economic to bring in what could not easily be grown at home it was difficult to specialise completely. Farmers needed stock for manure, and pastoralists needed to grow crops for the feeding of their family and their stock. As John Fitzherbert, the agriculturalist, had put it at the end of the sixteenth century 'Hardly or not at all can the Husbandman attaine to the excellence of thrift, onely by his Corne, unlesse he have other cattell: neither by Cattell, unlesse hee have Corne...'[3] Against this background it seems probable that arable farming was secondary to stock rearing in the seventeenth century, but that nevertheless substantial amounts of crops were grown in Warton parish. The work that follows tends to confirm this.

Probate Inventories

Some twenty years ago a detailed analysis of agricultural goods in the probate inventories of Warton parish between 1580 and 1680 was undertaken by members of the Mourholme Local History Society [4]. These inventories listed a farmer's holdings of grain, either in store or 'on the ground'. Among the matters investigated was this very point of the ratio between livestock and crops. The total value of livestock and crops given in 104 inventories for the period was first calculated as accurately as the primary evidence of the inventories allowed. Livestock was taken to include any mention of cattle (including oxen), sheep, horses, pigs, poultry and bees, but not slaughtered meat. Crops included any mention of oats, barley, wheat, peas, beans, hemp, flax, hay, straw or grass, but not processed grain such as meal and malt. The ratio between the two was then calculated. For the whole parish over the period 1580 to 1680 the ratio of the value of stock to crops was 59:41. There were variations between the individual townships. Silverdale and Borwick showed the highest ratio of stock to crops and Priest Hutton and Yealand Redmayne the lowest.

It would be of interest, at some future date, to extend this work to include the whole of the seventeenth century. As a preliminary the 27 inventories for the last decade of the century were studied on a rather simpler basis. Only cattle (including oxen), sheep and horses were included as stock, and only oats, barley, wheat, peas and beans as crops. The ratio of the values of stock to crop was found to be 65:35. The findings, allowing for all the problems of using probate inventories as evidence are at least consistent with the general conclusion that mixed farming continued throughout the seventeenth century in Warton parish, but with an increasing bias towards pastoral farming. Indeed the emphasis on pastoral farming by the last decade of the century may be underestimated since, by chance, there are an undue number of wills from the Yealands, an area which, earlier in the century, was growing more crops than other townships.

Marriage and the Seasons

There is one line of argument which might help throw light on the type of farming in Warton parish. It has been suggested that in rural England in earlier times people married when they were not too busy with work on the land. That is to say, in arable areas, people married after the harvest in late autumn and winter, while in pastoral areas marriages in the spring and early summer, after lambing and calving, predominated. In the early part of the century neither pattern prevailed in Warton parish. From 1661 to 1700 there was a slight predominance of marriages in April, May and June.[5] This would fit in with the findings in the rest of this chapter which seem to suggest that, though mixed farming continued, stock rearing was of increasing importance.

Climate Deterioration

Then, as now, the climate was of importance in deciding what crops were feasible and profitable. The deterioration in the climate of the British Isles, which had begun in late medieval times, continued into the seventeenth century. The climate from 1550 to 1700 was probably the coldest since the end of the Ice Age ten thousand years before. It was in fact the climax of a 'Little Ice Age'. In the last decade of the seventeenth century the growing season in England may have been five weeks shorter than it had been in medieval times [6]. Accompanying this colder climate, and perhaps more difficult to adjust to, there was an increased variability in temperatures year by year, which made it difficult to predict harvest outcomes and placed strains on inefficient storage systems.

In the north of England this shortening of the growing season would have had an even greater impact. Warton was at least low lying, and would have suffered rather less than the surrounding upland areas from the effects of climatic cooling.

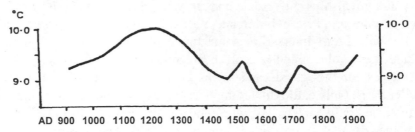

The average yearly temperature in central England from 900 to 1900AD

None of the surviving Manor Court records mentions crops directly, but it is plain from them that only spring sown crops were grown in the Town Fields. Each Court made regulations fixing the day when the Town Fields were to be 'driven', that is cleared of grazing animals, so that crops could be sown. It was always in the spring. The animals were allowed back in the autumn. There is nowhere any suggestion of arrangements to allow for the Town Field being kept clear for winter sown crops. What people might grow in any fields they held in severalty is another matter. Wheat, as is shown below, was grown in Warton, though very much in second place to oats. If it was the usual winter-sown variety it was presumably grown in individually owned fields, but there was a spring sown variety known at the time.

Favoured Crops

The implication seems to be that the Town Fields in Warton and Silverdale, the two manors for which there is the fullest documentation, were being used as 'half year lands' fallowed in winter and sown in spring. There is however a description by Lucas of the husbandry of four Town Fields in Carnforth which suggests something more akin to the Scottish Infield/Outfield system. He wrote that in the largest field, known as Huwthwaite, 'every Man plows or mows his part as he judges most proper; and so this field is never pastured'. In the other three fields however:-

> *The Proprietors plow one of them for three Years, then laying it, they plow the next for three Years, and afterwards the next; so that they are alternately three Years Corn and Six Years Pasture. He that has a Part in one of these Fields, has generally an equal Share in the other two...*[7]

The only other hint of this system found is that the Town Field enclosed in Yealand in 1746 was named as the Infield.[8]

Oats

The inventories are not sufficiently detailed to allow any numerical estimate of amounts grown. It is possible, however, to go through them and count how many times a crop is mentioned, and in this way to get a rough estimate of the relative frequency with which different crops were grown, or to be more precise held, for except where they are listed as 'on the ground' one can only assume that they were grown, not purchased. There is also a problem because of the number of times the non-specific terms 'corn' or 'grain' are used. The figures, for what they are worth, are set out in Table 3.2.

Table 3.2 Main crops in Warton Parish inventories 1600-1699			
Crop	No. of times listed	% age of inventories listing	
	1600 - 1699	1600 - 1649	1650 - 1699
Oats (or haver)	129	52	57
Barley	122	52	46
Peas	92	41	30
'Corn' & 'Grain'	79	33	30
Beans	55	22	28
Wheat	28	6	20
Rye	4	0.5	3

Oats plainly head the list with barley a close second. Then peas followed by beans (ignoring, that is, the non-specific 'corn' and 'grain'). Wheat seems to have been a much rarer crop and rye hardly gets a mention. To try to see if there was any change over time the first half of the century has been contrasted with the second. By chance, there are more surviving inventories for the first half of the century than for the second half so no direct comparison over time can be made. The percentage of wills mentioning a given crop can however be calculated for each half century and this makes some sort of comparison possible. The only changes that seem to be of significance are the marked increase in the percentage of inventories in which wheat is mentioned, and possibly the increase in rye grown.

Wheat

Lucas confirms the increase in wheat growing. He says:-

OF WHEAT This valuable Vegetable...was about forty or fifty Years since...a Stranger in this Parish...; but it has since been cultivated here with good Success[9].

However wheat does best where the rainfall is below 30 inches a year and the average July temperature above 60ºF [10], conditions which are hardly likely to have prevailed in the 'Little Ice Age' of the seventeenth century. It was perhaps changes in consumer taste which made it worth while to grow a more chancy crop. By the eighteenth century wheat bread was taking over. What had once been the luxury of the rich was being demanded by all classes.[11] The trend was less noticeable in Lancashire, where oats remained a staple food well into the nineteenth century.[12] Nevertheless even there wheat bread was probably an increasingly used luxury. By the late eighteenth century John Holt, the writer on the agriculture of Lancashire thought that '...the consumption of oat-meal is not so general at present as it was formerly; yet the quantity still used is very considerable...'[13]

Beans and peas would have had a number of uses. They may, to some extent, have been eaten green as we do, but would mostly have been gathered when black and ripe, and used as food for horses and cattle, or, in bad years, ground as meal for a very inferior bread.

Newer Crops

Both peas and beans, as legumes, would have helped put back nitrogen into the soil. The seventeenth century farmer would not have expressed it so, but the value of rotation of crops was understood. The newer crops, praised by the agricultural reformers of the period, are almost totally absent from the inventories. There is no mention of grass-seed, vetch or clover. Turnips are not mentioned in the inventories. Potatoes are

Inventory of John Banke of Silverdale, 1605 (Ref. WMW/K). Reproduced by kind permission of the County Archivist, Lancashire Record Office.

only mentioned once. Thomas Clarkson of Brackenthwaite Farm in Yealand Redmayne, a fairly well-to-do yeoman, died in 1686. His inventory mentions 'onyons and potatoes', but since they were only valued at one shilling, they were probably grown in his garden rather than his fields. He is the only one known to have experimented with potatoes, though by that time they were already common in other parts of Lancashire. In 1680 Wigan had a special potato market. Dame Sarah Fell of Swarthmore Hall bought seed potatoes in 1673 and 1674, and in 1686 the Rector of Croston successfully sued his parishioners for tithe on the potatoes they had grown.[14]

The impression certainly is that farming remained conservative in Warton parish. Andrew Blackie, the Scottish farmer mentioned in the preceding chapter, is said to have commented on this conservatism. While riding from Kendal to Burton, round about the beginning of the eighteenth century, he noticed good land 'well-cultivated for turnip, but no great quantity shown'. Then he came to 'Ellond', his spelling of Yealand, where he spent the night. He saw one estate well farmed, but the example was not followed by others. 'They are wedded to their own customs and will not be easily persuaded out of them'.[15]

Oxen

It seems impossible to leave the subject of Warton's arable fields without quoting further from John Lucas. He after all had seen what went on. On the matter of draught animals he says:-

> In this Parish they do rather plow with Oxen (Six whereof I have often seen drawing a Plow, without a Horse before them) than Horses, not only because of their turning to a more certain Profit, and having less of Hazard in them; but for their steady Draught, their stony land requiring it...[16]

This would have been nothing unusual. It was still common practice throughout England to plough with oxen, either alone or in a mixed team with horses. Oxen had the advantage that when they were too old for the plough they could be used for beef, presumably what Lucas meant when he spoke of the 'more certain profit' of oxen. They were held to be cheaper to feed, since they did not require the oats and grain needed for horses. Lucas mentions some particularly good Warton meadows down by the shore, 'which bear an herbaceous sort of Hay, and in good plenty too, which...is usually kept for the Use of their Oxen in Plow-Time'.[17] The oxen were shod:-

> The Ground of this Parish being stony...they shoe their oxen against Plowtime, which they do after this Manner; they cast them with a Rope fastned to two of their Legs, and so soon as they are down, they tie their four Feet together, which they put upon an Engine made of two Pieces of Wood placed Saltirewise and lined with Leather, and then they apply two little thin Plates of Iron to each Foot, which they fasten with three or four Nails, which are clenched upon the Side of the Hoofs, as they do those which fasten Horses Shoes...[18]

Fitzharberts
BOOKE OF
Husbandrie.

DEVIDED
Into foure feuerall Bookes, very ne-
ceffary and profitable for all forts
of people.

And now newlie correctted, amended, and
reduced, into a more pleafing forme of
English then before.

Ecclefiaſt. 10. ver. 28.
Better is he that laboureth, and hath plentiousfneffe of all
thinges, then hee that is gorgious and
wanteth bread.

AT LONDON,
Printed by I. R. for Edward White, and are
to be fold at his fhoppe, at the little North doore of
Paules Church, at the figne of the Gunne.
Anno. Dom. 1598.

Title-page of the 1598 Edition of Fitzherbert's Book of Husbandrie

The Inventories confirm that oxen were held in each township, but they were expensive beasts. For instance in 1633 eight oxen, belonging to John Pleasington of Borwick were valued at £41, more money than many farmers could have raised by selling everything they possessed. Very few farmers owned as many as eight or even six oxen. Many did not own any. If they ploughed with oxen it must have been co-operatively. This is implied in the Arbitration of 1658 between the tenants of the Yealands and Sir George Middleton. Any tenant who kept 'a draught to plowe his owne Lands' was to use them for a day a year on the demesne, but 'in case twoe or three or more Tenants joine to make one draught or plough for their owne ground', then they were to owe one day jointly.[19]

John Lucas on Weeds and Winnowing

Weeds were a perpetual problem. Till Jethro Tull invented his horse drill in the next century sowing was inevitably done broadcast and there were no convenient rows of seeds to hoe between. There was nothing but repeated ploughing and harrowing and back-breaking manual weeding to keep the crop in any way free of weeds. Lucas says:-

> They weed their Corn about the latter End of May or beginning of June, with an instrument like a Pair of Smith's Tongs, which they call a Pair of Gripes, jagged like a Rasp on the inner Sides, to take the firmer Hold...[20]

Lucas gives two further small insights into local farming practices. Millhead, the little rise above the Keer at the southern end of Warton was used, he says to winnow the grain. Winnowing meant tossing seed to rid it of chaff. A breeze was needed to blow away the chaff. This was often achieved by leaving opposing doors of a barn open to get a through draught, but probably the small rise at Millhead served as well. Indeed almost too well, for Lucas says it was only used 'in calmer weather'.[21] Elsewhere he describes the harvest.

40

When the corn is ripe, which is in August or September, they
shear it all, except the Bands, which they pull up by the
Roots...and mow none. [22]

To shear is to cut with a sickle, to mow to cut with a scythe. Both scythes and sickles are found in the inventories, but sickles much more frequently.

Woodlands

So far only crops sown by man have been dealt with, but the point has already been made that in the seventeenth century no produce of the land could be wasted and all land was utilised. If the soil was too shallow for agriculture it could be grazed. If it was protected from browsing animals, it would grow a natural woodland cover. Woods were not seen, as they tend to be to-day, merely as a source of timber trees to be clear felled and replanted. They were managed as a renewable resource by coppicing and pollarding and only some trees were left to grow for large timber. According to management, coppiced wood could be of any size; withies and stakes for fence making; wood for carts and ploughs; poles and balks suited for house building.

Leaves from the trees were a most important source of fodder for animals in the winter, either fed as lopped branches or by using the woodland as wood-pasture, that is the deliberate grazing of farm animals in tree land. [23] Though this latter was a declining practice after the Middle Ages it seems to have survived in Silverdale at least till the sixteenth century. In 1563 the tenants said they had always had 'libertie of Common...in a certain ground sometyme planted with trees called Sylverdale Wood...', but the timber was felled by a Richard Washington and 'ever since the Spring [the new growth] thereof hath been so eaten and kept down with their [the intruders] Cattell that the same is in effect destroyed...' [24]

Weeding tongs: artist's reconstruction based on a description in Lucas's History of Warton

Timber Rights

The right to use some of this wood for their own purposes was one which belonged to tenants by 'Ancient Custom'. There was a clear distinction between this small 'wood' and 'timber'. Timber might be reserved for the Lord of the Manor, but the tenants had varying rights (called bote or boote) to the smaller wood. In Warton, tenants had to buy timber for repairing houses, but had a right to all ash wood growing in their quickset hedges 'to maintain their husbandry gear withall'. [25] By agreement with the Lord of the Manor, Silverdale tenants had the right to both 'timber trees' and 'other wood' provided it grew on their tenements or on the common and was only for their own use and not sold. [26]

The tenants of Yeoland had a right to both timber trees for building and other wood for use as 'Plowboote, waine-boote, Cartboote, fireboote & hedgboote' but again not for selling off the manor.[27]. Sir George Middleton, Lord of the Manor of Silverdale and of the Yealands, fell foul of the regulations on timber trees.In Warton the Crown was Lord of the Manor. Middleton tried to grow trees on land he held there. He was found in 1649, by the Commonwealth commissioners who had taken over the manor, to have 'growing upon a parcell of Ground called Flea Garth containing by estimate 7 acres...about 306 oaks and several beeches worth £143-9-3d'. Sir George failed to prove that he had any right to sell 'crown' property.[28]

Peat Mosses

The peat mosses were another resource that was exploited. In many other parts of the country the seventeenth century saw the beginning of the drainage of wetlands to produce more arable land. Huge areas of south west Lancashire - Chat Moss, Martin Mere, Halsall Moss - were reclaimed from marsh. Warton parish seems to have valued the peat too highly as fuel to do this. The arrangement of the township boundaries ensured that each community had access to a peat supply. The steady accumulation of peat over thousands of years was described earlier (see Chapter 1). In the seventeenth century it was the most important local fuel source. Many tenancies in the parish included peat dales, where the tenant had the right to 'grave' peats for his own use. Over half the inventories compiled during the period 1600 to 1699 record that the deceased had a stock of turves or peats.

Peat-digging tools

Lucas describes in detail the diggings on Warton (Storrs) Moss.[29] The diggers, he says, usually 'fey off', that is reject, the upper layers. The firmer peat below was dug out in spring and laid upon the bank above '...then Women or Children carry them in small Wheel-barrows and spread them like Bricks to be dryed in the Wind and the Sun'. When perfectly dry the turves '...or rather Torff, as the Inhabitants here pronounce it...' were carried home. Properly stacked the dry turfs could be left out of doors, though some preferred to '...lay them under Hovels and standing on Pillars and cover'd with Thatch...' The extraction of the deeper layers of peat required careful drainage measures, and there are frequent references in Manor Court records to the need to keep ditches cleaned out on the mosses. At one moss at least (Longhaws Moss, by Carnforth) the danger of the sea flooding the peat-diggings was countered by the construction of a valve system in the tidal channel.[30]

Worthing

Anything that could at all be used to enrich the soil was conserved and used. There were no fertilisers to be bought in from outside and dung was a most precious commodity. According to the Oxford English Dictionary the contemporary name for it, 'worthing' may even derive from 'worth'. The value of the worthing held was seldom omitted from an inventory. It was so coveted that Silverdale tenants were forbidden to gather manure from the common 'except it bee within three rood of his own ground'.[31] The right to 'cowleing' i.e. raking the Backlane in Warton was given to Thomas Ward as a 'benefitt'.[32] No compostable material was wasted. It can be accepted as given that human ordure went on the dung heap. There were also 'brackens', or bracken as it is now called. Lucas describes how people:-

> ...strow them in the Highways near their Houses for Litter which mixt with other Manure makes an excellent Compost for their arable Ground.._[33]

There was also sea-weed or 'wrack'. In the 1670s just south of Warton parish, in Bolton-le-Sands:-

> ...about the sevnth month yearly the high tides brought the sheep's dung and sea tangle to the side, which was gathred by the inhabitants, evry house at the sand side knowing how far their liberties for gathring extended.[34]

Silverdale Manor Court records include similar careful regulations for the equitable allocation of the 'dirt' washed up on the shore there. It was so valued that tenants were even fined if they neglected to collect their ration.[35]

All these additional resources were put at risk by every attempt to replace Ancient Custom by a more modern, capitalistic, view of land as an individually held asset. The fear of their loss added fuel to the bitter battle fought between the tenants and the Lord of the Manor on the major issue of the tenure of their land, an epic battle which is described in detail later (See Chapter 5). There was, finally, one resource which has so far not been touched on, that is the right of pasture on the manorial commons. This was a resource so valuable that its consideration must be postponed to the next chapter.

FARMING: Livestock

Stock rearing in the seventeenth century and before had to be managed without imported feeds, so that winter feeding always presented a problem. It is no longer held that farmers got round this problem by slaughtering and salting down most of their stock in autumn. '...a community of cattle dealers would think twice before indulging in textbook massacres, and an overwintered young beast gained in market value...'.[1] One way or another the breeding and rearing stock would be kept going through the year, though it is probable that many animals were undernourished, and hence underperforming, by modern standards.[2] Doubtless some culling of unwanted and older beasts took place, and these could be salted for later consumption. Salting down was certainly used for salting tubs and 'flesh tubs' appear in some 15 per cent of probate inventories of the period.

Grazing Land

There were various sources of winter feed within the parish. Land available might be roughly divided into 'good' and 'poor' land in the way suggested in Table 4.1 below. (Farmers from richer arable lands might suggest that no land in Warton parish was really 'good', but these things are relative.) On the good land were both the arable fields and the meadows, but the distinction in usage was not absolute. The arable Town Fields were also used for winter grazing. Even in summer animals might be permitted to feed, or 'bait' there provided, for obvious reasons, that they were properly tethered or tended.

> *Whatsoeu[er] they be that doe bayte theire Cattell in Barleyside tyme...that can be p[ro]vede, eatinge pease oats, and not tendinge of them to pay xijd...* [3]

Table. 4.1		Land Available in the parish of Warton		
GOOD LAND Deep soil, mainly needed for arable use. Essential for food crops and hay.		POOR LAND Thin soil, rocky ground and peat mosses. 'The Manorial Wastes and Commons'. Unfenced		
Townfields (Shared) Ring fenced in growing season.	Enclosed fields (individual tenancies) Permanent walls, hedges or fences	Thin-soiled, grass, shrubs, some trees. Common grazing and browsing. Wood, timber nuts, berries game	Rocky areas mainly wood land.	Peat mosses dug for fuel

The grazing may have been on grassy balks dividing strip from strip, though some scorn has been poured on the notion that these dividing balks were a regular feature.[4] Certainly they would have been a wasteful use of good land. Nevertheless there must have been early patches of stubble, footpaths and awkward corners where the plough could not go, especially on hilly ground, where there was enough grazing to be useful. Moreover ley-farming was a well known method in the seventeenth century for improving worn-out arable land. It could be used even in open fields. Arable strips could be laid down to temporary grass and used as added pasture, thus effectively resting and dunging the land. When the soil had recovered the strip could be put back under the plough. It might be done by general agreement among the tenants (and in a way this is what the Carnforth tenants were doing in the Huwthwaite fields (see Chapter 3)), but it could also be done strip by strip at an individual's choice, provided he tethered any beasts that grazed on it. It is reported that the tenants of Fulbeck in Lincolnshire tethered as many as three hundred cattle in this way.[5]

Meadows

Also on the good land were the meadows where hay could be grown. In Warton, for instance, a swathe of fields along the banks of the River Keer and up round the coast are marked on the 1846 tithe map as meadows. Where a Common Field system prevailed such meadows would have been open as pasture to all tenants after the hay was got in. Tenants had holdings, called 'beastgates' in these meadows as they did in the Town Fields, and like the arable holdings they could be bought and sold. Naturally, as with strips in the common field, some tenants acquired many holdings, others were poor and held few or none. It is important to realise that 'The common field in Lancashire was never common to all and sundry'.[6] The common field system offered some protection to the poorer members of the community, but it certainly did not put all tenants on an equal footing.

The Common

There was a further source of pasturage in the manorial commons and wastes, features which are now gone from the parish since the last of the commons were enclosed in the nineteenth century. Tenants in the seventeenth century had 'common of pasture' on such land, that is the right to pasture their own animals there, though again in proportion to the amount of their holdings in the Town Fields. This was Ancient Custom and was also written into the sixteenth and seventeenth century legal agreements with the Lords of the Manor in Silverdale, Warton and the Yealands. These commons lay on so called 'poor land' (Table 4.1), but even poor land was not wasted in the village economy. The right to pasturage on the commons and waste land was of importance to the economy of all tenants, but most of all to that of smaller holders, those whose holdings were only just large enough to be viable. To them the possibility of pasturing on the common a few sheep for profit, and a cow for its milk, might make the difference between keeping a modicum of independence and having to sell up and become a landless labourer. It was six cottagers, that is very small landholders, who objected in 1676 when Sir Robert Bindloss, Lord of the Manor of Borwick, enclosed an acre and a half of common land. All the other inhabitants accepted the enclosure, presumably because it was made for the reputable purpose of compensating the unpaid constable for time spent on the job.[7]

Animal diseases/Animal breeding

There was a down side to this common of pasture. Since all animals grazed together, the possibility of controlling disease or improving breeds was limited. Manor Court books suggest that seventeenth century farmers were at least aware that there was a problem. Warton was not unusual in making regulations to fine those who put 'notoriously scabbed' horses on the Common. In 1677 John Hadwen was fined for putting an 'vnlawfull horse' on the common 'which doth cape the mercs'.[8] Both Warton and Silverdale made orders about rams.

> *wee order that noe tennant shall lett any rigalts run at*
> *liberty between Michaellmas and Martinmas.*[9]

A rigalt was a male animal with only one testicle, either by nature or by imperfect castration. A form of this word, rig or rigg, is still used locally. Whether it was feared that these unfortunates would sire poor offspring, or whether they merely interfered with the chosen ram - it was presumably rams that were being referred to because of the season - it is plain that some attempt was being made to control breeding.

The Town Bull

The value of a good bull was also recognised. It was the usual practice for a township to keep only one, the town bull. It was part of the agreement between Sir George Middleton and his Yealand tenants in 1658 that the Lord was to :-

An 1820 illustration of a Lancashire longhorn cow (Rural History Centre, University of Reading)

> *...keepe or cause to be kept one good Bull, to which the said*
> *Tenantes & every of them shall bee free at their pleasure to bringe*
> *their kine without anie thinge payeinge for the same,*
> *acquaintinge the Lord or some of his family with their cominge.* [10]

The only bulls mentioned in the inventories, other than Sir George's, were both in Warton township, suggesting that the distant crown did not feel obliged to supply a town bull there. Presumably the tenants would have had to pay a private owner for his bull's services. At about the same time Sarah Fell of Swarthmore was paying 6d a time 'for cow bulling'. [11]

Longhorns

The inventories make no mention of the breed of animals kept, though they carefully record age. Different breeds, or perhaps more exactly different types of cattle and sheep did exist in different parts of the country and new stock was sometimes brought in from abroad, but the age of improved breeds did not really come in till the eighteenth century, and even later than that in more isolated parts. An eighteenth century Cumberland farmer is reported to have said, apparently in good Mummersetshire, when asked about the breeding of his flock, 'Lord, Sir, they are sik as God set upon the land; we never change any'.[12] The cattle in Warton parish would probably have been of very mixed type, with probably the old longhorn type prevailing. They were smallish animals, hardy but slow growing. Fair milkers, but also strong enough to be worked. It was from such beasts that the later improved Longhorn, for which Lancashire became famous, was developed.[13] Whether shorthorns such as were found in Yorkshire or the black cattle from Scotland, that were coming down to northern England on the drove roads, were beginning to make their appearance in Warton parish there seems no way of knowing.

Silverdale sheep

The sheep of the Lancashire and Westmorland border were, it seems, mainly of the usual north country horned, coarse wooled sheep, the Linton. They remained unimproved even into the eighteenth century. Lancashire sheep were described by one agricultural writer as '...half starved creatures upon the mountains'.[14] There was however, in the nineteenth century, a separate local breed, the Warton Crag or Silverdale sheep. Arthur Young, the eighteenth century agriculturalist, noted it with approval in 1793 in one of his peregrinations around England. 'In our way from Kendal to Lancaster ...we saw a better kind of sheep, both in point of shape & quantity of wool, which go by the name of the *Silverdale breed*. Agreeably to our information, that breed is native, at least has not been lately introduced...'.[15] A year later the breed was being described as 'horned, white-faced, and close-woolled. They are said to be native, and are much superior to the common sort, in regard both to fleece & carcass'.[16]

One of the last Silverdale sheep breed. A ewe photographed in 1900. (From 'Westmorland Agriculture 1800 - 1900' by F.W. Garnett)

Whether the distinctive breed existed in the seventeenth century is not clear, though the fact that it was thought to be 'native' and 'not lately introduced' suggests that it may have. Other pockets of close-wooled, so-called 'Heath sheep', like the Whitefaced Woodlands,[17] are known to have occurred naturally. Indeed such a type was ancestor to the great breed of Cheviot sheep.[18] Lucas, talking about Warton and Yealand crags, says

48

'These Places yield a sweet and cleanly Herbage, which feeds a Breed of small *Sheep*, whose Flesh is much commended and esteemed...'.[19] Certainly the 'sweet and cleanly' limestone grassland and the sea-washed coastal turf in Warton parish would have provided excellent grazing for sheep. On the marsh not only is the grass of good quality, but it is also free from the parasitical trematoid worm which causes liver fluke disease in sheep. Since the quality of the grazing can affect the quality of the wool produced [20] sheep from this good grazing ground would be likely to be of superior market value whatever their breed.

Still less is known of the horses, pigs, poultry and geese that were kept. The breeding of horses by at least one inhabitant of the parish is discussed below. Pigs appear in many inventories, but in such small numbers that they must have been fattened for domestic consumption only. In Warton there were manorial rules that they must be ringed at all times, and in summer yoked as well, that is fitted with a wooden triangle to prevent them pushing too easily through gaps. Presumably, therefore, they were expected some of the time at least to forage for themselves. As for poultry all that can be said is that they were commonly kept. Perhaps their status is best summed up by the entry in a 1633 inventory 'poultry about the house'.

Overpasturing

There are indications that the commons and wastes, so important for the pasturage of all animals, may have been becoming less than adequate by the seventeenth century. There was encroachment on them by enclosure (see Chapter 2), and at the same time strong incentives, as is discussed below, to over-pasture whatever common there was left. Officially the commons in the Warton townships were 'stinted', that is the number of animals a tenant could pasture was limited, the limit being in proportion to the size of the holding. Even the number of geese a tenant might send to forage on the common was limited and an eye kept on those who contravened manorial rules. 'We are further agreede that Richarde Jackson al[ia]s bownes shall keepe no geese but iij gese & a stegge [gander]...'[21] and tenants were fined if they overstepped the limit, for the period quite sharply. Both Silverdale and Warton had a general rule that no inhabitant was to keep more sheep on the common in summer time than they could feed within the manor in winter time. Since the rule had to be re-iterated throughout the century it seems probable it was being evaded. At the end of the century the Warton Manor Court jury, before repeating the regulation once again, noted that '...greate complaint is and has been made concerning the abuseing and overcharging of our commons in Summer time...'[22]

Pigs in Tudor Times
(Rural History Centre,
University of Reading)

The townships do seem to have tried to deal with over-pasturing on the commons. Twice a year Warton and Silverdale commons were 'driven', that is the animals were rounded up, to allow the barleymen to check what animals were out there. The whole township was expected to turn out to help

49

> *...the By-law-men shall...give overnight notice to the Freeholders and Coppie holders, within Warton to goe along, and assist them in soe doing, and what house, and when to meet them the next day, and not any to depart till they have been their full circuit upon paine of Everyone offending herein three shillings four-pence.* (23)

The barleymen were to put all 'unlawful' animals found in the town pinfold and 'Impounde theim vntill the owneres thereof hav payde the sayd Barleymen for the sayd gudes and cattell...'(24) Similar orders were made throughout the century, but it does seem that despite manorial attempts at control the system was beginning to break down. Even the barleymen seem to have been reluctant to enforce the orders against overstocking, for the order just quoted about impounding unlawful animals finished by threatening to fine the barleymen if they did not do their duty. The matter was further complicated since not all animals found on the common which did not belong to manor tenants were strictly 'unlawful'. A right, within limits, to let one's Common of Pasture to outsiders was recognised, but any one with 'priveledge, freeledge and Com[m]on-of-pasture vpon the common' who let the right to an outsider was still to be responsible for any overcharging of the common with animals even when this came about by natural increase.(25)

The Salt Marshes

There was a further source of pasturage on the coastal marshes. To-day it is easy to forget the nearness of the sea. The flat and muddy shore, though it has beauties of its own, is not a blatant tourist attraction, and the villages, except for Silverdale, tend to turn their back on it. In the seventeenth century the sea was important, not only for the food provided by fishing, and the sea-wrack for manure, but also because the sea marshes were an important source of pasturage. They were, however, a fluctuating asset, since they are periodically eroded away by the River Kent as it changes its course through the sands. In the 1670s the marsh had been very extensive, but from 1677 the sea inundated the marsh which crumbled away with great loss of grazing land. At the same time new salt marshes appeared on the other side of the bay south and west of Cartmel (26). A hundred years before there must have been a similar disaster threatening at Warton, for a survey of the manor found that:-

> *...the Common of Pasture and Turbary...called Warton Marsh [is found] to be much wasted and decayed by reason of the rageing Seas dayeing [sic] overflowing and washing away the same so that in...time the same might be utterly wasted to the great Loss and impairment of the said Tennants...* (27)

Queen Elizabeth, as Lord of the Crown manor, denied any responsibility towards her tenants. They were never, her commissioners laid down, to require any abatement of rent because of the action of the sea.

Salt-marsh at The Cove, Silverdale

Stock marketing

The animals fed, legally or illegally, on the commons could have been disposed of fairly easily. Warton parish had easy access to two large markets for disposal of surplus products. Kendal, thirteen miles north of Warton village, was a considerable town, with a population of about 2,500. [28] Though it is believed to have been depressed in the 1630s it remained an important centre of the textile trade throughout the seventeenth century with wide-spread trade connections. Eight miles south of Warton village lay Lancaster, probably somewhat less prosperous than Kendal, but still an important place, especially for marketing livestock. By the 1690s Lancaster was becoming a centre for the growing trade with North America.[29] Warton parish actually lay astride the packhorse route between Kendal and Lancaster, and the important cross-sands route to Furness lay on the western edge of the parish. In 1665 a market was established at Burton-in-Kendal, only three miles from Warton village, making local trading even easier.

Wool

There is little evidence of surplus arable crops for sale, though some barley probably went to the malting trade in Carnforth. In fact the only firm evidence for a marketable surplus is the comment by Lucas that hemp seed produced in the parish was much sought after and commanded a good price.[30] Animals and animal products were another matter. There was evidently an extraordinarily high number of sheep and lambs reared which could be traded at the local markets, and there was also a very large wool crop. Most people, it is true, had only a few sheep, perhaps intending to provide themselves with a small supply of wool and meat. Many of these, no doubt, found that possession of a few sheep was the most convenient way to utilise manorial rights of grazing on the common lands. Several people had large flocks of sheep, numbering into the hundreds, with Sir George Middleton in the lead with a flock of 380 sheep 'old and young'. The 'Wool Book' for 1631,[31] a record of the tithes paid on wool and lambs in that year, implies that there were some six thousand fleeces produced in 1631 and each of these would weigh about three pounds before sorting.[32] Such a yearly output is of a size to suggest that more sheep were being kept than can have been needed locally. Much of the wool must have been sent off to the local markets where the relatively high quality of the wool would make it very competitive with the Rough Fell and Herdwick wool from nearby upland areas.

Horse Breeding

There seems to have been some trade in horses. Where water was available the limestone grassland was very suitable for rearing horses. The lime content of the grass makes for good bone formation, and the relatively slow rate of growth of the grass prevents the problems that can arise when horses indulge in overlush grazing.[33] Lancaster was an important centre for the horse trade, and Sir George Middleton at least may have been gaining money that way. His inventory lists 58 horses, surely more than an elderly gentleman would need for his personal use? In fact Lucas says that the

51

Middletons enclosed a large piece of ground near Brackenthwaite in the north of Yealand Redmayne which they used for raising horses.[34] This land, known as Colt Park, was probably the 'large portion' of common land already mentioned as having been contentiously enclosed by Sir George's father early in the seventeenth century (see Chapter 2). A modern day survey of the ground suggests that this 'large portion' was as much as 85 acres.[35] The land was limestone pasture, well suited to horses, with spring water and a small lake, Little Hawes Water.

A number of other people had four or five horses, mostly including mares and foals. The inventories would not necessarily make clear how much trading was going on. The 1600 inventory of William Williamson of Borwick only listed two horses, worth £6 between them, but his will includes details of fourteen transactions involving horses. Most of these involved people who lived locally (Dalton, Lupton, Whittington) but one who owed him money lived in 'Wensedall'.

Cattle Droving

It is not clear how far Warton farmers were involved in rearing cattle for the market. Perhaps a lack of water in the limestone pastures limited how many cattle could be held. What is certain is that Warton parish was on an important droving route. Specialised rearing of cattle for urban markets, both for beef and for dairy products, was a growing trade in the seventeenth century. Cattle were imported from Ireland in large numbers until 1667, when the Irish Cattle Act put a stop to the trade. Scottish cattle however continued to be driven south. One droving route passed through Keswick, Kendal and Burton-in-Kendal to Lancaster, so touching the eastern edge of Warton parish. Another droving route lay across Kent Sands to Hest Bank. Some of the cattle that were driven across the sands are believed to have been brought ashore at Cow's Mouth in Lindeth. Presumably this landing-point was favoured because there was a good watering-place on the common at Lindeth, namely Woodwell. Perhaps the fine suffered by John Waithman of Lindeth for '...alteringe the watercourse...'[36] there indicates that he was in the cattle trade and was trying to arrange the cattle-watering at the well to suit his own requirements.

For Warton township there survives a lively account of what happened when the cattle reached the township and came to drink at Senset Well. As early as 1593 the Warton Manor Court laid down that a good gate was to be installed on Well Lane, 'for the saftie of our feeldes'. Two men were appointed to keep the gate, and two more to see the drovers paid for going through the fields. They were 'to imploye the saide monye for the profitte of the towne, as by the most parte of the Tennantes shall be thought most needful...' Then when the droves actually came through the whole township was called on to help.

> *And further that when any Droues of Cattell, doe come to the Towne the saide keep[er]s to call fo[r] everye Tennante of the Towne, every house to sende one, to carie them through the feeldes..*[37]

Cow's Mouth, Lindeth, was used by cross-Bay cattle drovers. Drawing based on a painting in the Gaskell Hall, Silverdale, with the permission of the Management Committee.

Cross-sands route

There is little evidence that Warton parish farmers were directly involved in droving, or even that they were fattening drove cattle. The inventory of Robert Hodgson of Carnforth (1614) shows that he was owed 4s-4d. by a drover, but this may have been payment for grazing rather than a matter of trading in cattle. Perhaps the marriage of Edmond Cort of 'Lindell in Cartmel', referred to in the marriage bond as a 'cowhird', to Mary Hadwen of Silverdale in August 1688 was a happy by-product of the cross-sands cattle trade.[38] William Stout in his autobiography implies that the cattle trade was not a very reliable business to be in. Commenting on his brother Leonard's activities in the 1690s he says 'He would also buy and sell cattle, which is a dangerous employ: and to get him out of such business and company we were desirous he should marry.'[39]

Size of Herds

The size and constitution of the herds of the time suggests that on the whole Warton parish farmers were not into cattle trading in any big way. Table 4.2 shows the holdings of 145 individuals in Warton parish who are recorded in the inventories as owning cattle (the large herd of Sir George Middleton has not been included with the tenants' herds). One third of the individuals holding five or fewer animals in fact held a single animal only. The small herds of ten or under were made up of fairly even numbers of cows, heifers, stirks and calves. They would have been well balanced for a little milking, for the home consumption of the beef and also for the replacement of the plough teams. Draught oxen were put to work at three years [40] and their working life was perhaps four more years [41] so that a number of young cattle must have been dedicated to this purpose. In fact herds which include oxen are larger on average, about fourteen animals as against the general average herd size of seven. Ownership of cattle was very widespread, which is not surprising considering the number of useful products they provide - milk, butter, cheese, meat, leather, hair, tallow, - as well as their use for ploughing and for haulage in general. From the inventories it is known that butter and cheese were made in Warton parish, and that beef was stored both salted and 'hung'. Presumably some of these products were sold, but there is no evidence, except for one entry in Warton Manor Court

Table 4.2 Size of herds in inventories of Warton parish 1600-1699		
No. of animals in herd	No. of owners	% age of all owners
1 - 5	74	51
6 - 10	39	27
11 - 15	20	14
16 - 20	4	2
21 - 25	5	5
26 - 30	3	2

Book which seems to imply that meat was being brought to a market of some sort in Warton. [42]

There were three exceptionally big herds. Mr Thomas Kitson, a rich gentleman of Warton, had a herd of 22 beasts in 1638 made up of 8 kine, 1 bull and 13 'yonge cattel'. Richard Mason of Carnforth had 20 beasts (4 cows, 2 steers, and 14 stirks). He too seems to have been exceptionally well-to-do, dying worth £304-5s-6d. From the number of young cattle listed it sounds as though these two might have been rearing for the beef market. As for Sir George Middleton, he had a herd of 85 beasts (25 kine, 30 steers and heifers, 22 yearlings, 6 sucking calves and 1 bull).

Specialised farming

The picture that emerges is of a land of subsistence farming just moving into the beginnings of specialisation for the market, at least in cattle and wool. Town Fields and manorial control of agricultural practices were reaching the end of their life, but farming was still both more public, and perforce more co-operative than later. A farmer's beasts grazed on public land and watered at public watering places. As a manorial tenant a farmer had to co-operate with his neighbours on a detailed day-to-day basis. It was a system where there was perhaps too little room for initiative, too much petty interference, too much sticking to old ways simply because they were old. Yet the custom-bound, traditional way of life offered some support to tenants in the form of background rights and perquisites. The breaking of old custom, the enclosures, the engrossing and consolidating of holdings and the growing economic pressures to specialise were beginning to do away with traditional supports. The poor, the unfortunate and the bad managers were in danger of being pushed out. Once a tenant could no longer pay his customary dues, or was persuaded into selling, there was little for him, if he stayed in the parish, but the life of a landless agricultural worker and the frail support of the poor law system. He and his family might eke out their living by weaving, spinning and other 'by-employments' (see Chapter 14), but the opportunities were not great in a parish which remained almost entirely agricultural.

Manor and Tenancy

The previous chapters have stressed the overriding importance of land in the economy of the townships of Warton parish. It was natural that, where so much depended on land, anything threatening security of land tenure should meet with opposition. People valued security very highly, not unreasonably in a world which must often have seemed very insecure. The realities of near starvation, of overwhelming plagues and of civil war are discussed in later chapters. There was little, except pray, that could be done about such catastrophes, but there must have seemed a possibility at least of resisting attack on the right to hold land and pass it down to one's heirs. Four of the townships of Warton parish, Silverdale, Warton and the two Yealands, are known to have put up a fight against attempts to alter the system under which land was held.

Land tenure

The system of land tenure in Warton parish and elsewhere in England is unfamiliar to us to-day. The unit was the manor, the old Norman one, but the system of villeinage had been gradually modified. Though no longer serfs, most of the tenants still had a quasi-feudal relationship with the landlord, and this was expressed through the Manor Court and the 'custom of the manor'. The manor was based not on statute law, but on Custom, which ruled the relationship of lord and tenants. In theory custom could not be changed, but had existed 'from the time to which the memory of no man is to the contrary', as the phrase went. It was enforced through the Manor Court, which again was not based on statute law or royal charter, but was the private court of the Lord, though not owned by him. It existed to declare and enforce the ancient customs of the manor, which were binding on both lord and tenants and would be upheld in the royal courts.

Ancient Custom

The powers of the Manor Courts had accumulated over the centuries and were multifarious and confusing. Contemporary jurists produced a theory which attempted to systematise them. They held that there were two courts, the Court Baron and the Court Leet, with slightly different functions. In practice there was almost always only one court. In so far as it was the Court Baron, the 'private' court of the Lord, all tenants had to attend or be fined for failing to do so. In so far as it was the Court Leet, a public court of petty jurisdiction, all males resident in the manor had to attend. The business of the joint court was carried on by a sworn jury, normally of twelve men, sometimes more. The principle of selection of the jurymen remains unclear, not only in Warton, but everywhere. The functions of the court were to deal with changes in tenancy, to appoint manorial officers, to make by-laws binding on all tenants, to decide minor disputes and to fine offenders. In fact there was continual gradual change and there was little legal precision and, as a result, disputes were endemic.

Copyholders and Leaseholders

There were, in general, several kinds of tenure by which manorial tenants could hold their land of the Lord. There were, first, free tenures. In the past these had been of various types, such as 'Socage' and tenure by 'Knight Service'. By the seventeenth century such tenants were simply known as freeholders. They were still tenants of the Lord and had to attend the court to account for their tenure, 'make suit of court' as it was called, and they had to pay a small fixed rent, but they had complete security of tenure. Then there was customary tenure, about which there will be more to say. 'Copyhold tenure' was a form of customary tenure, but with the difference that the tenant held a copy of his entry in the court roll, which he could produce in evidence in the King's courts if his right to the property was questioned. Copyhold gave almost as much security as freehold and it was quite usual for a tenant to hold some of his land by copyhold and some freehold. Copyhold property, like freehold, could be sold. The new tenant had to be 'admitted' by the Lord in the Manor Court, but by custom the Lord could not refuse to do so, provided all manorial dues had been paid. Sometimes a copyhold property was held 'in inheritance', which meant it passed on to the heir. Sometimes it was for life only, or often three lives (usually tenant, wife and heir), after which the Lord could renew on his own terms. Finally there was leasehold, the least secure of the tenures. At the end of the term of a leasehold the landlord was under no obligation to renew.

Fines

A feature of the system was the 'fine', not a punishment forfeit as we know it to-day, but a payment made by the tenant when the property changed hands; a 'particular fine' on the inheritance or sale of the tenancy, and a 'general' fine on all tenants on the death of the Lord. These fines were based upon the Ancient Rent, usually some simple multiple of it. Ancient Rent would have been fixed 'time out of mind'. The value of money had been falling since long before the seventeenth century, so that these fixed rents had became relatively very small. Since custom did not allow rents to be raised, landlords could only increase their returns by increasing the fines. The status of these fines was variable. Sometimes they were 'certain', that is there was documentary or other evidence of what multiple of the rent they should be; sometimes they were 'at the Lord's pleasure'; more often the matter remained open to argument. It is no wonder that disputes were frequent and recourse was had to Chancery or provincial courts. In 1966 R.G. Blackwood made a study of the situation in the north-west in the seventeenth century. He concluded that in these parts landowners '...seem to have stressed their rights over, while denying they owed any obligation towards, their tenants'.[1] More recently John Breay has documented in considerable detail such disputes in many of the northern dales.[2]

30 March

This Booke begunto be —, written for the use of kheeping a Court Leet & Court Barron —, within the Mannor or Lordshipp of Warton by the Sands in the Counly palatine of Lancaster.

Front paper of the
Warton Manor
Court Book

Boons and Heriots

There were many complications of the basic struggle. There was the matter of the 'heriot', the right of the Lord to claim the tenant's best beast from the heir. There were 'boons' owed to the Lord over and above the rent, either 'boon days' that had to be given to working on the Lord's private demesne, or 'boon gifts', chickens, eggs or such like, which the tenant had to give the Lord. He was generally obliged to use the Lord's mill, a matter dealt with more fully in Chapter 6. There were reciprocal rights which the Lord owed his tenants, such as the right to use timber and stone from manorial land. All these rights and duties could come into the dispute.

Rapid Change

Ancient Custom was not a concept well-adapted to deal with rapid change, and the sixteenth and seventeenth centuries were times of very rapid change in various ways; a continuing growth of population, monetary inflation and the beginnings of town growth and industrialisation to name but a few. New markets were opening up to feed the town population. Subsistence farming began to give place to specialised farming for the market. For these and other reasons land was more and more in demand. Landlords, who had once valued land as supplying prestige and men to fight in their train, now began to see it rather as a potential source of increased income. Some behaved oppressively in demanding higher and higher fines, sometimes forcing the tenant to give up his tenure. With land in such demand it was likely to be easy to find a new tenant prepared to take the tenancy on the terms demanded. Thus the landlords were hoping, not only for an immediate gain from increased fines, but also to push tenancies down from copyhold to leasehold, and from long leases to short. Tenants, on the other hand, would hope to establish their fines as 'certain' and their tenure as protected.

Tenant-right

In these northern parts 'tenant-right', a particular form of customary tenure, was a feature. It stretched from north Lancashire to the Scottish Border, an area where warfare with Scotland had persisted over a long period. Tenants were required to equip themselves with horse and armour for border service. The exact nature of tenant-right had never been clearly defined. Some held that it involved the descent of land to male heirs, though others held that the land was held during the Lord's will and pleasure only. The crown valued the military aspect and supported the tenants when threatened with eviction. In 1571 an Act of Parliament confirmed the status of tenant-right, set fines at six times the ancient rent and said that, beyond that, there were to be no charges. Arbitrary fines were declared detrimental to the state which depended upon these tenants for its defence.

Title page of the Custom of the Manor of Warton. Reproduced by permission of the Librarian, Lancaster Public Library.

James 1 and Tenant-Right

The Union of the Crowns removed the need for border service. James I reversed the previous crown policy by declaring that his tenants in the border country were merely tenants at will. He would be graciously pleased to re-grant them their land on new terms at double the old rent, though with the concession that fines, at double the improved rent, would be made 'certain'. When individual landowners followed the example of the crown there was angry opposition from tenants. Just over the border from Warton, in Westmorland, tenants in the Barony of Kendal put up a lively struggle. They met in the winter of 1621 in Stavely churchyard and, with the help of the Vicar of Kirkby Lonsdale who was present, drew up a remonstrance to be sent to King and Parliament. It was a radical document which spoke of an axe that had '...a sharp edge when it looked towards the poor tenants, cutting up the tree by the root, but when it looked toward the landlord was so blunt as it was not able to cut down the Boughs and the Branches...'[3]

A Lancashire schoolmaster, Jasper Garnett, wrote a play which was acted in Kendal castle. In the play there was a pit where ravens were supposed to be feeding on sheep. One of the characters says 'Ravens, quotha...no...its false landlords make all that croaking there, and those sheep we poore men, whose right these by their skill, would take awaie, and make us tenants at will, and when our ancient liberties are gone theile puke and poole, & peele us to the bare bone'.[4] The case dragged on into the next reign but the ultimate decision of the Star Chamber was in favour of the tenants whose estates were declared to be copyhold in inheritance and their fines 'certain'.

There was no necessary identity between manor and township, but it chances that, roughly speaking, the two coincided in Warton parish in the seventeenth century, except that Silverdale Manor had been divided into two 'moieties', or halves, at least from the sixteenth century. The Yealands had at one time come under three manors, Redmayne, Conyers and the once important manor of Yealand Storrs, but by the seventeenth century, when the Middletons of Leighton Hall were Lords of all three, their business was carried on as though they were one manor. Most land in the parish was held by customary tenure though, at least in Warton, there was a fair sprinkling of freeholders. There were 58 freeholders listed in a rental of Warton Manor in 1649.[5] The distinction is blurred, however, by the fact that 31 of the 58 also held copyhold land. The Township of Warton had at one time also had land held as 'burgage plots'. These were a survival from the days in the thirteenth century when Warton had been made a chartered borough and forty-four burgesses had been created and given burgage plots.[6] The borough did not flourish and its charter status lapsed.[7] Nevertheless at the beginning of the seventeenth century there were still 43 tenants listed as holding by 'Burgage Free rent'.[8] There is no evidence that any special status was bestowed by the tenure, and in the 1649 rental quoted above they are not mentioned separately. In 1572 it was specifically stated that Warton Manor had no farmers 'that did hold by Lease or Term of Years.'[9] No mention has been found of tenants holding directly from the Lord by leasehold in the other townships, though it does seem that some manor tenants were sub-letting their land in this way.

Warton Manor

Discord between landlord and tenant seems to have been particularly bitter in north-west Lancashire. Warton parish was no exception, and for Silverdale, Warton and Yealand Manors the struggles are fairly well documented. In the seventeenth century Warton Manor was unique in the parish in that the Lordship was held by the Crown. Warton's tenants were also the earliest to get written confirmation of their rights. Their struggle can be followed through the pages of an eighteenth century copy of the relevant documents, entitled 'The Custom of the Manor of Warton' and now held in Lancaster Reference Library.[9] In 1572 Queen Elizabeth's government had appointed a commission of five gentlemen from neighbouring parts to enquire and survey the Manor of Warton. They gathered twenty-four '...of the most ancient and Sage men inhabiting in...Lordships next adjoining to the said Manor of Warton'. These ancients took their oath '...that the Tennants of Warton and their Ancestors time out of mind had had, and then had an ancient Custom there called Tennant Right...'

The commissioners accepted that this confirmed inheritance to the next heir; a certainty of fine on the death of the tenant of two years rent; that every tenant paying a yearly rent of twenty shillings or more ought to keep a horse and armour '...to attend at all times when need is upon the Sea Coasts or otherwise...' and that those with lower rents should be ready to serve the Prince '...at Commandment...'. Further each tenant had to repair his property at his own cost, and owed suit of court to the Lord; must pay all fines assessed in the court and obey all lawful demands of the court. A widow had the custody of the heir until he or she reached the age of sixteen and then the heir '...be it man or woman to enter to the one half of the said Tenement...'; the other half to remain with the widow '...during her pure Widdowhood and if she commit fornication and otherwise miscarry contrary to the Custome of the said Mannor then she to forfeit her widdowright and the heirs to enter into the whole Tenement'. Heriots are not mentioned. The existence of this document proved enough to save Warton tenants from further disturbance, as in 1618 when the Attorney-General gave the opinion that the decree of Chancery had settled the question and the Lord Treasurer accepted this. Again in 1649, during the Commonwealth, a survey of 'the late King's possessions' was carried out and this confirmed that fines were certain at twice the rent.

Yealands

The Yealands were not so fortunate. Having no written custom, they were in a weak position in dealing with the Middletons of Leighton, who had been Lords of the Manor since the sixteenth century. J. Rawlinson Ford, a local historian who lived at Yeoland Manor before the war, collected and published the evidence of the battle that ensued.[10] In the Easter term, 1642, the tenants of the three Yeoland manors laid a complaint in the Duchy Court of Lancaster against George Middleton, the new Lord of the Manor, alleging that Thomas, his father, had levied a 'general' fine of seven years ancient rent, and very heavy 'particular' fines (i.e. on change of tenancy), namely 10, 16 and even 30 times the ancient rent. From some of the poorer tenants this meant he extorted the whole of their tenements. Thomas Middleton, the tenants further complained, had been demanding a fine from widows who inherited, which was against custom, he was also entering into the inheritance of an heir under age and taking the profits for himself, and when the heir came of age he would demand an unreasonable fine as if he had not enjoyed such profits. If the heir was a daughter he sometimes took and kept two thirds of the property. He had been refusing to admit an heir who had come of age to the property unless these unreasonable conditions had been met which, the tenants said, '...would quite overthrow the ancient customary estate of the inheritance'.[11]

Furthermore, said the tenants, he had enclosed with a wall certain common lands; stopped up rights of way to church and market; debarred them from the use of several wells and furthermore kept his park overcharged with red and fallow deer, and allowed these to eat his tenants' crops. Since the death of Thomas Middleton, his son George had demanded even higher general fines of 12 and 14 years ancient rent, being twice as much as his father had extorted. He was demanding a heriot of every tenant, though it was only widows who had to pay one. He continued to demand, as his father had, particular fines of 16, 20 and 30 years rent and terrified his tenants with threats of forfeiture if they refused to pay.[12]

In the same complaint to the Duchy Court the tenants expounded what they considered Ancient Custom to be. They claimed that they held their tenements by 'inheritance descendible', that is to say passing automatically to the heir as long as the customary rents and fines had been paid; that, although fines were arbitrary, they had only been at 2 to 4 times the rent and that anything more was 'very grievous because of the poverty of the country and the barrenness of the land'; they allowed that they paid every ten years a 'town tack' of double the annual rent; they claimed that a heriot should only be paid by widows and that, in return, she was allowed to enjoy her late husband's land without a fine.

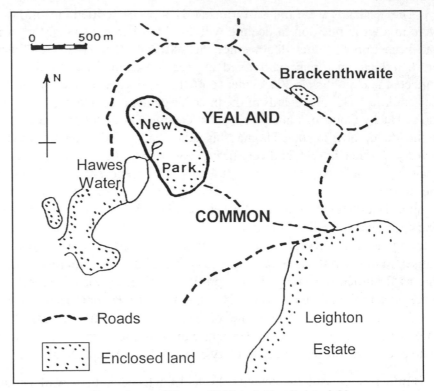

The enclosure of Thomas Middleton's New Park took 85
acres of commonland grazing from the Yealand tenants.

Sir George Middleton

In a bill of complaint to the Duchy Sir George Middleton put his side.
He said that, since the death of his father in 1640, many of his tenants in
Yealand, Silverdale and Lindeth were refusing to pay their fines at all. He
may have had a case. This was a time of civil war and tenants may well
have felt emboldened to resist what they saw as unjust claims by a landlord
who had espoused the losing side. Sir George however went much beyond
complaints of mere irregularities. He denied that tenants had any customary
rights and claimed that they were, in his own words, 'tenants at will without
any obliging Custome',[13] which meant that in his view the heir had no
automatic rights, and the Lord could admit him on any terms he chose to
impose. Sir George was not alone in this more modern view of land as the
absolute possession of the landlord for a number of others in north-west
Lancashire seem to have been moving in the same direction. Sir George,
moreover, wanted it both ways. If his view of land ownership was modern,
his view of what his tenants owed him was old fashioned, since he was also
demanding that his tenants pay him boon gifts and boon day service,
personal services which on the whole were being dropped from manor
tenancies by that date.

62

Arbitration of Five

The matter was referred to the arbitration of five Lancashire and Yorkshire gentlemen and in 1658 they made their decision.[14] The tenants had their claim to tenant-right confirmed, with admission of the heir being automatic and the right to sell the tenement. They were awarded fines certain, both for general and particular fines. But the level of these fines was fixed at 8 years ancient rent. They lost the argument about the heriot, for it was settled that all tenants, not just widows, must pay a heriot. Moreover they had to make a single payment of 22½ years rent within the next year and certain manorial duties were specified, including the obligation for tenants to do a day's ploughing and send two men to help with the shearing on the Lord's demesne. They were also bound to grind their corn at the Lord's mill. A rent roll, apparently from the next year, since it includes the 'Compasicion Fine' of 22½ years ancient rent, shows that after the agreement Sir George cleared £1,135-2s-9d from his tenants, of which only £34-19s-9d was from current rent, and the total did not include the extras from boon hens, boon capons and the value of boon day shearings and ploughing.[15]

The Middletons

The Middletons were not easy landlords, but in noticing their grasping attitude it is well to remember that, the one as a Catholic recusant and the other as a royalist 'malignant', both Thomas and George Middleton had to pay heavy fines to the state. Nevertheless the legal thinking behind the arbitration is not clear. If the tenants had been correct in saying they held by tenant-right, why did they have to pay such a heavy fine to the Lord of the Manor? It is true that Sir George may have felt he needed some compensation if some tenants had really, as he claimed, been withholding rent, but 22½ years rent from all tenants still seems out of proportion. It is interesting, that under the Commonwealth, a known 'malignant' was able to obtain his rights, and possibly rather more than his rights, through the legal system. Possibly there was more sympathy with him from the five gentlemanly arbitrators as a wronged landlord than disapproval of his politics.

Silverdale Manor

The Silverdale struggle was similar to the Yealand one, though less is known of the preliminary stages. In 1671 an 'Award' [16] was drawn up mediating between the two parties, namely the tenants of Silverdale (or rather that moiety of Silverdale Manor which had not been sold by the Crown to Lord Zouche in 1605) and Sir George Middleton, Lord of the Manor (the Middletons having acquired the Lordship some time between 1635 and 1654).[17] The Award was subsequently ratified in the Court of Chancery of the Duchy. The tenancies are referred to as 'Customary estates of Inheritance and Tenant right' and fines fixed at two years ancient rent 'forever hereafter'. Tenants were allowed a copy of their entry in the Manor Book, but they had to pay twelvepence for it. Widows, and widows only, owed a heriot (or money in lieu). In return for this the tenants had to make a single payment of 55 years ancient rent.

It is not easy to clothe these legal and financial details with any feel of the human aspect of living in these manors in the seventeenth century. Not everyone living in the townships would necessarily have been actively involved in the struggle, for it was of vital importance only to those who held their own land as direct tenants of the Lord of the Manor. An attempt is made later (see Chapter 12) to assess what proportion of those earning their living from the land were in this relatively fortunate position, and what proportion were farm labourers working on other men's land. Yet there must have been a lot of insecurity and sometimes real hardship as peasant farmers tried to hold on to their inherited lands and support themselves and their families. The arbitrators of the Silverdale Award expressed a wish that the parties should be 'Lovers and Friends as in Christianity they ought to be', but that was before the fine of 55 years annual rent had been mentioned.

Mills and Milling

When this book was being put together there was discussion about where the information on mills and milling should go. Did it belong with arable farming? Or with information about trades and crafts? In the end it was felt that the most logical place was after the discussion of the manorial system. Throughout the middle ages that system had given to milling a special and privileged place. In the days before easy transport each small community necessarily had its own mill, and by long standing custom ownership of the mill had come to belong to the Lord. They were 'soke mills', a soke meaning a right of local jurisdiction, or the area over which the special jurisdiction was exercised. Within the soke no other mill might be built, and the inhabitants could be compelled to bring their grain to that mill only. Even the use of hand mills at home was contrary to soke principles and if the owner of the soke chose to search them out and destroy them he would be supported in a court of law [1] (though two people at least in Warton parish had hand mills openly shown in their inventories). Naturally a soke mill was a profitable possession. Rather naturally, also, such a monopoly came to be viewed with suspicion by the tenants, and 'Ancient Custom' recognised that some control was needed. In principle at least it was accepted that, in return for the privileges of his mill the Lord was held bound to consider 'the convenience of the tenants'[2].

Throughout the whole of the Middle Ages a favourite expression of the practical piety of men of wealth was the bequest of a mill with all its rights to a religious house. Much of our knowledge of early milling comes from the careful ledger books of religious houses. The information is relevant to lay-held mills, since monastic mills like all other mills were generally maintained on the soke system.[3] At the time of the dissolution of the monasteries the monastic mills came to the crown. Such a 'King's Mill' would be retained as a valuable source of revenue for the royal coffers until it was found necessary to sell it to raise cash. In 1609 King James I, short of money as always, began selling off mills in a big way.[4] A mill-owner did not usually work the mill himself. He would either employ a miller or more likely lease the mill to a working miller who would then expect to recoup the rent by charging the tenants for grinding their corn, or on occasions over-charging them, knowing they could not go elsewhere. One can see why stories and sayings tended to depict millers in a poor light.

Mill Sites

The sites of four mills in Warton parish have been identified. Warton mill, Carnforth mill, Capernwray mill and Whitebeck mill. Nothing is known about the mechanics of these mills except that they were all water-mills. Windmills were being used at the time in the Fylde, but none are known around the Warton area. It is true that on the Warton tithe map of 1846 a 'Little Windmill Field' is marked, but nothing has been found of its history. The fact that the four water-mills were in the east of the parish is simply a reflection of the availability of water-power. There are no streams on the limestone areas, and even in the east of the parish the watercourses have very low gradients, offering no obvious sites where water-power can be readily exploited.

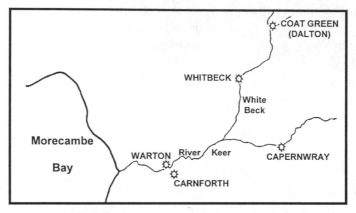

Sites of mills in Warton parish in the seventeenth century

Warton Mill

Warton mill was the only royal mill in the parish. There is a suggestion that it may have been one of those that came into lay hands at the Dissolution having formerly belonged to the monastery of Syon, but the evidence is not conclusive.[5] It may simply have belonged to the crown because it was part of the crown manor of Warton. It was disposed of by James I, along with so many other mills. Lucas says he had heard that the king gave it to one of his courtiers, who then sold it off, which sounds plausible.[6] The rental of Warton manor, 'late parcel of the possessions of Charles Steward late King of England' which was prepared for Parliament in 1649 only says that a Leonard Washington '...did purchase the rent of the said Milne which formerly was about £4 per annum of the King but...the rent hath not been paid these 20 years'.[7]

The mill continued to function and remained subject to the control of the Manor Court. In 1668 a certain Christopher Charnley was found to have converted the mill into a cottage. An order was made by the Manor Court 'that he remove his wife, children, and goods from thence...upon paine of offending therein Five pounds'.[8] In the same year there had been 'severall sad, and grievous complaints' against Charnley for taking excessive toll. It was therefore ordered that in future the miller was only to take one peck of grain in every twenty from Warton tenants. Presumably he could charge more to outsiders. According to Lucas the general going rate at the beginning of the eighteenth Century was one sixteenth part.[9]

Warton mill was still there in the eighteenth century, for it was marked on Yate's 1786 map of the County Palatine, where it is shown lying on the Warton side of the River Keer, very close to the road (still known as Mill Lane) that runs from Warton down to the Keer Bridge. The exact site of the mill is not known, but it is very likely that it was built very close to the road for ease of access. The Keer provides a strong flow, but the gradient on its lower reaches is only about one in four hundred. As there is no preferential position to site a weir to take water from the river it would have been sensible to place the mill where it was most convenient of access and then tailor the mill-race to fit in. The position of the weir, given by field-names such as 'miln dam meadow' on the tithe map of 1846, was just below the confluence of the Keer and the White Beck (or in modern terms 1½ Kilometres north of Junction 35 on the M6). The great length of the mill-race is confirmed by Lucas who says that the water was 'brought down the Meadows to the Mill in a Chanel above half a mile in length...'.[10] No doubt the exact position of this large watercourse (in which Lucas nearly drowned when he was a boy) could be found with further research. As it passed through the meadows north of the Keer it would collect additional water from the streams that originate in such springs as the Wheelhole and Senset Well in the south of Warton township.

Carnforth Mill

Much less is known of Carnforth mill, though its position is fairly accurately given by Lucas. It lay one hundred yards east of a house at the Carnforth end of the bridge over the Keer below Millhead. He is sure of the position of the house because it was the one *in quâ vitales auras primum hausi,* in which he drew his first breath.[11] Lucas also makes it clear that it was not powered by water from the Keer. It drew its water from three small springs on the north edge of Carnforth. They were inadequate it seems for, at the end of the seventeenth century, the miller, one Thomas Ward, made two attempts to improve the water supply. He thought first of an aqueduct over the Keer to bring the water from the Carlepot, a very profluent spring in Warton. His second idea was to draw a 'goit', a water-course, from the Keer above his mill. That project too failed [12], perhaps because the weir constructed for Warton mill left a much impoverished flow in the lower reaches of the Keer. Carnforth mill may also at some time have tried to obtain water from the Nether Beck, since that stream is diverted westwards along a deep ditch some 900 metres east of the probable mill-site. Despite these difficulties in finding an adequate source of water the supply must have been considered good enough to make the mill a viable business proposition. At any rate Mr James Lucas, cousin of the historian, thought it worth while to buy the Carnforth mill as well as the Warton one sometime at the beginning of the eighteenth century.[13]

An example of what is thought to be a contemporary mill mechanism taken from a 17th Century English Edition of Viruvius treatise on mill construction.

Yealand mill

The Whitbeck mill in Priest Hutton was bought by the Middletons in 1605 from the Bindlosses for the considerable sum of £80 down plus £3 annually.[14] All Yealand tenants had to use it, as confirmed by their legal agreement with Sir George Middleton in 1658. They did however manage to get it written into the agreement that they only needed to use his Whitebeck mill while the miller remained honest. If not, or if he did not serve them in 'due time', they could go to other mills 'till the Lord have reformed what is amisse, & then to return againe'.[15] The mill at Whitbeck became a flourishing affair. The Middletons and their successors diversified into malting, no very surprising development in view of the malting trade developing in near-by Carnforth. Already in 1676 it was being described as 'Whitbecke milne and Kilne'[16] By the early eighteenth century it had become a 'water corn mill, kiln, malt kiln, malt house and malting'.[17] White Beck Mill was still there in 1759 when it was the subject of a petition to the Lord Keeper of the Great Seal.[18]

As its name implies the mill is on the White Beck, a tributary of the Keer. Though the Beck has a reasonable gradient (1 in 80 overall) the volume of water is small and the mill required a pond about 70 metres long. Whitebeck Mill and its pond are shown on a plan, a photocopy of which is held in the archives of the Mourholme Society. Although the source of this plan is not known it was probably made for the Lancaster Canal Company in about 1791-2, when details of the canal's route were being worked out. It was possible to carry the canal 40 miles northward from Preston to Tewitfield on a course so level that not a single lock was required. At Tewitfield construction came to a halt for some twenty years while money was found to complete the more expensive extension to Kendal, which required locks. In the meantime the canal needed a feeder, to keep its water topped up, and the White Beck was seen as ideal for this purpose. Taking over the water-supply would have meant that the mill's working life would come to an end, and the canal company had to buy the mill out before constructing a short length of feeder channel to divert the stream into the canal.[19]

Borwick Mill

Of the history of the mills used by the other three townships almost nothing is known. Sir Robert Bindloss of Borwick Hall, Lord of the Manor of both Borwick and Priest Hutton in the seventeenth century, is said to have owned 24 mills. [20] They were not necessarily in the neighbourhood, for he was a rich man with extensive property, nor does it necessarily mean that he owned that number of mill buildings. A mill was essentially the two grindstones, so there might be two or more 'mills' in one building. One mill at least must have been in Borwick. When a Thomas Chorley, miller of Warton, made his will in 1698 he made Thomas Chorley, miller of Borwick, an executor. Lucas mentions this mill, and also another at Capernwray.[21]

The latter still survives as a dwelling house below the aqueduct which takes the canal over the river Keer, but nothing seems known of its history before the canal was built in 1792. Then the millrace from a weir on the river Keer had to be taken by pipe through the aqueduct. This was not benevolence on the part of the canal company. Had the mill's water supply been cut off the company would have faced a large bill for compensation. An earlier mill-race, higher up the valleyside and over a kilometre in length, is recorded on the old Ordnance Survey sheets of the area, but most of this has now been obliterated on the ground. The eastern end of this race is at Keer Bridge, Capernwray, but it is not known when it fell out of use. It is yet another detail that would repay further research. Capernwray Mill survived as a corn mill till about 1913, and then continued for a few more years as a saw mill.[22]

Heron Corn mill 1740's

Silverdale Mill

Little can be found of any mill for the use of Silverdale tenants. A water-mill within the township itself would hardly have been a practical proposition since there is no suitable water supply to turn it. At the beginning of the eighteenth century a list of strict 'charges', that is instructions, to the Manor Court jury was drawn up by the steward.[23] It lists thirteen things the tenants are, or more usually are not, to do. After the twelfth charge there is a heading, 'Lord's mill'. Nothing follows. Heron Corn Mill, at Beetham, is not only in a different township and parish, but in a different county. It would also have been difficult to reach from Silverdale. There is one source of water power, within reasonable reach of Silverdale, though just over the boundary into Yealand Redmayne; the Leighton Beck, where later the Leighton Iron Furnace was sited,[24] but no evidence has been found to support this piece of pure speculation. There is another possibility. Silverdale may have had a windmill. In the sixteenth century a certain Thomas Kitson is said to have died holding 'sixteen messuages and half a windmill' in Silverdale.[25]

By the beginning of the eighteenth century the privileges of the soke mill were being eaten into. The custom had been growing of buying ready-ground meal or flour. Millers took on the new trade and became 'Merchant Millers'. Large batches of corn were ground in fewer mills, and the less profitable mills fell out of use.[26]

Where to live and what to wear

A number of later seventeenth century houses have survived in the seven villages of old Warton parish, but almost all earlier houses have vanished. This is a common finding throughout England; everywhere the backward sequence of surviving houses tends to come to a sudden stop. Earlier buildings are simply not found, apart from a few chance survivals. Around this point there must have been a quite rapid replacement of older houses. W.G. Hoskins coined the phrase 'The Great Rebuilding' to describe this change from the now vanished medieval style of domestic house to a newer style which has proved capable, in many cases, of remaining in functional use to-day.[1] In southern England the change came from the mid-sixteenth century on, particularly in the years between 1570 and 1640. In the north of England the change came later; for Westmorland and Cumberland perhaps as late as the end of the seventeenth century.[2]

Datestones

For houses in South Lonsdale there is the evidence of 'datestones'. In Warton parish, as elsewhere in Lonsdale, it was a pleasing custom to adorn a house with an engraved stone, often over the doorway, which bore the date, along with the initials of the original occupier and his wife. The detailed work of Emmeline Garnett on these datestones shows that '...the most vigorous activity recorded by extant datestones was in the years 1670-1700'.[3] Miss Garnett has recorded 21 authenticated stones dating from before 1700 in the townships of Warton parish. Two date from before 1600, neither on ordinary domestic houses, one being on the Hall at Borwick, and one on Archbishop Hutton's School in Warton village. (The latter stone has moved with the school and is now kept in the modern school building in Back Lane though, from lack of funds, it has not been possible, at the time of writing, to put it on display.) Among the nineteen stones from the seventeenth century there are ten dating from before 1670 and nine after. Whether this excess of early stones means re-building really was relatively early in Warton parish, or is simply the result of chance vagaries of survival is impossible to say with so small a sample.

A co-ordinated study of houses in the area would undoubtedly reveal more surviving seventeenth century houses. The Lancashire County Council, as part of its duties under the 1971 Town and Country Planning Act, brought out a booklet on the Warton Conservation Area.[4] It lists houses built in the seventeenth century in Warton, but does not cover the other townships. The booklet does not go into architectural detail. Nor has there been any co-ordinated study of barns and other agricultural outbuildings. If such buildings are not mentioned in this book it is not because their importance in an agricultural community has been overlooked, it is simply because information on them has not been found.

A co-ordinated study of buildings throughout Warton Old Parish would help us to discover more about the living conditions of our forbears. Such a study however remains to be done, and until it is we shall have to be content with what can be deduced from general observation, from documentary sources, and from the work done on comparable houses elsewhere. Of particular relevance is the work of R.W.Brunskill of Manchester University on vernacular architecture, for almost all the housing in Warton parish would have been of the type Brunskill has defined as 'vernacular', a type he opposes to the 'polite' architecture of the bigger houses of the gentry.[5]

Houses in the vernacular style would be built by a local craftsman, whether himself the owner or not. He would be guided by a series of conventions which had grown up locally. He would use local materials, and give functional considerations dominance over the aesthetic (which is not to say that the result was not often aesthetically pleasing). Such a building would reflect both local resources and local traditions. Only two houses in Warton parish in the seventeenth century stood outside this vernacular tradition and could be categorised as, at least partly, of the 'polite' type of architecture; Leighton Hall and Borwick Hall. (There was also the Old Rectory in Warton township, a fourteenth century manor, which must have been a 'Big House' in its day, but by the seventeenth century it was already a ruin, though part of it was still habitable.)[6]

Big Houses

Borwick Hall, which still survives, had been built in the 1590s by the Bindloss family, rich wool traders from Kendal. It was a stone built house of some architectural pretensions. It is still recognisably itself to-day, though it had almost fallen into ruin by the beginning of this century, before Fuller-Maitland, music critic of *The Times*, restored it.[7] Leighton Hall, in Yealand Conyers, was the home of a catholic gentry family, the Middletons, who feature largely in the history of Warton parish. The present house is the product of the eighteenth and nineteenth centuries.[8] In 1697 Celia Fiennes described it as 'an old timber house',[9] but she only saw it from a distance as she rode through the park. Lucas, who must have known it better, says 'The House, which is an old one...is much like the

The Old Rectory, Warton, with
Warton Parish Church in the background.

Houses in Paris, which...are all of Stone, Walls, Staircases, Floors and all...'.[10] The difference would be resolved if Celia Fiennes was talking of the earlier house and Lucas of the re-built eighteenth century house, except that Lucas specifically says that the house he is describing is 'an old one'.

The Cruck Frame

What can be discovered about the housing of more ordinary people in the seventeenth century? In particular what can be found about the older dwellings that were replaced in the Great Rebuilding? None have survived, except perhaps as a hidden framework under a newer shell. The invaluable Lucas tells us something. When he was writing his *History of Warton Parish* at the beginning of the eighteenth century, he described the houses there as '...all of Stone, strongly laid in, and well roughcast with good lime, which makes a substantial, warm and not unhandsome building'.[11] Further on, however, he adds that at Hazlehead in the south of the township of Warton 'Several humble Cottages are to this day inclosed with Walls of Hazle wattlings dawbed with a coarse Morter made of Loam and Straw; and the Partition Walls in many better sort of Houses are of the same material...'.[12]

Wattle and daub, that is woven withies daubed with clay, dung, horsehair etc, were a universally available and cheap way to infill the spaces between the weight-bearing timbers of a frame constructed house. The frame carried the weight of the roof and upper stories and redistributed it to the foundations. Cheaper non weight-bearing materials could then be used to clad the frame. Wattle and daub was an entirely adequate material to use. Indeed, wattle and daub continued to be used for internal walls as Lucas said, and as many a house-owner in the parish to-day can testify.

The frame, in the north-west, was usually the 'cruck'. In this design the roof load is carried to the ground by inclined timbers. According to Brunskill these 'A-frames' would have been assembled on the ground and then each reared into the vertical and tied together by roof and side purlins. The simplest building thus produced consisted of a central ground floor multi-purpose room open up to the roof timbers. Sophistication could be added either by flooring over the ground floor room to make an upstairs chamber, or by building out extensions between the crucks.

Chimneys

Lucas describes just such simple houses in Carnforth which were still standing when he wrote in the early eighteenth century. 'Some of them are unlofted open to the Roof, and One..is yet without a Chimney, the Smoak being left...to find its Way out at a little slooping Hole on each Side of the Roof'.[13] In that house the hearth was against the wall, but in the same passage he describes a house he had seen when young in Over Kellet, a nearby village. There the fire had been made 'according to the most ancient Custom, on a hearth; against a little Wall about 1 Yard high and 1½ long, in the middle of the room'.

Wattle

73

Once, such chimneyless houses had been the norm. In the 1580s William Harrison could write, in his *'Description of England'*, that among the things most astonishing to the old men of his time was 'the multitude of chimneys lately erected whereas in their young days there were not above two or three, if so many, in most uplandish towns of the realm...'[14] In the north country most houses were likely to have remained as chimneyless as the two that Lucas describes until well into the seventeenth century. Chimney design developed gradually. At first it might be no more than a projection from the gable wall to keep smoke and heat from the thatch.[15] There is an example of an early type of chimney, a mere projection from the gable end, still to be seen in Yealand Redmayne at 23 Silverdale Road. The refinement of a pot atop the chimney did not, on the whole, come till the eighteenth century.

Houses of this type could be extended by adding further supporting cruck arches. There is a survey from the 1580s of the houses in the town of Hornby further up the Lune valley. It lists the number of 'bays', that is spaces between two crucks, for each house. The largest had fifteen bays, a number had only one. The commonest size was four bays. Almost all the houses, even those with only one bay, were extended by 'outsetts', or extensions.[16] No comparably detailed survey has been found for any of the townships of Warton parish, though there is a survey, made in 1609 for King James I, of his crown manor of Warton in which brief mention is made of some disputed properties. Amongst these were two dwelling houses, one of five bays and one of four, and seven cottages each of two bays.[17]

Roofing

To-day houses in the area are all slated, flagged or tiled. In the seventeenth century thatch would have been the usual roofing, even for the later stone-built houses. Lucas, speaking of Carnforth, says that 'The Houses in this Town (two or three excepted) are...even Gentlemen's houses not excepted, covered with straw Thatch...'.[18] His only other comment on roofing is to say that the 'poorest sort' of people thatched their houses with bracken.[19] He makes no mention of roofing in any other township, but then he is pleasantly far from being a systematic writer. Thatch was universally available at no great cost. In the near-by village of Clawthorpe thatch was being used even within living memory.[20] Other roofing materials, slate, stone and tiles, were becoming available, but their use was limited because of the difficulty and cost of transporting such heavy materials. Right at the end of the century, in 1697, there is one possible mention of slate, or at any rate of slate-like material. John Cumming of Hilderstone, in Yealand Redmayne had among his inventoried goods 'Slate Flagg and Bees'. The whole item only came to to £1-5s, which seems small for roofing a house. It is possible he used the slate flag to make a bee-bole to shelter his bees.

17th century stool

The Interior

It is not easy to find out about the internal arrangement of the houses, either old or new. Some were certainly extremely primitive. One that was built against the north wall of Warton Old Rectory survived long enough to be described in 1976. 'It consisted of one living-room from which a ladder led up to a wooden platform covering part of the ground floor to make a half-loft for sleeping accommodation'.[21] The cottage was never accurately dated, and indeed such simple houses are difficult to date closely. It was apparently considered to be 'modern' and demolished when the Old Rectory came under the care of the Ministry of Works.[22] Fortunately a plan and elevation of the Rectory, made in 1973, exists.[23] It shows a cottage against the rectory in the correct position though it looks rather more elaborate than the one described. The cruck arch which supported the roof was preserved and can still be seen in the rectory grounds. Whatever the actual date of the building it probably would have given a fair idea of the simple cruck buildings of the early seventeenth century, and it is a pity that it was demolished without record.

That some houses were more elaborate can be deduced from surviving probate inventories[24] which sometimes mention the room in which the inventoried goods lay. Unfortunately, even more often, both will and inventory are silent on the subject, so that no general conclusions can be drawn. All one can note is the difference between the first and the second half of the century for the 49 inventories in which rooms are mentioned (25 before 1649 and 24 after). In the first half of the century almost all the rooms mentioned are described merely by their position in the building, usually in relation to what was called the 'bodystead' of the house (or sometimes the 'firehouse', or simply the 'house'), that is to say the main room. The house itself might be distinguished into 'upper' or 'lower' (which probably meant inner or outer, rather than above and below). More definitely indicative of more than one floor were phrases like 'the little chamber beneath' or 'chamber over the house'. Cellars and lofts get a few mentions. Only four rooms are defined by function, two butteries, a word at that time implying a store room, one parlour and one bower. Parlour and bower were functional descriptions in that, unlike the all purpose word 'chamber' they came to imply an inner living-room offering more

A view of the Old Rectory, Warton,
showing the cottage that used to stand at the north end.

75

privacy than the main hall. Parlour seems to have been the usual word in Warton parish, bower was the common word for the same type of room in the Lake District.[25]

In the second half of the century rooms are still defined by their position, but rooms designed for a particular function appear more frequently; not only butteries, but kitchens, a milk house, parlours, a bed chamber, a bed parlour and a wash house. Fifteen such specialised rooms are mentioned. (The rooms in Leighton Hall described in Sir George Middleton's inventory in 1672 have not been included as they would skew the comparison. The Middletons had so many rooms they had to be defined by who slept in them, or the colour of the decoration, as well as by function; a dining room, a nursery, a kitchen, Mr Blackburn's chamber, the Red room, a dairy, a brew house, a bake house and more besides.)

This increase in the number of rooms designed for a particular purpose was common to the whole country. It began in the fourteenth century in Great Houses and spread down through the social scale. By the sixteenth century, in the south country, it was common in the houses of even the moderately well-to-do, but was slower to reach the north country. In Cheshire farmers are said to have kept to the fire in the centre of the 'house' till the early seventeenth century, and of Lancashire it has been said that '...observers of the past and present have commented on the extreme simplicity of building methods and living standards'.[26]

Furniture

A study of the surviving wills and inventories suggests that most of the houses were furnished very simply; something to sleep in, something to sit on, something to cook with and something to store goods in. Even in the second half of the century life seems to have been scarcely less basic.

Beds of some sort feature in inventories throughout the century. Bedstocks or bedsteads, both meaning the frame of a bed, are most frequently mentioned, but trundle beds are also a feature. These were low beds which were stored during the day under a higher bed, or 'stand bed', and brought out at night. Only six cradles are mentioned, so one can assume that babies slept with their parents. On the bedstocks went the 'bed', feather beds being plainly superior to chaff beds.

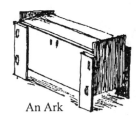
An Ark

It is difficult to judge how basic these bedsteads were, but almost certainly many of them were four-poster. So natural was it thought that a bed should have curtains that when George Fox had a travelling bed made it was furnished with posts as can be seen at Swarthmoor Hall. Four-poster beds with curtains were most desirable, not only to exclude draughts, but to allow privacy in houses which still had very limited numbers of individual rooms. The inventory of John Backhouse of Yealand (1690) mentions a tester, or canopy, which implies it was a four-poster. One of his other beds had curtains listed among its furnishings. He was described as yeoman, and was fairly well-to-do, nevertheless, despite the four-poster bed, the family had only chaff beds, no feathers. In 1684 Thomas Robinson of Priest Hutton left '...unto my sonne Lanslett one bed standinge in the Chamber with Curtaines rodes & Compleat bedinge now belonginge the same: with...one little chist wherein my writings Lyeth & one little box with all the bookes in it with one table and a forme...'. The curtained bed must have conveniently allowed the use of the room as a writing room in the day.

Tables and tableware

Tables feature in only 21 per cent of inventories in the first half of the century, the figure rising to 60 per cent in the second half. One might reasonably assume that, instead of tables, many people used a simple board supported on stools, or still better on trestles, the 'trests' which appear in a number of inventories. John Cockeram of Borwick's inventory in 1611, listed a 'frame for a table...in the parler'. Such tables could be conveniently put aside to make space. For keeping table-ware on, people had shelves, even 'a table with shilves', and 'dishboards' or dressers.

The settings to go on the table were mainly pewter or wood. Ordinary spoons, presumably of wood or horn, hardly get mentioned, but silver spoons do, usually only one or two in a household. Agnes Hadwen of Carnforth left two pairs of silver forks in 1620, the only mention of forks in all the inventories. The dining tables, even if only rough boards on trestles, could also be made elegant with table cloths and table napkins, though the use of these was restricted. Out of 157 inventories only 15 list table cloths or table linen, and only 11 list napkins. Not that napkins were necessarily for use at table. At that date the word was used for any small hand towel. It should perhaps be noted that the word 'towel' occurs in only four inventories. Of course bathing was not a regular part of life. Only Sir George Middleton of Leighton Hall is known to have had a bathing tub, but still people must have washed hands and faces at least. It was perhaps unusual to have a named piece of cloth for drying oneself.

Chairs

Chairs, stools and forms occur in most inventories. The impression is that they were functional in design with mere support in view, rather than comfort. Only very occasionally is something less basic described, as a 'long settle form' and 'an old man's chair'. The latter was Francis Jackson's in 1670, but he was the vicar and also had a desk and a dressing-table and a 'chamber over the house' to put them all in. George Hodgson of Yealand Conyers also had a desk in his 'little chamber' in 1699. One wonders if it was the same one.

What people did have, to increase their comfort were plenty of soft furnishings, particularly bedding - sheets, coverlets, blankets, bolsters and pillows with 'pillow beares', or as we would say pillow-slips, to cover them.

Around the house there were cushions, which are listed in a third of the inventories, usually as 'quishons' or some similar spelling. Curtains are mentioned less often and it seems usually, from the context, to have implied curtains for a bed.

Chests and cupboards

Of all pieces of furniture chests are the most frequently mentioned, being listed in 85 per cent of the inventories. There is very little to indicate how plain or elaborate they were. Arks, mentioned in 47 per cent of the inventories, were bins for storing flour or meal, made of split planks wedged together and pegged, but able to be taken apart for cleaning. Barrels, tubs, knops (a north country word for a tub), coffers, trunks and boxes were also used for storing. Almeryes (variously spelt) and cupboards occur in only 15 per cent of the inventories. Almeryes were a type of cupboard, often with a pierced door, in which to keep food. Thomas Greenwood of Warton had a 'Cat mallison', a cupboard to keep cheese and meat in (maleson was a curse, which is presumably what the cat said when it couldn't get in). On the whole though it seems that people still tended to keep their goods in containers with lids like chests, rather than in containers with doors like cupboards. A chest of drawers would have been known at the time, but they were not common. There is no mention of one in the inventories.

Kitchen-ware

Salt cupboard by the hearth at 5 Silverdale Road, Yealand (illustration by kind permission of Mr and Mrs Jury)

Cooking was done over a peat or wood fire using iron utensils. Very often all the pots and pans are listed together in the inventories as 'iron geare', or 'iron stuffe in the house', but we also find spits and griddles, cauldrons, skillets, frying pans, and dripping pans (placed beneath roasting meat to catch the dripping). Cauldrons were suspended on adjustable hangers called rackencrooks. In nearly half the inventories a 'brandreth' appears. This was a three legged iron stool on which a pot could be set over or beside the fire. Ovens are not mentioned, but since they would have been built into the hearth they were hardly a chattel to be listed in the inventories. They may in any case have been less important in this part of the world where oat-cakes largely took the place of bread. For making those the skillets would have been more suitable.

Luxuries

There are a few indications of little luxuries among people's possessions, but very few. Two people had a clock (one of them admittedly Sir George Middleton). Watches begin to be mentioned in the second half of the century. Silver objects are mentioned in 12 per cent of the inventories, often no more than a silver spoon, but sometimes a substantial platter or bowl. Though what Margaret Hadwen of Carnforth, who died in 1632, did with a 'piece of silver called a silly penny' is more difficult to guess.

'Silly' could have been a form of the older word 'seely', meaning something blessed or fortunate, in which case the silly penny would have been merely a silver coin kept because it was felt to be lucky. It is to be presumed that men smoked, though the only evidence is the mention of a tobacco box in two inventories. One of these belonged to Francis Jackson the vicar; amongst his silver was 'a tankard, tumbler, two spoons and a tobacco box'. One rather sees him settling down comfortably in his 'old man's chair' in 'the chamber over the house', to his drink and his pipe.

The only surviving inventory showing anything really approaching luxurious living was that of Sir George Middleton (the will of Sir Robert Bindloss, an even richer gentleman, has not been traced). Sir George had possessions like pictures worth £9, curtains on a rod at his windows, a 'glass with a frame', a map *and* the bathing tub. He also had carpets, though the wording of the inventory implies that the carpets were not on the floor, but on tables as one sees them depicted by painters of the time. Altogether the contents of twenty-one rooms are listed (probably many of them heated since he paid hearth-tax on twenty-four hearths).

Amenities

That however was the house of a great gentleman. The houses in the townships, even the better ones, would have been very lacking in comfort by modern standards. The downstairs floors would mostly have been of beaten earth, though perhaps a parlour floor might be boarded over.[27] If even Middleton did not put his carpets on the floor they would have been an unlikely find in any smaller house. Rushes were a cheaper and renewable form of matting. Houses were likely to be very cold in winter. It was not without reason that the main room in the house was called the 'firehouse', for the hearth tax returns for the 1660s[28] show that the majority of houses had only one hearth. Smaller chambers, if any, would have had no heating except perhaps a charcoal brazier. Draughts must have been everywhere, particularly where the 'bodystead' of the house, the room with the fire, was still open to the roof timbers. Even if it was lofted it might be only with removable planks.[29] Boards and loose wood 'about the house' often feature in the inventories. They doubtless had many uses, but the inventory of William Sander of Borwick in 1676 specifies 'loose bords & Guist for lofftin with all'.

A 17th century hearth

Dunghills

One scarcely needs to mention the lack of running water or sanitation. Dunghills would serve as the depository for human excrement as well as animal dung. Large and permanent hills lined the streets, and presumably bred clouds of flies each summer. In 1699 Elizabeth Burrow had a dung hill '...at the uper end of the weend [Crag Road]'. It stood before her barn and was '...3 yards in Breadth and 4 in Length'.[30] John Dawson, a gentleman of

Warton, bought a '...Dung hillstead at the street side Lyinge under the Garden wall.' it was still there 25 years later.[31] It seems, however, that even our ancestors' noses could be tried beyond endurance. Certain tenants were admonished to '...keepe open theire Pooles, and pittes, adioyninge to the highway w[hi]ch is very noysome, and vnsavory to all passengers...'.[32]

Public Buildings

So far only domestic buildings have been described. As in any village there were others. Mills, the school house, dissenting meeting houses and the church are described each in their appropriate place. There was also a cock-pit sited, as is said to have been customary, between church and school, the two institutions which provided the most constant patrons. A circular ring of earth still identifies the site on the south side of Crag Road.

Then there were the inns. Lucas, rather surprisingly, does not mention any of them. They certainly existed, though many of them were probably no more than ale-houses set up in someone's dwelling house. Ale house keepers had to be licensed by the Quarter Sessions, and the Justices of the Peace tended to think of a license to sell ale as a cheap way of supporting a poor woman who might otherwise have come on the rates. Such women would be likely to be too poor to bother to make wills, but Alice Godsalve of Borwick might

The Red Lion Inn, Warton.
Now known as Windsor House

be an example of one who did. When she died in 1607 her inventory shows that she had three pigs, some poultry, her clothes and some scanty household gear. She did have, however, 'ale pottes' and chairs, stooles, quishions and an ale bench'. There was at least one inn in Warton township early in the century that was big enough to house a meeting of the Manor Court.[33] It was said to be sited near the school house. No name is given, but it may well have been the Shovel, or a predecessor on the site, for it is known that the Shovel was used at a later date for Manor Court meetings. Indeed the very last Manor Court met there in 1902.

When a survey was made in the reign of James II of possible stabling and accommodation for military personnel Warton was written down as having 17 'guest beds' and 12 'stabling places', Carnforth as having four of each, Borwick three guest beds and five stabling places and Silverdale as having two of each.[34] The provision was not large (Lancaster at the time had 308 guest beds and Kendal 279), but it does suggest that a substantial number of people were using Warton as a through route, very possibly after crossing the sands from Furness.

Clothing

Dress, in the seventeenth century, was not a mere matter of personal choice. What one wore depended much more than to-day on who one was. At the end of the twentieth century anyone can wear what pleases them within the limits of what they can afford. In the seventeenth century there was, in addition, another type of restriction. Social inferiors, it was strongly held, should not ape the dress of their betters. By the seventeenth century the 'sumptuary laws', restricting dress were falling into disuse, but the underlying thought, that of clothing 'suitable' to a person's rank, persisted.

Economic necessity, however, probably did more to ensure moderation in dress than sumptuary laws which had always been difficult to enforce anyway. Clothes were not cheap. In the inventories the deceased's 'apparel' formed a very real part of their assets. As might be expected the cost of the apparel tended to vary with the wealth of the deceased, though not as widely as the wealth itself. The apparel of Sir George Middleton of Leighton Hall was valued at £50, that is some 5½ per cent of his total inventoried assets of £870. When Elizabeth Drinkall of Borwick died in 1638 her apparel was valued at only eight shillings, but this was still about 15 per cent of her total assets of two pounds and twelve shillings.

Dress in Borwick

It is difficult to know how typical these findings are. Apparel was too frequently costed along with other items for it to be possible to reach any very exact knowledge of how much it cost. As a rough check seventeen surviving inventories for the township of Borwick made between 1600 and 1649 were studied. Fifteen give the value of the deceased's apparel. The average value of apparel as a percentage of the value of all inventoried items for the same individual was 8.9 per cent. In the inventories of the five richest people it was 3.6 per cent. For the five poorest it was 17.9 per cent. There are many reasons why not much emphasis should be placed on these findings. For one thing one suspects that those with the smallest estates may have been the elderly who had already given away much of what they once possessed except, naturally, the clothes they wore.

The figures do suggest, though, that clothes were relatively expensive. It is not surprising that they were considered worth handing on in wills to friends and relations as well as servants. A man or woman's clothing would be itemised and bits left to different legatees. William Williamson of Borwick, when he died in 1600 left his blue jacket and brown jerkin to his son, his buckskin breeches to one William Bower, a pair of black breeches to William Thornton, his leather doublet with the brass buttons to Leonard Graveson and to Richard Bacchus his working-day leather doublet, a grey jacket and even 'the pair of leggstalls that are on my leggs'. In 1614 Robert Ingleton of Warton left to his wife 'One pair of breeches to make her an upperbody of'. In 1632 John Banks of Silverdale left his breeches, jerkin, hat, shoes and petticoat to his brother (a petticoat at that date, as part of a man's attire, was a 'petty', or short, coat). In 1633 Thomas Turner of Priest Hutton left his 'flaxen apparel' to his son-in-law, while to his son he left 'coloured carsey to be for him a suit of apparel'. It was, it seems, to be a hard-wearing suit. Carsey (or Kersey) was a coarse woollen cloth, usually ribbed.

Men's clothes

These garments form what had come to be the standard dress of men of the period, namely a 'suit of clothes'. It consisted of breeches (usually knee length and of varying fullness), a jacket (the medieval tunic had gone out of fashion and the smock for farm work had not come in) and a new garment, worn over the shirt and under the jacket, the waistcoat.[35] Terminology might vary a little. A rougher type of jacket might be called a jerkin and a waistcoat might be termed a vest or a doublet (though this latter was essentially a padded garment which might, for warmth, be worn over the waistcoat). There were stockings to cover the legs below the breeches (a separate stocking for each leg had replaced the earlier joined 'hose').

Women's Clothes

Women's clothes mentioned in the wills and inventories include coats, petticoats, aprons, waistcoats, smocks, cloaks, hats, gowns and 'bodies'. Also girdles and 'sleeves' (which were at times a separate item of dress, not attached to jacket or bodice) and one mention of a 'safeguard' (a wrap around skirt worn, as when riding, to protect ladies' clothing from mud and dust). Women's clothes also were long-lasting enough to be bequeathed at death. In 1600 Ann Turner of Priest Hutton left to Thomas Turner's wife a red kirtle and chamlet overbody. However in 1603 Jenet Addison preferred to leave to her daughter ten shillings towards buying a new gown. Again all these named articles of clothing add up to the standard dress for women; a skirt (often called the petticoat), a bodice or 'body' (the earlier one piece 'gown' had given place to this two piece form) and an 'overbodice' the equivalent of a jacket. The skirt was worn over a shorter underskirt, and could be kilted up over it for ease of movement. Under the bodice and skirt came a full-sleeved chemise, smock, or shift.[36] An apron was a constant part of women's dress, worn by all ranks, not just a working protection as it was for men.

Fabrics

Yet though the range of garments was common to all ranks, the finished appearance would naturally vary enormously according to the material used, and the money put into shaping and ornamenting, as can be seen in the illustrations in these chapters. The materials mentioned in Warton inventories mostly sound fairly work-a-day; serge, flannel, linen, canvas, fustian (a coarse cloth, later of wool and cotton mixed, but at this date more probably of wool and flax), karsey or cersey, and harden, a tough hempen

Country man or artisan 1670

cloth. Such materials would have been suitable for working dress (though laundering must have presented a problem). There are mentions of somewhat finer cloth, chamlet the fine wool already described, muslin (technically a fine cotton, a possibility at this period, but there was also a light wool cloth that went by this name), say (a fine textured serge) and even silk, though only in the form of a 'silk girdle' and a 'silk hat'.

Etceteras

Of course these were only the basics of what men and women wore. There were all the etceteras. There is at least one mention among women's wills in Warton parish of a ruff, stockings, bands, kerchief, cap and a belt, but this is not a fashion book and no attempt is being made to keep up with the changing fashions over the century. Under-garments are not mentioned, unless this is what such phrases as 'linen garments' and 'muslins' refer to. Equally uncertain is whether the wig found its way to Warton parish. It probably did. In 1663 Samuel Pepys was considering whether to buy one of the new periwigs and after wondering if he had 'the stomach' for it, he did so. Wigs soon became the wear for anyone with any pretensions to standing.

Making Clothes

Where did the men and women of Warton parish get these clothes? The age when clothes were of necessity all home-made from the spun fibre to the final putting together was past. Much thread was spun in the parish, wool and hemp (though certainly not silk), but relatively few people wove it into cloth, a matter discussed more fully in Chapter 14. This fits in with the findings from elsewhere. Sarah Fell, daughter of Dame Margaret Fell, kept an account book for the household while her mother was in prison for her adherence to Quakerism. It has survived and is helpful on how she obtained clothes for her household. There was hemp grown on the property and sheep kept for their wool, but she regularly paid to have it spun and woven, and then paid again to have the cloth dressed and then dyed in Kendal. The accounts show regular payments to a tailor (a local man from Ulverston). She payed also to have stockings knitted and when they wore out to have them 'footed'. She sent to shops in the town for such items as hats, gloves, buttons and shoes. She even sent as far as London for gloves.[37]

For poorer people it must have been a choice between spending working time on making clothes, or earning money and paying for someone else to do it. One does not know where the balance lay. There are specific references, even as early as the sixteenth century, to establishments very near to Warton parish which stocked ready made articles. James Backhouse of Kirkby Lonsdale, for instance, was a general dealer. In his 1578 inventory there were, among his goods, many lengths of cloth and of linen, hats and hat-bands, sword-girdles, hose, a pound of pins, sugar and spices and other provisions (and even 'arsnyck').[38] Christopher Harrison of Abbot

Hall, Kendal had in his inventory over 300 pairs of stockings. Kendal was a place that knitted stockings, and Harrison evidently dealt in them. There were stockings of ash colour, white, seagreen, clay-coloured, blue and white, purple and mulberry.[39] The colours came from natural dyes and, despite their vivid names, might seem insipid to our eyes which are accustomed to synthetic equivalents. But the Kendal dyers could provide a wide choice of colours, some from locally grown plants such as Dyer's Greenwood and some from dyestuffs imported from other parts of England and abroad.[40] There would have been plenty of other dealers to be found in Kendal, besides James Backhouse, and many in Lancaster, too. One did not even have to go to the town to buy, for there were at the period a great variety of pedlars who went round the villages calling at houses both large and small.

There is one slight hint that there may even have been a dealer in clothes in Warton parish itself. In 1610 Ann Burton of Silverdale had one gown, four red coats, two 'threewhaters' (whatever they were), three pairs of sleeves and a cloak worth thirty shillings. She also left eight smocks, two kerchiefs, three 'muslins', six bands, five aprons, three caps, two hats, two belts, a pair of shoes and 'other linen'. The whole lot came to some £2-13s out of a total inventory value of only £7-8s-8d. Of course she may simply have liked to be well-dressed, but it seems excessive for one not very rich woman.

Dearth, Disease and Demography

In this chapter an attempt is made to estimate not only the changing size of the population of Warton parish, but also its experience of death, of birth and of movement in and out of the parish. All this must, of course, be viewed against the background of general population changes in the country. The population of England and Wales rose during the seventeenth century from something over 4 million in 1601 to about 5¼ million in 1701, but the rise was uneven, steep in the first half of the century, with a slowing and then a decline in the second half. [1]

Demographic Trends, Warton parish

The vital statistics of Warton parish in the same period have been very fully studied by Speake.[2] This chapter draws freely on his work. He used the information from Warton Parish Registers, to set out the statistics of baptisms, burials and marriages from 1611-1800 in a markedly spiky graph which is reproduced here as Figure 8.1.

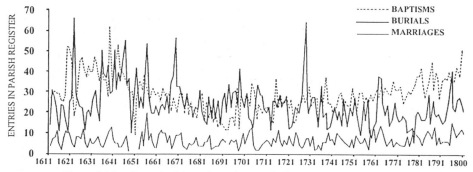

Figure 8.1 Baptisms, burials and marriages, Warton 1611-1800.(From R.Speake, 'The historical demography of Warton Parish before 1801', Trans. of the Historic Society of Lancashire and Cheshire, vol. 112, 1960, p.53.)

Speake's findings are consonant with the trends found for Lunesdale as a whole,[3] and both are broadly similar to the findings for England as a whole. There were three phases in recorded births and deaths in Warton (or rather, since neither of these events was recorded, in the baptisms and burials which stand surrogate for them). In the late sixteenth and early seventeenth centuries there was an excess of baptisms over burials until about 1637 with the 1623 'mortality peak', which is discussed below, a devastating interruption. Then followed a period when baptisms and burials were more or less in balance, both dropping from the late 1640s until, almost at the end of the century, there was an excess of burials recorded, though the excess has been magnified because (a point discussed below) there was more under-registration of baptisms than of burials. This excess of burials continued well into the eighteenth century when, from 1730 on, baptisms rose more than burials, resulting in a natural increase in the population.

Census 1801

These variations in baptisms and burials over the century cannot, however, give information on the actual size of the population. In attempting to work this out it has to be accepted that precision is not possible. The first definitive population figure resulted from the 1801 census enumeration, which put the population of Warton parish at 1,574.

Population Estimates 1563 and 1664

It is possible however to make estimates of earlier population. What is considered a fairly close approximation to the population figure for 1563 can be worked out from the Ecclesiastical Return of Households. In that year the Privy Council had required all bishops to make a return for their dioceses, which was to include the number of families in each. In Warton parish there were 284 households. Various workers have used different multipliers, varying from 4.2 to 4.5, to convert household numbers into population numbers. The figure used here is 4.25. This gives a population estimate for Warton parish in 1563 of 1,207.

Table 8.1 POPULATION OF WARTON TOWNSHIP estimated from the 1664 Hearth Tax Returns		
Township	Numbers	% of whole
Borwick	128	10
Carnforth	174	14
Priest Hutton	170	14
Silverdale	106	9
Warton-with-Lindeth	366	30
Yealand Conyers	165	13
Yealand Redmayne	124	10
Total	1,233	100

The Hearth Tax[4] imposed in 1664 revealed that there were 290 households in Warton parish which, using the same multiplier, gives a population of 1,233 (distributed among the seven townships as shown above in Table 8.1). These two results suggest an almost static population over the hundred years. Perhaps it is prudent to view this conclusion with some scepticism. Though the two population figures, a hundred years apart, are close anything could have happened in the years between.

Rickman's multiplier

With some ingenuity, and using a limited number of assumptions, the Parish Registers can be used in a third way to estimate population. Whereas the above two simply give a snapshot of the population in a specific year this third method attempts to chart the population over the century, though it has to be accepted that precision is not possible. John Rickman (d.1840), who was involved in the 1801 National Census and in preparation for the one in 1841, suggested this statistical method on the basis of surveys and study of Baptismal Registers. He divided the 1801 census population figure by the average number of annual baptisms for the previous decade which gave a figure of 38.7. To find the population in any given year he applied this multiplier to the average number of baptisms for the decade preceding that year. Many, using his idea, round the multiplier up to 40, but there seems no reason not to use 38.7.

As a check this multiplier might have been used to obtain the Warton population for 1563. Unfortunately the Warton Parish Registers only begin in 1568. The best that can be done is to find the annual baptism averages for the period 1570-1580, which is 31.4. This gives the population for 1580 as 1,215; very close to the figure of 1,207 based on the *Ecclesiastical Return of Households*. The baptismal average for the decade before 1664 being 31.2, use of the same multiplier gives an estimated population of 1,207, slightly lower than the estimate of 1,233 from the 1664 Hearth Tax returns.

Under-registration of baptisms

Speake thinks that under-registration of baptisms occurred in the parish, mainly because of separate Quaker registration later in the century. Other protestant non-conformists in the area being, he held, so few in number that they would have had a minuscule effect and, by contrast with the Quakers, it was 'unlikely that the presence of Catholics in the area would have affected registration to any appreciable degree'.[5] Formal Catholic registers were not kept until 1782. To correct the baptismal figures for presumed under-registration it has been advocated that the baptismal figure should be increased by 15 per cent before calculation.[6] If the 1664 population is recalculated by inflating the baptismal figure in this way the population figure is 1,397 and suspiciously high. In fact during the decade 1661-1670 Quaker registrations were equal to only 5.3 per cent of total registrations, though higher in subsequent decades (1671/1680 7.8 per cent; 1681/1690 6.9 per cent; 1691/1700 15.5 per cent).[7] Using the correction of 5.3 per cent gives a figure of 1,275 for 1664 which is close to the Hearth Tax derived figure of 1,233. The population figures for the whole century, calculated after making adjustment for Quaker registration from 1660 onwards, are shown in Figure 8.2 and Table 8.2.

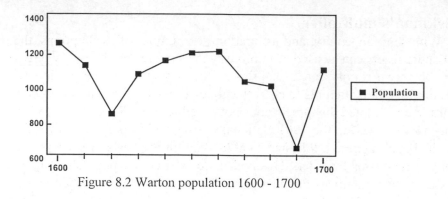

Figure 8.2 Warton population 1600 - 1700

Table 8.2 WARTON POPULATION 1600-1700 (After adjustment for non-registration by quakers)										
Year	1600	1610	1620	1630	1640	1650	1660	1670	1680	1690 1700
Nos	1260	1134	861	1089	1164	1209	1218	1049	1025	672 1118

The 1620 and 1690 figures in Table 8.2 are bizarre. The only explanation which comes readily to mind is that there was some exceptional reason for under recording baptisms over limited periods, such as an inefficient incumbent. But leaving aside these aberrations, it looks as though the parish population hovered around 1,100 to 1,200, being rather lower in the second half of the century than in the first. Speake was able to cite another authority which gave the population of Warton parish in 1701 at around 1,200.[8] The parish had 11,100 acres, so that the density of population was a mere one person to nine acres. In 1991 the population of the same area was 9,822[9] or one person to the acre (though since 5,150 of this population are congregated in Carnforth, which developed into a small town in the mid-nineteenth century, the density of population in the more rural parts of the area of the 'Ancient Parish' must be more like one person in 2 to 2½ acres). The figures show that in trying to get a proper perspective of Warton parish in the seventeenth century we have to remember how sparse the population was, spread as it was over seven townships.

Migration

Not all changes in population came about through changes in the ratio of births to deaths. Warton parish was not a closed community. There was migration in and out. Marriage registers for the parish from 1638 to 1700 record the place of origin of the parties (the register of marriages is too incomplete and unreliable before that to be used). They show that 30 per cent of recorded marriages involved a partner from outside, mostly not more than 20 miles away.[10] Regular and consistent movement of people in and out of the parish over short distances, especially east and south was the order of the day (See Table 8.3). There might be a presumption that there tended to be net outmigration given the relatively large number of males from outside marrying and presumably carrying their partners off and having families elsewhere, but this apparent excess of bridegrooms from outside could equally well be because even in the seventeenth century it was more common for a marriage to take place in the parish of the bride.

Table 8.3 MARRIAGES IN WARTON 1638 -1750			
	No. of Marriages	Brides from outside	Grooms from outside
1638 / 1647	69	6	17
1651 / 1700	292	33	52
1700 / 1750	319	25	67

Civil war

The record of births and deaths given in the parish register is not only a source from which changes in population can be estimated. It can also offer insight into matters of health and social welfare affecting our seventeenth century forbears. Before considering these, some thought must be given to war as a cause of death. It was, after all, the century in which a civil war occurred. The vital statistics given in the Parish Registers for Warton, covering the war period and some years after are given in Figure 8.3. Certainly burials rose from 1640 to 1642, dropped again, but reached a peak in 1647; baptisms behaved in the opposite way. But perhaps the most striking feature was the surge of marriages in 1656. It would be interesting to know what caused this. Perhaps the fact that in 1655 some ten to twelve thousand soldiers were disbanded [11] could be relevant, though it is not known how many men from Warton entered the army. Almost the only bit of

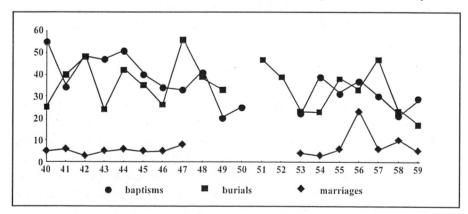

Figure 8.3 Baptisms, burials and marriages, Warton 1640-1659.
Figures are missing from the records for certain years.

information is that some of Sir George Middleton's Yealand tenants followed him to war despite their long-standing battle with him over tenancies.[12] Warton parish was never, however, directly fought over. It seems likely that the other factors, discussed below, had far more influence on mortality than war casualties.

Death rates and Mortality Crises

The Warton Parish Registers show, in the years up to 1750, that unusually high death rates occurred in the years 1574, 1586, 1587, 1592, 1623, 1642, 1647, 1670 and 1728 (figures are missing from 1594 to 1612).Three years stand out. These are 1623, 1670 and 1728, in each of which burial rates were unusually high. These were each years when a 'mortality crisis' could be said to have occurred. Historical demographers are most interested in such mortality crises. These are defined as occasions when yearly burials occur at twice the average rate for the period.[13]

Malthusian Theory

Earlier historians, following the teaching of Malthus, favoured famine as the probable cause of such mortality crises. In 1798 the Rev. Thomas Malthus produced a theory to explain the dynamics of population change. It was based on the idea that, unchecked, population would inevitably increase faster than food production. At a certain point food would run out and further increase in the population would be checked by famine. Revisionists then elevated disease to prime place above famine as the killer (though in fact even the most convinced Malthusians had granted that when plague, the 'Black Death', stalked the land it had primacy). The debate has been long-running, swaying one way and another. Among those favouring disease as the main cause of excess deaths there was at first a tendency to blame plague as the disease responsible for any mortality crisis which occurred. Plague had appeared in epidemic form in the fourteenth century and then became endemic, that is to say it was to be found somewhere at all times, with epidemics breaking out from time to time. Towards the end of the seventeenth century plague, for no reason that has ever been satisfactorily explained, suddenly almost died away and smallpox took over the role of demon.

It has even been claimed that plague '...was the only epidemic disease of great significance till the mid-seventeenth century'.[14] To-day, as we confront disease organisms endlessly adapting themselves to make war on humans, it is difficult to believe this. It is known that there were significant outbreaks of other diseases, some identifiable, such as typhus, influenza, dysentry and smallpox, others which have not been properly identified. At the time they were given non-specific names like 'epidemic catarrhs' or 'hot agues' (ague usually, but not always, indicating malaria, which was endemic in England at the time).

Disease

In 1551/2 the Sweating Sickness made its last appearance after causing five epidemics since its first appearance in the fifteenth century.[15] We know that syphilis and other venereal diseases were taking a hold. There are great difficulties in deciding what diseases were implicated at a given time, or in a given place. Conclusions are easier to reach when contemporary accounts are still extant, as in notes in parish registers or in diaries, though even then it is often difficult to interpret seventeenth century descriptions of symptoms with sufficient accuracy to make a firm diagnosis. In the absence of such documentation, reliance may have to be placed on the seasonality of the burials and the favoured target of the disease (by age group and sex) all of which give strong clues, a fact which is discussed further below.

Famine

The other postulated cause of excess mortality, famine, must be reckoned with in the seventeenth century. Poor harvests were common and though the idea that a total lack of food in the country might be responsible for high burial rates is now viewed with some scepticism, it does seem that in times of scarcity, very often people's incomes were too low to allow them to buy sufficient food from elsewhere to sustain vigorous life. There was a telling local example in 1649. In that year *"The Moderate"* of Newcastle carried harrowing reports about Cumberland and Westmorland.

> *All the poorer sort are almost famished and some really so...many have died in the highways for want of bread...no less than 30,000 families...had neither seed nor bread corn, nor monies to buy either.(16)*

Crises of subsistence

When food was scarce because of a harvest failure prices rose. Many people's incomes would be too low to buy sufficient food at these inflated prices. There has been a tendency to describe the problem not as famine, but as a 'crisis of subsistence'. Probably it is fair to say that a consensus has developed around the view that there may have been occasions when virulent disease scythed through populations of both vigorous and frail, and other occasions (especially in earlier times) when starvation occurred, but most often there was a combination producing a famine-related crisis in which malnourishment resulted in opportunistic infections carrying off weakened people.

Mortality crisis in 1623

The year 1623 is the the best documented example of a mortality crisis in Warton parish in the seventeenth century. There were 71 burials, though the average for the decade was 26. The monthly burials are shown below (Figure 8.4). The Warton Registers tell us little about the age, sex and social status of the victims. The year 1623, however, has been much studied·

and there is relevant information from other parts of the north-west. A high mortality has been found in many parishes throughout Cumberland, Westmorland and north Lancashire. It has been estimated that 5 per cent of the Lancashire population died, mostly in the winter of 1623 and the early spring of 1624. [17] Some have considered that such a very high death rate must indicate plague, but this peak of deaths in winter is not the characteristic pattern of deaths from plague. That typically causes deaths to peak in the hot months. There were contemporary references to scarcity and the Registers of at least one parish in the north-west, Greystoke in Cumberland, explicitly record deaths from starvation in the Burial Register. There are entries such as 'a poore hungersterven beger child' and 'a poor man destitute of meanies to live'.[18]

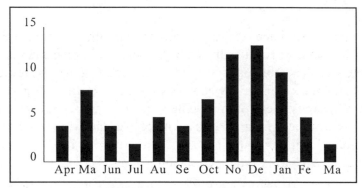

Figure 8.4 Monthly burials in Warton 1623-24

It would add further proof if it could be shown that the prices of foodstuffs had indeed risen because of scarcity. Average prices of, for instance, wheat are known, but there is a lack of precise figures for the north-west, though the Privy Council admitted that they were especially high there.[19] Comparison of the prices of wheat against burials in Warton does not seem to show any clear relationship. It should be said that wheat was not the major grain used in the north; oats and barley figured much more.

One feature supports the idea that a lack of proper food underlay the mortality crisis. In times of severe malnutrition conceptions tend to fall alongside the increase in deaths, and then rise again sharply afterwards.[20] Different explanations have been offered, such as anovulation in women, reduced sexual activity, early miscarriages and stillbirths. In Ashton-under-Lyne, most unusually, abortions were recorded in the Register; they reached nearly 7 per cent of births in 1623.[21]

Looking at Figure 8.5 one can see that for the period 1620 to 1639 the process appears clear in Warton parish. Baptisms were high in 1622 while burials were low; fell steeply in 1623 as burials rose abruptly to a peak and remained unusually low in 1624 and 1625 before rising again to a sustained

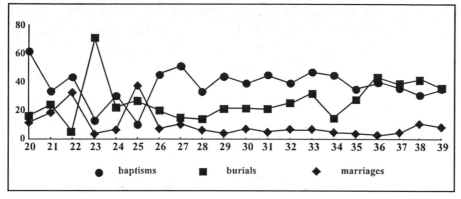

Figure 8.5 Baptisms, burials and marriages, Warton 1620-39

high level. Taking all the evidence it seems fair to conclude that Warton in 1623 was suffering the same 'crisis of subsistence' as so many other parishes in the north-west.

Mortality Crisis in 1670

When the Parish Registers are examined for the period 1660 to 1679 the year 1670, with 62 burials against a decadal average of 32.67, stands out. The monthly burials (Figure 8.6) show a different pattern from that of 1623/4. It has been suggested that when an excess of burials occurs in a given year, and 50 per cent or more occur from June to October, it is very suggestive of plague; and that if 66 per cent occur from July to September it is certain.[22] In Warton, 35 of the 62 deaths in 1670/71, more than 50 per cent, were recorded between June and October, but the second plague indicator, 66 per cent between July and September, was not satisfied.

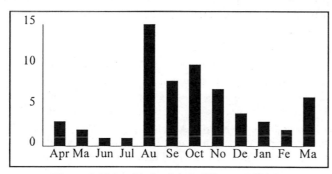

Figure 8.6 Monthly burials in Warton 1670-71

It is also possible to show that the relationship of baptisms to burials is different from the corresponding years centring on 1623. Baptisms do not fall in 1670/71 as deaths increase, nor is there an upswing after the crisis year. Perhaps it was because adults in this crisis did not suffer famine-prejudiced reproductive physiology, but were suddenly and severely culled. On the face of it, then, an outbreak of plague was possibly implicated, Warton being involved in a late flourish of this malign pestilence, but the evidence is incomplete. No mention of plague has been found in any record.

Plague typically kills adults and children equally, unlike other summer plagues such as epidemic diarrhoea. The register of burials does suggest that some of the dead may have been children, as for instance where they are entered as 'son of' or 'daughter of' someone else, but there is no exact record of ages.

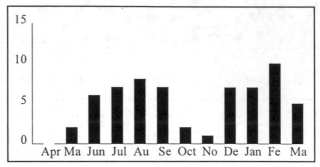

Figure 8.7 Monthly burials in Warton 1728-29

Mortality crisis, 1728

Going somewhat beyond the seventeenth century, the intriguing year 1728/9 is reached. There were 63 burials in Warton; the second highest total after 1623 and all but twice the decadal average of 32. Figure 8.7 shows two distinct humps, one in summer and the other in the following winter/early spring. Among these burials there were three stillbirths, twenty children, eight widows and one pauper (an analysis made possible because the eighteenth century registers record such details). Such a high proportion of deaths among these vulnerable groups suggests again a 'crisis of subsistence'. We also have the advantage of a contemporary account of affairs in this region at that time in William Stout's *Autobiography*. He writes of 1728:-

> *It was a very sickly summer [1728], and great mortality in the plain country, much more than in the towns; and burials were double this year to what they were last year, and corn proved dear - wheat 20s, barley 10s, oats 7s, beans 13s, oatmeal 14s a windle and potatoes double what they were last year, and linen manufactury very low and spinning one third less than last year so that the poor have had a hard year.*[23]

Ever Threatening Sickliness

What Stout meant by 'sickly' we cannot tell. There is one epidemic fever so closely associated with famine that it has been called 'starvation fever', and that is typhus. Typhus is louse borne, attacking all but the very young, particularly during the winter and early spring. It might have been the cause of the the winter bulge in deaths in the above graph. The summer bulge could be due to 'summer diarrhoea', dysentery or perhaps typhoid. Full evidence is not likely to be forthcoming.

Each of these years is an example of a mortality crisis in Warton, but represents a different community experience. 1623/4 might be described as a 'crisis of subsistence' with famine the predominent problem. A case can be made for thinking plague was the reason for the excess deaths in 1670. In 1728/9 the population perhaps endured a double misfortune, with very lean times with food in short supply and on top of that a microbial epidemic in the summer. The causes of the mortality crises are interesting. To-day the the major causes of death in England are heart disease and cancer, as they are in other developed countries.[24] Seventeenth century Warton parish was still, it seems, in the position of poorer countries to-day, and of this country any time up to the beginning of the century, with infectious disease (often on a background of poor nourishment) the major cause of death.

ALL SORTS AND CONDITONS OF MEN
The Gentry and the 'Middling Sort'

Warton parish in the seventeenth century had, as has been shown, a small population and almost all who lived there earned their living from the land, but the picture this might call up of a rural haven of egalitarianism would definitely need correction. It was not only that incomes varied enormously. Sir Robert Bindloss of Borwick Hall was said to enjoy an income of £3,240 a year.[1] The paupers in the almshouse received £3-6s-8d a year.[2] Nor was income the only difference. There was, it was held, an ordained order in these things. Some were high, others low and each should be content in their state.

Gentry

The difficulty began when attempts were made to define ranks. All agreed that at the top were the gentry, but what made a man a gentleman was harder to pin down. Unless a gentleman happened also to have a title there was no legal definition. There was a feeling that it was, or ought to be, a rank a man was born to, yet simple genealogy was not really the answer. Families could move in and out of gentility as fortune favoured them or not. On the whole it had to be accepted that a gentleman was essentially one who kept up the life style of a gentleman, who wielded the authority proper to a gentleman, and who also, and importantly, had the wealth, preferably landed wealth, to keep up his standing. The use of the masculine pronoun here is deliberate. In the seventeenth century a woman took the rank of her father or husband. In other chapters the difficulty does not arise, since women's real rôle and not their formal rank is being discussed.

However gentility was defined, all were agreed that only a small minority of the population, perhaps two per cent or so, rated as gentry. Lancashire was no exception. Figures of 3.2 per cent at the beginning of the century and 1.8 percent towards the end have been suggested.[3] Warton parish in the seventeenth century had something over a thousand inhabitants. Accepting that in Lancashire the gentry constituted from 2-3 per cent of the population only, one would not expect more than 20 to 30 inhabitants in a parish the size of Warton, or some five to six families, to rate as gentry.

The Bindlosses of Borwick Hall

There is no difficulty identifying the top two families, the Bindlosses of Borwick and the Middletons of Leighton. Their pedigrees can be found in the Victoria County History and are of some interest in that they exemplify two of the ways by which gentility could be achieved. Between 1567 and 1590 a Mr Robert Bindloss bought up the manors of Borwick and Priest Hutton.

It was accepted practice at the time for men who had achieved wealth to expend some of it in acquiring landed property and so facilitating the family's upward movement towards gentility. It is not known why Mr Bindloss chose Borwick. Perhaps it was merely on the market, but it could also be that he had an eye to land in Warton parish as relatively profitable. He also acquired and much enlarged Borwick Hall. [4] It seems accepted that the money originally came from the cloth trade in Kendal, where a Christopher Bindloss Esq had been 'Dealer in Kendall Cottons, and Chief Alderman...of that corporation. A° 1579...'. [5]

THE ACQUISITION AND DISPERSAL OF THE BINDLOSS ESTATE

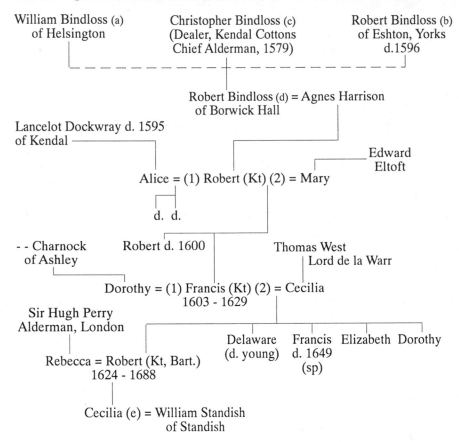

(a) This is the name given in the Visitations of Westmorland

(b) This is the name given in Hopkinson's Pedigrees of Lancashire Gentry (quoted by Lucas).

(c) This is Lucas's own preferred pedigree, as given in his *History of Warton Parish*. Lucas makes an ingenious attempt to combine the last two pedigrees by suggesting that Robert Bindloss of Eshton was indeed the father of Robert of Borwick Hall, and that Christopher Bindloss of Kendal was his younger brother and chose to leave his money to his brother's son to purchase Borwick Hall. There seems little doubt that the Bindloss fortune came from the cloth trade.

(d) Bought the manor of **Borwick** in two moieties in 1567 and 1590. In 1590 he bought the manor of **Priest Hutton** from Lord Mounteagle. Sometime in the 1590s he greatly enlarged **Borwick Hall**.

(e) On the death of her father Cecilia inherited the estates which thus passed to the Standish family, and through them to the Stricklands. It was never their main residence. In 1854 the Hall and estate were sold to George Marton of Capernwray.

The fact that Christopher Bindloss was referred to as Esquire, meant that the family was already moving up into the ranks of the gentry before Robert Bindloss rounded off the process by acquiring a country residence. He himself was knighted as were his son and grandson. By 1641 the latter had also been created a baronet. He was also probably the richest gentleman in Lancashire.[6] In politics Sir Robert can perhaps be described best as a cautious royalist. That is to say that up until 1649 he was prepared to serve on the County Committees under the Commonwealth, but he was among those who ceased to serve after the execution of Charles I.[7] He did not go so far as to support Charles II materially when the latter marched with his Scottish supporters in 1651, though Lucas retails a story that he entertained Charles himself at Borwick Hall when the rest of the army were encamped at Carnforth.[8] At any rate he joined in a Loyal Address to Charles II on his restoration. He was, Lucas adds, '...the last Gentleman, in this Part of the Country, that took Pleasure in and frequently practised Falconry...'.[9]

The Middletons of Leighton Hall

The Middletons were already established as gentry in the fifteenth century when a Geoffrey Middleton married, in 1438, the heiress of the Crofts, the big local family of the day. Over the next two centuries they acquired, along with much other property, the manors of Yealand and Silverdale; also Leighton Hall in Yealand Redmayne as a residence. The Middletons' position as the big Catholic family of the neighbourhood is discussed later (see Chapters 15 & 16), here they are considered merely as gentry. There was nothing positively bad or disreputable about them, but they seem to have had the trick of attracting odium. Historians still quote them as examples of grasping landlords, though they seem to have demanded no more of their tenants than many other Lancashire landlords did. They managed to be fined more heavily as recusants than almost any other family in Lancashire, a county which was generally lenient to recusants. They were profoundly disliked in their own neighbourhood. This comes out not only in the concerted, legal opposition of their tenants (see Chapter 5), but also in a number of less legal harassments.

Borwick Hall

According to Sir George his tenants dug up his best meadows for turf and peat.[10] His father, Thomas Middleton, had made just the same complaint against the inhabitants of Warton township. They did him much wrong, he said 'in digginge and gettinge his mosse & turbarie in warton mosse in crosspassinge taking awaie of his mosse & turbarie at their pleasure with cart & barrowe at all tymes & seasons of yeare...as also in killinge of his deare in his parke & demanes & in other of his grounds & lands'.[11] After the Restoration, Sir George put in his claim for compensation for all he had suffered from his loyalty to the Stuarts. Like so many other

THE ACQUISITION AND DISPERSAL OF THE MIDDLETON ESTATE

(The Middletons of Middleton near Kirkby Lonsdale)

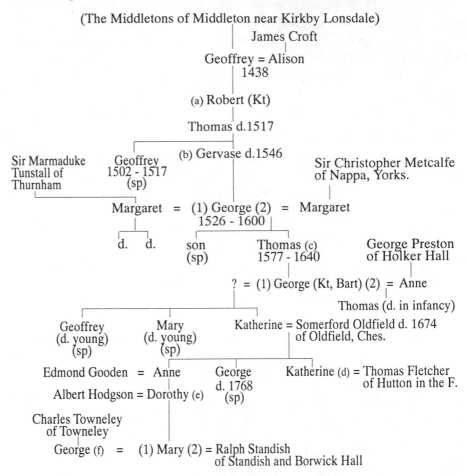

(a)   Inherited, through his Croft mother, the manors of **Yealand Conyers, Yealand Redmayne, Yealand Storrs** and **Leighton**.

(b)   Acquired a moiety of the manor of **Silverdale**, and c.1539 the "manor" of **Tewitfield**.

(c)   Died holding the manors of **Leighton** (with the park), **Yealand Conyers, Yealand Redmayne** (with the New Park), **Tewitfield** and **Silverdale**.

(d)   Inherited the **three Yealand Manors**. In 1713 she and her husband sold the manors to Charles Gibson of Preston.

(e)   Inherited **Leighton Hall** and the demesne lands.

(f)   Died without children. The Leighton Estate passed to a nephew, John Towneley of Towneley who sold it c.1790 to Alexander Worswick son of a banker of Lancaster, whose son Thomas, after the failure of the bank, sold the estate to Richard Gillow of Lancaster.

aggrieved Royalists he did not get a farthing, but he claimed for £38,350.[12] In this he included £7,000 for damage to his property and £9,930 spent on legal battles with his tenants who were, he alleged, inspired by his Parliamentary enemies among whom he named Thomas Fell of Swarthmoor. It would be interesting to know more of this unexpected tie-up with George Fox's protector.

There were other gentry families in Warton parish. Little is known of them, but they do illustrate that gentility was not a permanent status. Croft, the name of a once important family, was no longer a gentry name in the seventeenth century. The name of Kitson also fell from gentry rank, again for unascertained reasons. There was a Thomas Kitson, styled 'gentleman' in his will in 1638, but by the beginning of the eighteenth century Lucas was referring to the Kitsons as has-beens. There was, he said, a house on the north bank of the river Ware which 'was formerly the Seat of the Kitsons, a family which flourished here in great Repute for many generations'.[13] He thought they were related to a Sir Thomas Kitson, Sheriff of London in 1533. If so, the Kitsons have a claim to fame that Lucas knew nothing about. Margaret, the sister of Sir Thomas, married a John Washington of Tewitfield in Warton and became the ancestor of the first president of the United States.[14] One small individual act of Mr Thomas Kitson can be learnt. He took care of his mother. In his will he wrote '...I will that my mother shall be sufficiently keep'd with meate, drinke, Lodgings, Apparel & a Maid to attend on her...'.

The Washington family

Then there were the Washingtons. Lucas calls the family '...ancient and yet credible in the Town...' At the beginning of the seventeenth century the Leonard Washington who held the mill was described as a gentleman.[15] On the whole, though, many of those with the name of Washington seemed to be slipping out of the ranks of the gentry. References to them suggest a certain raffishness. There was Elen Washington who was bound over in 1635, for reasons unstated, not to keep an ale house or sell any beer or ale.[16] This, probably, was the same Ellen Washington who had in the same year to be bound over to keep the peace with the blacksmith.[17] In 1642 the Washington family had a set-to, women and all. Laurence Washington complained to a J.P that Ellin Washington, Thomazin Washington and Alice Washington and two male Washingtons had come to his door and dared him to meet them '...on the field and they will either have his life or he should have theirs and doth alsoe kneel downe upon their knees and did wish Gods curse to light upon him...'[18] Even Leonard Washington, the gentleman who owned the mill, may have been something of a *mauvais sujet*. In 1629 a Leonard Washington threatened to kill John Dicconson of Docker and in 1631 he and an Anne Washington, spinster, were in trouble for threatening a John Harling.[19]

Lady's formal dress 1670s

Nor was a later Leonard Washington of the high truthfulness of the great George Washington who could not tell a lie. When, in 1676, Leonard Washington was accused by his neighbour, Bryan Bland, of chopping down his tree he denied it categorically. It was, he said, Bland who had chopped down his, Washington's, tree. The court believed neither and fined them both for defamation.[20] How he was related to the Leonard Washington who had compounded for his estates as a recusant in 1632 [21] has not yet been clarified, nor is it known how they stood in relation to the Catherine Washington who was listed as a recusant a number of times between 1668 and 1680.[22] Among the Washingtons the christian names, Leonard, Lawrence, Alice and Ellen are repeated too frequently over the generations to make identification easy, even with the help of the genealogical trees drawn up by Mr Pape in his study of the Warton Washingtons.[23]

Gentlemen helped keep the local world of the townships in contact with the bigger world of the County and of the central government that lay behind it. Both Bindlosses and Middletons served on the Commission of Peace and both Sir Robert Bindloss and Sir George Middleton served as Sheriff of the county. In 1645 Sir Robert represented Lancaster in Parliament. Yet both families were also much involved with their neighbours in ordinary day-to-day affairs. This is particularly clear in the records of the Crown Manor of Warton. Sir Robert Bindloss, Sir George Middleton and Mr Thomas Kitson were all tenants of the manor in 1649, the former holding his land by freehold, the latter two as ordinary copyhold tenants. All three were fined at various times for infringing manor regulations. The Bindlosses had the right to pasture a flock of sheep on Warton Crag, a privilege that went with ownership of Borwick Hall [24], but their status did not prevent Sir Robert's grandfather from being fined when he was found 'overchardinge of our Common agaynst our Custome'.[25]

The Middling Sort

Below the gentry came 'the middling sort', a description of even vaguer definition than gentleman. In a rural area such as Warton parish yeomen and husbandmen formed the vast majority of 'the middling sort'. A yeoman or a husbandman might also exercise a craft, but that did not alter his status. Yeoman and husbandmen were both, essentially, those that farmed their own land whether they held it by freehold, copyhold or leasehold tenure. Husbandman was an occupational title describing all who 'husbanded', that is tilled, the soil. Yeoman was an honorific title, of obscure origin, applied to certain husbandmen. Whether a man was called yeoman was essentially a matter of local decision. Wealth came into it, but was not decisive. On the whole, yeomen were better to do, but they were also older and possessing '...a certain preheminence and more estimation' among the common people.[26] There has tended to be a feeling that yeomen held their land freehold, but records do not support this distinction. Many men called yeomen were freeholders, but many were copyholders or held land by a variety of tenures.[27]

Man's dress 1674

One might say that these middling sort are the people this book is mostly about, for they are the ones whose records have survived to be studied. It was from the ranks of yeomen and husbandmen that the jurymen were chosen for the manor courts. Their tenancies are recorded in the manor court records. They were the ones with enough possessions to make it worth while to have a will drawn up. It was from among them that the men came who organised, and presumably paid for, the fight for tenant rights. Yet in another way we know very little about them. We have, for instance, the names of twelve men from the Yealands, and twenty three men and one woman from Silverdale who took part in the legal battle against Sir George Middleton, but little knowledge of who they were, how old, how wealthy, how related to each other. For some communities family historians have worked together and, with the aid of computers, achieved a 'reconstruction' of the total population at a given time in the past. For a community as relatively small as Warton parish this should be a feasible undertaking and one which could throw more light on just such matters as who these village Hampdens were who fought for their rights.

A little can be deduced about the lives of such people from a general knowledge of the period and from such records as chance to have survived. The 'middling sort' covered a wide range of wealth. At the top were men like George Townson of Borwick and Halton. When he died in 1638 he was described as a yeoman, but his inventoried goods were valued at £315, in the same range as the £358 of possessions of Mr Thomas Kitson, gentleman, who died in the same year. A certain difference in their style of living is possibly hinted at in their inventories.[28] George Townson merely had more of everything than other tenants. His single sign of ostentation was a silver bowl worth £2-13s-4d. Thomas Kitson had, over and above a good supply of every-day goods, plate worth £17, a 'light horse, wth sadle & bridle' worth £12, and £17 worth of gold and money lying about the house.

Deference

George Townson even if he did not keep up the gentlemanly style which he could have afforded would have had his own standing in the neighbourhood. He could expect deference from those less fortunate, just as he would show outward deference to the gentry. It was, after all, the duty of every parish priest to see that young men and women knew their catechism, in which they were taught that it was their duty 'to order myself lowly and reverently to all my betters'. It seems that, by and large, people were ready to accept that they did have 'betters' who had to be treated in a special way in face to face contacts. What a man or woman thought about any particular representative of their betters is another matter. It seems that one can say of Warton parish that any outward deference to the gentry was not inconsistent with bloody-mindedness towards an individual gentleman. Nor, as has been shown in an earlier chapter, did deference prevent the yeomen and husbandmen acting in concert against oppressive landlords.

When Sir Robert Bindloss's father, Sir Francis, overstepped the limits of upper-class joking, the victim took him to court. Sir Francis was acting as Steward of the Crown Manor of Warton. At some uncertain date before his death in 1629 he called together the court, but did not name the place. Most of the tenants, including the deputy bailiff, went to the school house where the court was usually held. Sir Francis meanwhile, with a few of those in the know, went to a 'Bye alehouse' and held the court there. Because the bailiff was not in attendance Sir Francis set a fine of £5 on him and would not remit the fine even though the bailiff turned up at the ale house within half an hour. If it was a joke there was a nasty edge to it, for £5 was a swingeing fine at that period. The outcome of the case before the magistrates is not known.[29]

The Middletons, it has been seen, complained that the men of the township killed their deer. There is one record in the Quarter Session papers which illustrates the sort of difficulty they may have had in getting evidence from an unwilling tenantry. In 1640 four deer disappeared from the park, and turned up, dead, in a house in the village. Other deer had been missed before, one reported to have been carried to 'Parson Fetherstone howse' (a cleric not so far identified). The two witnesses, both of them described as yeomen, put up a firm denial of knowing anything about anything. They had never even heard of anyone owning a gun with the intention of killing deer, nor anyone with greyhounds. Indeed the second witness finished up by comprehensively denying '...that he ever knew aney of Mr Middeltons deare killed or aney other of aney mans else...' [30]

A Royalist Plot

In 1654 local people got another chance to get their own back on a Middleton. It was the year in which Oliver Cromwell was establishing himself as Lord Protector and royalist plots were in the air. Sir George and Leighton Hall seem to have been at the centre of a potentially serious royalist rising.[31] Information was laid against Sir George. Eleven men and one woman gave their names as witnesses '...with manie others if neede required'. They seem to have done their best to bring damning evidence against Sir George but, whether deliberately or not, they contrived to throw a slight air of farce over Sir George's alleged conspiracy. He had collected a band of some fifty or sixty men at Leighton, but what did this band do according to the witnesses? Sir George '...did deryde my Lord Protector and called his swyneherd Oliver Cromwell, and since my Lord was made Lord Protector hee calles that ladd my Lord and nothinge ellse, And he calles his Cowladd General Lambert And said the Land was ruled by a Company of Peddlers and Tynkers and Traitors'. Further than that we learn that the company ate well '...they did brew and bake every day, for six weekes together, killing of stall fedd oxen, and fatt sheepe'. They made a fine show '...they did sound twoe Trumpetts allmost everie night...and sounded all or the most parts of the poynts of Warr. And...fired their pistolls verrie often... Sr George himselfe shott several doggs and Catts with his pistolls...' It seems, however, that the most damage they did was to beat up some men in the fields till they were driven off with, one feels, some loss of dignity, by a group of women. (32)

Trades and Professions

There are two groups of the middling sort not yet mentioned, those whom to-day we would call professional, and those in mercantile occupations. They were little represented in a rural parish like Warton, as one would expect. There are indications that people from Warton parish did move into trade and the professions, but only by leaving the parish. In St Botolph's church in the City there is, or was, a memorial tablet to a Robert Tailor of Warton in Lancaster, described as a Draper of London, who died in 1577.(33) In the 1670s the Warton Manor Court records mention a number of city dwellers who became the possessors of land in Warton; Robert Croft, Merchant Taylor of London, bought a tenement and messuage in Warton from Thomas Hyndc, gentleman, also of London, and then two further acres of land from Elizabeth Clarkson, spinster of London. Robert Lamberson of Leeds, clothier, sold a couple of roods of land to a Warton inhabitant. George Middleton of Greys Inn bought land from John Washington of the parish of St George the Martyr and so on. It seems likely that these city dwellers, buying and selling land in Warton, had their origins in the parish.

On the professional side Lucas mentions Roger Dodsworth (1585-1654), a distinguished antiquarian and collector of manuscripts who had spent two years at Warton Grammar School.(34) Lucas himself left the parish to spend the rest of his life as a school teacher in Leeds. Most distinguished of all those who found fame elsewhere was Matthew Hutton (1529-1606). He was born in Priest Hutton, and ended his life as Archbishop of York (see Appendix 4). Of professional people who actually lived in Warton parish there were the clergymen, and any beneficed clergyman was *ex officio* a gentleman of a sort. Warton, moreover, was a fairly well-endowed parish and could expect to attract men of standing and education. There were also the Masters of the Grammar School, usually clergymen themselves. One might have expected references to members of the legal profession, for it was a very litigious age, but lawyers would normally live in towns. Lucas mentions *en passant* a Mr Dawson, Attorney-at-Law, who lived in Warton, but not why he chose to live in so out of the way a place.(35)

Professionals do not seem to have been much employed in the care of the sick. In 1690 the Churchwardens in their 'Presentments' stated 'wee have none that practise physick in our parish'. A statement that was repeated in 1698,(36) but whether these reports indicate that there had been practitioners before and the situation in the 1690s was unusual, or whether this was the usual position we do not know. Although, officially, anyone purporting to practice physick was under the control of the church and required a licence, it was a largely unregulated market place. As it said in the preamble to Henry VIII's first Medical Act in 1511-12:-

> *Physic and Surgery is daily within this Realm exercised by a great multitude of ignorant persons as common artificers, smiths, weavers and women who boldly and customarily take upon them great cures and things of great difficulty in which they partly use sorcery and witchcraft to the grievous hurt, damage and destruction of many of the King's liege people.* [37]

The Care of the Sick

One reference only to a doctor has been found. In February 1676 Dame Anne Middleton of Leighton Hall [38] paid 2d to 'doctor Kynean' for a 'by lester' (the word seems clear enough, but what it means is another matter, a blister? a clyster [enema]?). Nothing else is known of this doctor or where he came from. It is probable that, for the ordinary people of Warton parish, it was the women who cared for them, not through sorcery, but through accumulated experience and of necessity. We know at least that one woman made herself helpful to her neighbours, though she could hardly be called professionally trained. In 1689 Margaret Turner of Priest Hutton was in trouble 'for practising as midwife without Licence'. [39] Licence from the church that is, licensing by either fellow nurses or doctors was a long way off. Only at the beginning of the eighteenth century was there a resident doctor. The Rev. Dr William Aylmer became vicar in 1714 where, Lucas tells us, '...(having formerly studied Physic as well as Divinity), he was very serviceable to the Bodies as well as the Souls of his Parishioners...'[40]

The only direct information about the care of the sick deals with their financial support, not their medical treatment. There are a number of appeals in the Quarter Session records for financial relief from those caring for the sick. In 1657 Jenett Walling appealed for relief because she had the care of a 20 year old son 'Ideot, dumbe, lame, decrepite'. A remarkably clear clinical assessment of the degree of his helplessness was added. He was one 'who could never since his birth goe stand or speake or anyways helpe himselfe though meate were sett him'.[41] In 1673 Agnes Wraston asked for help because she was still caring for her dead husband's sister who was 'distracted' and also had the King's Evill',[42] (a phrase commonly used for ulcerating glands in the neck, probably mostly tubercular). In 1698 Bridget Winder petitioned for help because her 3 year old son had '...the distemper commonly called recketts'. She used to be able, the petition said, to lay him down and so had 'addled [earned]' something for her living. Now the boy was bigger and was becoming 'more humorsome and tedious' and could not be left. The petition says that 'like the woman in the gospel, she hath spent all her liveing and yet [he] is nothing bettered',[43] which rather suggests she did spend something on trying to find a cure. The one petition that mentions medical treatment is that of Richard Townson of Priest Hutton in 1653. He was troubled with 'the Evill' so that he was in danger of losing his arm. He wanted help in getting to London in the hope of getting a place in a hospital.[44] 'The Evil', as opposed to the King's Evil, could mean any disease or malady, and the description is too vague to allow of a diagnosis, so that one does not know what it was hoped the London hospital could do.

The petitioners would be hoping, not that the justices would find the money they needed, but that they would order the parish Overseers of the Poor to find it. But the work of dealing with the problems of the poor by the Overseers and by the parish whose officials they were is too complicated a matter to be dealt with at the end of a chapter. The poor and the poor laws form the subject of the next chapters.

ALL SORTS AND CONDITIONS OF MEN
Poor Husbandmen and Labourers

There was no sharp cut-off between the 'middling sort' and the landless poor. A small tenant might well be as poor as any labourer or servant. Indeed Sir Thomas Smith, a sixteenth century lawyer, had lumped them all together in a dismissive manner. Poor husbandmen, day-labourers and servants, he had written, had 'no voice nor authority in our commonwealthe...but only to be ruled and not to rule other...'.[1] However, Sir Thomas did allow that these men had some standing for at least '...in villages they are commonly made churchwardens, aleconners, and many times constables...'

How poor a poor tenant might be and what shifts he was put to to supplement what he could earn from his small holdings are matters discussed later (Chapters 13 & 14). Yet however poor such a man might be, while he held land as a tenant he had some status and some privileges denied to Sir Thomas Smith's next category, the day-labourer. Landless labourers, totally dependent on wages, were known before the seventeenth century, but their numbers were growing. An estimate of how many there might be in Warton parish is made in Chapter 14 and it was certainly not a negligible number. In this chapter the question of what such a day-labourer might earn, and how that wage matched up to his needs is tackled. Before entering on that a word needs to be said about the third group in Sir Thomas' list of those with 'no voice' in the commonwealth, namely servants.

Servants

Servants, often living-in, were an accepted part of life at any time up to the second world war, even for people of extremely modest means. Not that all people in the seventeenth century calling themselves servants were what we should mean by the term. People who nowadays would call themselves an agent, a secretary, a bailiff or a factor were content to call themselves 'servant' and their employer 'master'. Christopher Guy, bailiff, called himself Dame Anne Middleton's servant when he made up her accounts, but he was a man of standing in his own right, the

The Bailiff's House, Yealand Conyers

probable owner of the substantial house still standing on the corner opposite the New Inn in Yealand Conyers. It bears, on a date-stone over the door the initials CMG, appropriate for Christopher and his wife Mary and the date 1667.

There must, however, have been plenty of ordinary servants in the parish. Such men and women, if they lived in with the family might be better fed than they had been at home, but they were largely without effective rights. Servants it had been said, being without property '...have no reason to have votes in the institution of government'.[2] They counted as part of their master's household and he was held to stand in the place of a father to them as well as to his children. But, where masters failed in their paternal duties, servants had little redress. During the civil war and the turmoils before and after, new and radical opinions on all subjects were welling up. There were those who dared to question a system which kept large parts of the population with 'no voice'. This questioning found perhaps its most terse and memorable expression in the words of Colonel Rainborough, a parliamentary army officer, when he declared that '...I really think that the poorest he that is in England hath a life to live as the greatest.' To which Ireton, Cromwell's son-in-law retorted 'Honour thy father and mother, and that law doth extend to all that are our governors'.[3] Of all the political movements perhaps only the Levellers really tried to make Rainborough's claim a practical reality and even they, in demanding almost universal suffrage, seem to have excluded servants from their proposed franchise.[4]

Servants make little showing in the records of Warton parish, but such information as there is suggests that it was Ireton's view which prevailed rather than Rainborough's. Servants were to show deference to their betters, for they were to be fined if they '...doe uppon maliciouse minde defame or evill reporte any maried man or woman...', but they were also to be protected from bad ways, for the alehouse-keepers were forbidden to tempt them into their houses for longer than an hour, especially on the Sabbath day at the time of Divine Service,[5] nor were they to encourage them to play games of chance after ten o'clock at night.[6] All this is not to say that relations between master and servant were never happy, fitting in with the ideal of the servant as part of the family. A number of servants were left gifts in wills, both of clothes and money. Some of these servants seem to have been very much part of the household. In 1632 Jennet Walling bequeathed her servant Issabel Cornthwaite forty shillings 'which I borrowed of her'. In 1616 Robert Sander left all his 'moveable goodes' to be equally divided between his wife and his servant, Ellen Jackson. In 1675 Elizabeth Nicholson, servant to Bryan Bland, took the risk of opening the pinfold gate and letting out her master's cow that had been impounded for trespass.[7]

Wages

No information is available from Warton on wages either of servants or day-labourers, and very little that is relevant on the cost of what must be bought out of those wages. Such information is available from elsewhere, but in using general levels it must be remembered that Lancashire, in the seventeenth century, was a relatively poor county. In all tax assessments of the seventeenth century Lancashire, out of the forty counties included, always comes among the lowest sixth in wealth. (Though, as Dr Marshall has pointed out in the Introduction, there may have been some underestimation of wealth in this remote county.) Furthermore North Lancashire was unlike the other parts of the county, bearing an affinity in some ways to Westmorland which made a still poorer showing in the tax assessments, invariably coming among the last three counties assessed. An assessment at the end of the century shown in Table 10.1 gives an indication of how different the wealth of Warton parish might be according to whether it conformed to that of Lancashire or that of the more northern counties.

Table 10.1 Tax assessment of 1693 (From Thorold Rodgers [20])		
County	Total Assessment	Acres per £
Westmorland	£3,014	161,391
Lancashire	£21,300	57,240
Durham & N'thumberland	£25,147	74,433
Cumberland	£3,147	315,460

Quoted wages in other parts of the country may therefore not be applicable to Warton parish. There is, however, some information available for the north-west. The main sources used here are the accounts for the Shuttleworth family of Gawthorpe and Smithils,[8] for Naworth Castle [9] and for Hornby Castle.[10] These accounts range from the 1580s to the mid 1620s and so cover at least the early decades of the seventeenth century.

There are good records from the Naworth Castle estate which show wages for a range of jobs. A selection is listed in Table 10.2. Naworth lies in the north of Cumbria, east of Carlisle in what was then called Cumberland, not far from the border with Northumberland.

Some workers were paid piece rates and these are harder to interpret without knowledge of how long the job took. A dyer, for instance, was paid 4s-2d per dozen yards dyed, sheep-shearers 3d to 6d per sheep, and their assistants 1d to 3d. Weavers' remuneration depended on the cloth.

For harden they were paid 1d a yard, but for kersey 2d and for Linsey-woolsey 3d to 4d. One weaver was paid 7s for weaving 25 yds of fine linen, that is rather less than 3½d per yard.

Wages in the Lune Valley

The Hornby accounts, dealing as they do with an area in the Lune valley itself, would be of particular interest, but they deal only with the end of the sixteenth century and owing to their use of a different accounting method, it is impossible in most cases to calculate a separate rate for a particular job, though some entries allow it. There are entries, for instance, such as 'Re hay getting, paid to diverse persons for 34 days mowing meadow at priory at 8d per day to meat and wages, 22s.8d'. Another reads '... and to diverse persons for skayling [spreading, as of hay], raking, cocking and getting off the said meadow in hay for 62 days and a half at 3d a day'. Another entry reads 'for one day making a hay stack 4d'. The entries are few but wages recorded are comparable to those at Naworth.

The actual list of jobs at Hornby is, incidentally, of interest in its own right, by showing a range of tasks undertaken, which helps fill out the account of by-employments given in Chapter 14. Jobs such as making traps for the coney warren, shoeing oxen, mending yokes, getting spelkes [wooden pegs, as for thatching], thacking [thatching] houses, mending sacks, cutting wood and faggots, graving [digging] turves, 'warping the web', repairing the common pinfold, repairing the deerhouse and so on.

There are some entries in the Hornby accounts which do give some indication of the rates of pay per year of some of the servants of the Lord of the Manor. These persons are named, unlike the common labourers, and must have had some standing in the heirarchy of the manor. (Though the only woman mentioned is not given a name of her own, but is simply entered under her husband's name as 'Dollyer wife'.) It is not always clear to what length of service the payment applies, but for a certain John Fisher it was (in 1582) as much as 26s-8d a quarter or over £5 a year. By contrast 'Dollyer wife' only got 6s-8d for a whole year of making whitelights [candles].

Wages rose throughout the sixteenth and early seventeenth century (though falling in terms of purchasing power) and by the 1640s farm labourers in the south of England are reckoned to have been earning in the region of a shilling a day and rather less in the north, though figures for the northern counties are hard to come by.[11] The figures quoted in Table 10.2 seem to confirm this, suggesting that in Cumbria and the Lune valley only the most skilled could hope for such wages, and the run of labourers were earning only six pence a day, or thirty six pence a week when they managed to find work every weekday. Perhaps thirty pence a week on average, taking winter and summer together, would be a more likely assumption, but it must be an assumption because we simply do not know how regularly day labourers were employed.

JOB DESCRIPTION		£	s	d	
Bricklayer			1	0	(range 1s - 10d)
Carpenter	(with victuals)				
	(without)		1	0	
his man	(with victuals)			4	
	(without			10	
Cooper				6	
his man				4	
Gardener				10	
Glazier				8	
Haymakers	(men)			8	
	(women)			6	
Labourers	(ordinary)			6	
Mowers			1	0	(range 1s - 10d)
Masons			1	0	
Paver				4	
Plasterer				6	
Plumber			1	0	
Quarryman				4	
his boy				2	
Saddler				6	
Slater				6	
Thatcher				8	
his server				6	
Thresher				9	

Table 10.2 Wages (from the Naworth Accounts [9]) — WAGES PER DAY

What might thirty pence a week mean in terms of purchasing power? In particular can one find evidence that such a wage might be too low to ward off starvation in bad years? Many of those who hired out their labour for a wage would be working part-time to eke out what they could make from their small holdings. It would be an almost impossibly complicated task to balance what might be coming in to such households against possible outgoings in the form of tithes, rates, taxes and fines to the Lord of the Manor. The task is perhaps a little easier for labourers totally dependent on wages. It seems that wages, at any rate of farm labourers, were not tithable.[12] Day-labourers, not being tenants, had no fines to pay to the Lord. How much they had to contribute in Warton to rates and taxes is not known, but certainly they could be exempt from some taxes (See Appendix 2). Local Overseers of the Poor and the Vestry had powers to exempt inhabitants from paying rates [13] and certainly day-labourers would have been more likely to be receiving money from the Poor Rate than paying into it.

Out of his wages the labourer must of course, buy other necessities than food, but it has not proved possible to find prices of these. We have some prices for items of clothes, for instance, in the Gawthorpe accounts. Five pairs of children's shoes cost 4s-8d, seven and a half yards of canvas to make doublets for the children cost 8s-9d, three pairs of hose 'for the boys' came to 2s-6d. These clothes, however, were for the children of the gentry, and in the seventeenth century there was an enormous divide between the clothes of the rich and the poor. Clothing of this quality would have been impossible for labourers' children. Even such information on the cost of garments as can be obtained from the inventories of the inhabitants of Warton parish is of doubtful relevance to the poor, because they left neither wills nor inventories. The amount spent on rent or on equipping a house is equally unknown.

Cost of living

It is, moreover, a sad fact of life that the poorer the family the greater the portion of income that must go on food. It has seemed worth while to try to make some estimate, however tentative, of the cost of food, for there are prices for some foods, particularly cereals. From the Gawthorpe accounts we have prices of wheat. Gawthorpe is in Lancashire, near Burnley, and the prices, therefore, more relevant to Warton than the more generally quoted prices for the south of England. The accounts tend to be given in measures which are no longer current, such as a windle or a mette. Measures which, moreover, varied from place to place. Accepting that a windle of wheat round here was 210lbs or 3 bushels of 70lbs, and that a mette was the local term for a bushel it is possible to calculate some prices per pound from the Gawthorpe accounts which are set out in Table 10.3.

Table 10.3 Prices of Wheat (from Gawthorpe Accounts [8])	
Year	price/lb
1582	0.49d
1593	0.81d
1605	1.09d
1612	2.74d
1620	1.37d
1633	1.71d

The northern working family, however, did not rely on wheat as a basic food, but on oats. Both the Hornby accounts and the Naworth accounts record oat prices, mostly for a bushel or mette, a volume measure. The comparison with wheat prices is complicated by the fact that different grains have different weights per volume, and so a bushel of oats weighs only 56lbs against the 70lbs for wheat. A calculation of comparative prices is given below in Table 10.4.

Table 10.4 Prices of Oats and Wheat (based on figures from the Hornby[10] and Naworth Accounts)		
	Price/lb	
Year	Oats	Wheat
1581	0.21d	0.49d
1583	0.75d	0.81d
1612	0.66d	2.74d
1620	0.24d	1.37d

It is plain that oats came cheaper, but how much oatmeal would a man have to purchase out of his 30d a week to keep himself and his family fed? Oatmeal is relatively high in calories. In 1964 the Ministry of Agriculture estimated that an ounce of oatmeal produced 115 calories, and an ounce of wholemeal flour only 91.[14] Even in the nineteenth century Lancashire workers were heavily dependent on oats eked out by potatoes.[15] In seventeenth century Warton parish the latter were not yet available, (see Chapter 3). Plenty of other foods were eaten, beef, lard, butter, cheese, but it is likely that these were only occasional luxuries for the poor and that the main source of nourishment was oats. If this was so then to obtain 1000 calories a day (far less than a working adult needs) a labourer would need 8.7 ounces of oatmeal each day, which is 3.8lbs a week. Allowing his equally hard-working wife an equal share and two hypothetical young children the same amount between them, the man would need to earn enough to buy 11.4lbs a week.

Staving Off Starvation

The figures given in Table 10.4 cover 40 years of inflation and price variation. There are however figures for two years at the beginning of the seventeenth century which fall within eight years of each other. They must not be taken as giving the average cost of grain even for that decade, but they might be used as examples of years of low and high grain prices in the region. In 1620, with oats at 0.24d a pound the required 11.4lbs would have cost 2.7d a week. It sounds very little, though in fact it represents nine per cent of a weekly wage of 30 pence. In 1612 the cost for the same quantity of oats would have been 7.5d, or a quarter of the postulated wage.

To obtain 2,500 calories a day (a far more realistic figure to maintain health and vigour) then in 1620, with oats at 0.66d a pound, the hypothetical wage labourer would have had to pay out 6.8d to obtain his 11.4 lbs, which would be 22 per cent of his earnings, and in 1612 18.8d, or 63 per cent of his earnings. Allowing for the fact that the wife and children might also have been earning something it would be possible for the family to remain this side of starving even in a bad year, but an adequate diet would be possible only by ruthless cutting down on other items of purchase.

To have tried to live on wheat would have been another matter. To obtain even 1000 calories for the family the labourer would need to purchase 14.4lbs of wheat a week. Even in 1620 this would have cost 19.7d, representing 65 per cent of a 30 pence weekly wage. In 1612 it would have cost the impossible figure of 39.5d. Figures could be calculated for the cost of living entirely off wheat in a bad year, but they would have little meaning. A family in Warton parish able to buy that much wheat would almost certainly not be living on cereal alone, but would be enjoying a varied diet including meat, butter, cheese and so on.

These calculations are based on a very limited sampling of prices and wages and on assumptions about the average composition of a labourer's family and about his customary diet. They take no account of other necessities to be purchased and certainly of no luxuries like beer and ale. Not that these can be strictly considered as luxuries. Before the days of tea and coffee there was really nothing else for a poor man to drink (except water of course, and there is little comfort in that as one's only drink and, before piped water, not much safety). We know that at the beginning of the seventeenth century a quart of the best ale cost a penny.[16] Poor people would drink, not best ale, but 'small beer' which presumable came cheaper, though it would contain little in the way of either alcohol or calories. The inventories show that there were a number of moderately large-scale maltsters in Carnforth, but also that many people had small holdings of malt, so presumably home brewing was practised. But how much was drunk and how much it cost to keep oneself in small beer there is no way of knowing.

Incomers

It does seem, from the estimates of the cost of grain and probable wages that there cannot have been much left over for other needfuls after a labourer had fed his family even on the most basic diet of oatmeal, certainly nothing for luxuries. The calculations also support the generally held opinion that there would be years when an adequate diet, even of oatmeal would be hard to purchase for any labourer and impossible if he should fall ill or be unable to find regular work.

As has been said poor tenants might be materially no better off than day-labourers, but they did have a defined position which servants and labourers lacked. The latter might quite frequently not even be native to the parish. Servants were hired from elsewhere at hiring fairs (see Introduction p.3). Day-labourers might have come in seeking work. With the national population increasing there was a pressure on people to move to wherever there was any hope of a living. In some areas squatters came in and settled themselves on forest and wasteland. This does not seem to have been the problem in the Warton manors, where common land was more limited and manorial control strong. It was rather the manorial tenants themselves who were putting up cottages on the common and converting their outhouses into cottages for the use of outsiders. Or one may assume so since there were Manor Court orders forbidding the practice. The fine for this could be £10, a very large fine indeed.[17]

The fear was that the incomers would become chargeable on the parish. The offence was spelt out when Mrs Mary Oldfield built a house at Coatstacks in 1691, and the manor Court found that she had '...brought in an inmate chargeable to the township'.[18] In 1668 a general order had been made that no one was to receive any 'inmate....to dwell in any Dwelling-house, or out house' unless, and this was the nub of the matter, they were farming land worth £5 or more, or could give other 'good and sufficient security to the....overseers of the poor' indemnifying them against any charge which the township might incur.[19]

It is plain that, where wages were so low, the fear was justified. Servants, day-labourers, poor husbandmen, incomers without customary rights, servants, orphans, women left with children on the death of their husband, the old and the ill; these were the people who slipped down into the ranks of the really deprived, the sort of people who swelled the mortality figures in crisis years (see Chapter 8) and needed support from the rates. For during the sixteenth century it had become obvious that private charity alone, especially after the demise of the monasteries, was no longer able to deal with the problem of poverty and the state had stepped in. From the end of the sixteenth century a poor rate, levied on the parish, had come to supplement, though not to do away with, the need for charity. The problems of the welfare state had begun.

CHAPTER ELEVEN

HOW IT WAS

ALL SORTS AND CONDITIONS OF MEN

The Poor

The Poor Laws

Human nature being what it is, it was not only from charitable motives that help for the poor was organised by the state at the end of the sixteenth century. So many people, for various reasons, were without work and reduced to vagrancy, beggary or crime that it was felt law and order were threatened. The 'Poor Laws' which, in the sixteenth and seventeenth centuries, were enacted to try to deal with the problem would require a whole book to themselves to do any justice to their good intentions and their grievous failures. Perhaps from the point of view of this book only two points need to be made. The Poor Law, by the two great acts of 1597 and 1601, established a system of 'compulsory, rate-financed poor relief' and under this system every parish in England became responsible for its own poor.[1]

The parish had been a convenient choice as the unit of administration of the Poor Laws. It was, usually, small enough for the real needs of the indigent to be known. Already, under earlier legislation, it had a duty to co-ordinate charitable donations, not to mention the church's much older function as the natural centre, where public announcements were made, parish documents were stored, coroners' inquests and any other function requiring a large meeting place were held. Tudor legislators found it convenient to impose other new civil duties on it, such as maintenance of highways, though to call what resulted a 'civil parish' is to antedate events by several hundred years. Civil parishes were not established till 1894. In the seventeenth century it was the ecclesiastical parish that was being required to take on more and more secular functions. So there arose an anomaly that for civil purposes the parish was held to include all who lived within its bounds, even though an increasing number of parishioners were no longer members of the Church of England.

Vestries

The secular functions of the parish were controlled through Vestry Meetings. Who might attend these Vestry Meetings '...whether...all who actually resided in the parish, or those who owned or rented lands or houses within the parish...or merely the heads of households, or the adult men only...' was never generally determined by law.[2] Increasingly over the next century vestries became 'closed'; self-perpetuating oligarchies of the better to-do. It has not been found what the situation was in Warton parish in the seventeenth century, though it is clear that it had the necessary parish officers to carry out the duties laid on it by the various parliamentary acts. Churchwardens, Constables, Surveyors of the Highways and Overseers of the

Poor are all mentioned in documents. All the offices were unpaid, though there might be perquisites attached to the job, and all were compulsory upon whoever was chosen, usually for a year at a time, though the duties might be avoided by paying for a deputy.

Constables

It was the Churchwardens and the Overseers of the Poor who had the duty of dealing with money collected by the Poor Rate for the relief of the indigent, but it seems worth saying something first about the office of constable since this was an office that was held by poorer inhabitants, though perhaps less so by the end of the century when closed vestries preferred to keep all offices in what might by then be called middle class hands. It was a very ancient office, originally a manor appointment and only gradually coming under the control of the Vestry Meeting. The change was part of a general tendency. As the secular duties of the parish increased, the function of the manor courts decreased, and became limited to matters of the inheritance and transfer of land. For a time the powers of the two overlapped, or at any rate were not very clearly differentiated. In the early years of the seventeenth century the jurymen of Warton Manor Court plainly felt responsible for the constable. They fined Robert Waithman and his son for 'abuseinge the cunstable',[3] and Anthony Atkinson 'for not Obayeinge the Constable, and abuseing him when he com[m]anded him to keep the Kinges Ma[tes] Peace'.[4]

It was everywhere a much disliked office, involving as it did a great deal of trouble with one's neighbours and much ill-paid work. There is one surviving petition of a Warton constable which can afford some wry amusement. In 1665 the constable was given the task of conveying two impressed seamen from Warton to Lancaster. The constable found himself liable not only for all his own costs, but for feeding the two men and 'the persons appointed to watch them'. On top of this he was ordered to pay the seamen, for reasons which are not now clear, the sum of forty shillings which he had to find from his own pocket. Altogether he was forty-nine shillings down over the whole affair and had to petition the justices for repayment. The surviving records do not say if his petition was successful.[5]

It is not surprising that references to the constableship in the Quarter Session papers are mostly concerned with the attempts of individuals to evade service. The appointment had, by law, to be approved by the Justices, but it is not known how Warton chose the candidate each year. It may well have been, as it was elsewhere, that the job fell on the house rather than the person. There is an entry in the Warton Manor Court records for 1691 which says clearly that any tenant with at least four acres of land must take on 'all offices' within the township '...in the way of house row or neigh[bour]hood...'[6] Warton's four Bylawmen were certainly chosen this way. Two were to be chosen '... above and two beneath till they meete at the midde Towne, and so to revert agayne'.[7]; a division of Warton which can still probably be traced in the name Boon Town (above town) at the upper or north end of Warton.[8] Not only would poorer men be liable anyway to be made constable if the lot fell on their house that year, but it was known for the better to-do to pay poor neighbours to deputise for them in this onerous task.

Overseers of the Poor

To return to the Overseers of the Poor, although they were parish officials they were appointed by the Justices of the Peace from among 'substantial' householders, and were under their supervision.[9] The accounts and other records of the Overseers form a primary source of information on poor relief. Unfortunately Warton, like so many other parishes, has almost no surviving Overseers' records. There is a little information from Quarter Session records. The Justices of the Peace had been given the task of supervision and it was possible to appeal to them against a decision by the parish. There are too few of such cases to make up for the absence of local records and in any case Quarter Session records would be dealing with exceptional issues by their very nature.

From such little evidence as there is for Warton parish it seems that its practices were in no way unusual. There was, in the seventeenth century, no suggestion that people could not be given relief in their own homes. That only came when the whole system was re-organised in 1834. There is an entry on the fly-leaf of one of the Warton parish registers which says that in 1707 a total of £2 was paid to the poor of Warton in small doles. Five widows received five shillings each and 'Widow Nicholson's children' received a shilling between them.[10] Money from the poor rates could be spent on seeing that people were housed by paying the rent for them, or even by building houses for them.[11] In 1638, at the Session of the Peace in Lancaster, the petition of John Kitson to have himself and his family given 'houseroome' within the parish was accepted by the justices. The churchwardens and overseers of the poor were told there would be a fine of twenty shillings a month if they did not see to this.[12]

Settlement Act 1662

In the same way there is virtually no information on how Warton parish dealt with the Settlement Act of 1662. This was passed to try to solve the problem of people moving to another parish (often in search of work) and then needing parish support. Which parish was to pay ? The Act laid down that they were to be returned to the parish of origin. Great hardship might arise as indigent, helpless people were ruthlessly sent back to possibly distant parishes even when they were dying. Whether this happened in Warton parish is not known but it might be noticed that when Richard Townson, a clothier of Leeds, needed help to get to a London hospital it was Priest Hutton, where he was born, that was considered liable, not Leeds

Petition of Richard Townson of Priest Hutton 1653 (QSP 81/4).
Reproduced by kind permission of the County Archivist, Lancashire Record Office.

where he worked and lived.[13] In 1677 the Overseers of the Poor of Warton petitioned the Justices of the Peace in Lancaster. They sought their help against William Waineman of Carnforth who had promised 'to keep harmless' the town of Warton from any claim from a John Rippon. Since then Rippon and his family had become 'chargeable' on the town of Warton and Mr Waineman was not keeping his promise. The petition is briefly annotated on behalf of the Justices 'nothing'.[14]

Forgery in Yealand Redmayne

Not all those in need were entirely innocent, but one cannot help feeling for John Osliffe of Yealand Redmayne who in 1681 was in prison awaiting trial. He had been there since the last assize and petitioned to be allowed to go home on bail '...whereby he may endeavour to provide for his Family to kepe them out of Poverty'. He had been charged, by a William Foster, with forging a shilling ten years before. If he could not be allowed home, Osliffe finished, then could he please be freed 'from the Irones he has bene burdened wth ever since his confinement'.[15] The petition is again annotated 'nothing', which is not surprising, for forgery counted as high treason, punishable by hanging and quartering. Osliffe was not the only one in Warton parish involved in the alleged forgery. Another Yealand Redmayne inhabitant, Thomas Hobkyn, yeoman, was also named by William Foster as was John Lawrence of Warton, husbandman. The case was a notorious one, involving much of Lonsdale, and ended up with the hanging of William Smorthwaite, High Constable of the Lonsdale ward.[16] What happened to Osliffe, Hobkyn and Lawrence has not emerged.

Charities

Despite the attempts under the Poor Laws to organise relief there were still beggars, as there are to day. Lucas says that in Carnforth, when he was young, there were no beggars, or at any rate they were '...as rare here as...a Horse in the Streets of Venice...'[17], but he is talking of beggars 'belonging to the town'. The parish registers mention three paupers buried in Warton in the seventeenth century, all apparently from outside the parish. It does not say if they were begging, but probably. The children of two pauper women, each described as *advena*, that is a stranger, were baptised.

To save poor inhabitants of Warton parish from open begging there was not only the Poor Law system, there was also still charity. A small minority of the destitute would have been fortunate enough to find houseroom in the almshouse, the Hospital of Jesus, that Archbishop Hutton had endowed. There were at most six places for the whole parish and they were for men only. Hutton and his heirs had the right to select who should be admitted, and the almsmen were paid out of the Hutton estate a yearly sum which works out at something just over 2d a day,[18] not as poor a ration as it sounds when it is remembered that a man in work might be getting no more than 30d a week.

Others beside Hutton made charitable bequests. Thomas Mansergh of Borwick, who died at the beginning of the eighteenth century left an estate yielding £36 a year to be used to put poor children out as apprentices.[19] The charity still functions. Dr Sherlock, chaplain to Sir Robert Bindloss (see Chapter 16) left £10 to the poor of Warton parish,[20] a charity which also still survives. In 1669 John Hynd, clerk, left in his will ten pounds the interest of which was again to be used for apprenticing poor children, or else 'for buying cloaths for poore children'. In 1670, Francis Jackson, the vicar of Warton, left ten pounds the interest of which was to be disposed among the poor of the parish.

Others left more modest sums, usually to the poor of their own township. In 1669 John Bisbrowne left five shillings to the poor of Silverdale 'to bee Disposed to the moste needfull...' In 1680 Hugh Cornthwaite, also of Silverdale gave ten shillings 'to the poore within the hamlett of Silverdale'. In 1633 Jennet Heblethwaite left twopence to every householder in Carnforth. It was to be given to them '...att the bridge as usually has beene heretofore'. As it was to go to everyone it sounds more as though this was a form of the 'penny dole' which it was customary to give to those coming to a funeral (see Chapter 18). Jennet Heblethwaite may have been wanting to be sure it was paid to Carnforth people only by thus having it paid out as they crossed the Keer on their way to the parish church in Warton. These were the formal charitable gifts. Informal and passing acts of charity to unfortunate neighbours necessarily go unrecorded.

Attitudes to Poverty

It seems that the inhabitants of Warton parish had some compassion for the poor in their midst, but there is really not enough evidence to know how the poor were viewed. Were they pitied as unfortunate? Condemned as improvident? Or was poverty simply accepted as part of life? The implication of the small gifts to the poor of one's own township described above is that charity did not have to extend even to the whole parish, certainly not to the poor elsewhere. The Poor Laws, with their parish-based rates and their refusal to help any pauper from outside must have reinforced this feeling. Nor is it easy to know how the poor viewed themselves. Was there in any sense a 'sub-culture', to use a modern phrase, of the poor? Did a poor man of Silverdale see himself in any sense as more akin to poor men elsewhere than to his richer fellow townsmen of Silverdale?

It has been suggested that there were characteristics (other than lack of income that is) that differentiated the poor. That, for instance, 'the poor' rarely, in the seventeenth century or any time in the past, attended church. As William Perkins, the Elizabethan calvinist theologian had put it '...they join not themselves to any settled congregation for the obtaining of God's kingdom'.[21] But Perkins was talking about those he called 'rogues, beggars and vagabonds'. If the settled poor of a village were also non-church attenders then this would certainly be a differentiating characteristic in a period when religion was taken so seriously.

John Addy in his researches into sin in the seventeenth century is able to quote lamentations from Lancashire gentlemen, puritan and otherwise, about the tendency of the multitude to view Sunday as a day to make merry on. The Privy Council in 1593 commented on the emptiness of churches in the north-west on Sundays, though blaming 'bastards and drunkards' rather then specifically the poor.[22] Lucas certainly describes (see Chapter 16) a group of persistent non-attenders in Warton parish in the 1680s (other that is than those not attending on conscientious grounds), but Lucas does not say that these offenders were particularly found among the poor. They were simply people who preferred to loiter away the time in the churchyard or alehouse.[23] Lucas may have had the lower orders in mind when he wrote of irreligious behaviour, but he does not say so. Lucas in fact, though accepting without question wide differences in status, rights and duties between rich and poor, is not 'class conscious' in the modern sense of the word. He attributes bad behaviour to individuals, not to their level in society. Even in his description of a piece of vandalism there is no suggestion that the lower orders were to blame. It was simply something to be deplored. (The vandalism, one is relieved to learn, was not particular to Warton parish. Lucas assures us that it was a wide-spread practice throughout England.)

> ...I cannot but take Notice of...a beastly Custom of unclean and irreverent Persons, to pollute and bedaube the Walls (and sometimes the very Doors) of the Place where Almighty God is to be worshipped, with Piss or other more nasty Excrements; an Irreverence Travellers tell us not to be seen, or so much heard of in any of the eastern Nations... [24]

CHAPTER TWELVE

HOW IT WAS
Women and Children Last

Earlier in the book it was promised that an attempt would be made to do justice to the women and children of Warton parish. Women formed half the population, or perhaps slightly more if estimates of a slight excess of females in the era are correct.[1] Yet their lives have gone comparatively unrecorded. When one considers the status of women at the time this is not surprising. In Common Law an unmarried woman was subject to her father and after she married all her rights were so vested in her husband that she scarcely existed in law. She could not easily manage a business on her own since she could not sue (or come to that be sued) in the civil courts, except through her husband. Only as a widow could she exercise independent power. There is a good example of an active and managing widow in Warton parish. Dame Anne Middleton, widow of Sir George Middleton of Leighton Hall, seems to have taken a very active part in managing the property after his death in 1672, but she was perhaps in an unusually strong position because the estate had passed to a son-in-law, there being no surviving sons.

It was all but impossible for a woman to get higher education. They were not admitted to the universities. Grammar schools were either founded for boys only, or very rapidly dropped girls from the foundation. Even primary education was hard for women to acquire. Schools for girls did exist, but they tended to be industrial schools rather than places of learning. Even Christ's Hospital which did keep girls on the foundation did not give them access to the more advanced learning of the mathematical school. They were 'taught, besides reading, writing and arithmetic, all kinds of plain needle-work and to knit the boys stockings'.[2]

Husbands and Wives

These attitudes had good biblical authority. There were changes over the seventeenth century, some advantageous to women's independence, some not. The growth of Puritanism had rather mixed effects. In theory Puritan thinking emphasised God given male dominance, but it also stressed the need for mutuality in marriage, again with biblical authority. Eve had been, as it was often put at the time, created not from Adam's head nor from his foot but from his side, to 'be an help meet for him'.[3] It has been suggested that Puritanism also had an unexpected side-effect through its emphasis on the importance of individual conscience. If conscience must be obeyed then what about the conscience of women? Must they too not listen to it? Moreover within the Dissenting Churches women might find a rôle as preachers. Especially among the Quakers women were given much more equal consideration. George Fox, when he heard someone say flippantly that women had no more souls than geese, retorted with the words of Mary 'My soul doth magnify the Lord'.[4] In other ways women may have lost out over the century. Alice Clark, who in 1914, wrote an early classic on the working life of women argued that, while work had been carried on in the home, women and men could be partners in it. With the coming of a more capitalist organisation, the man worked away from home and the wife either had to be kept by him, or find such work as was compatible with home and children, usually spinning, which was notoriously ill paid.[5]

It seems likely however that such a change in the wife's position would be less marked in a rural parish. John Fitzherbert, a late sixteenth century writer on agriculture, gave an account of the working day of a farmer's wife which shows her as working very closely alongside her husband. Not only was she to do all her own housework (which included making butter and cheese, spinning the flax and making all linen and clothes) but she was also to milk the cows, feed the pigs and poultry, tend the garden. Then when the farm was busy she was to shear and winnow the corn alongside the men, drive the plough and even cart dung. On top of this she was to go to market to sell her butter and cheese, and finally render her accounts to her husband. At least he was to do the same to her, for if they were to thrive 'they must be true ether to other'.[6] The husbands of Warton parish who referred in their wills to 'my dear wife', or who asked to be buried as near to her as possible, may have all been using conventional formulae, but it seems more likely that they truly valued such a helpmeet.

Women and inheritance

Moreover, in a rural parish like Warton, customary law was of more everyday importance than common law, and under customary law women's status was perhaps marginally higher than under common law.[7] Inheritance was not only in the male line. There was no searching about for distant heirs. Under the Custom of the Manor of Warton, in the absence of a son, the eldest daughter inherited.[8] By implication this was also the case in Yealand Manor where it had been agreed that a tenant could take over when 'his or her' fine had been paid.[9] If a woman holding a manorial tenure married, her husband's right to her manorial property was not entirely automatic. There are entries in the Warton Manor Court records describing the process whereby a wife was questioned, first privately by the steward, then in open court. She then had to declare that she wanted her husband to be admitted to her property. What would have happened if she had said it was not her wish is another and unanswered question. It is not clear why the formula was only recorded for a few years in Warton Manor Court records. The matter seems to have been differently settled in different manors. In nearby Halton the husband 'is to have all her customary Lands during his natural life whether he has issue by her "Yea! or no" '.[10]

Under customary law the widow could be allowed half of her husband's property rather than the third that was her legally guaranteed right under Common Law. That this was so is spelled out in the 'Custom of the Manor of Warton' and implied in the terminology of wills in all the townships.

Under common law, according to Blackstone, the great legal authority of the time, a woman had no right even over her own children; her husband could dispose of their care as he thought fit.[11] Under Customary Law custody was hers and also the enjoyment of the property until the heir was of age - with one proviso as was spelt out in the Custom of Warton Manor.

That every Wife after the Death of her Husband to have Custody of her natural child being heir to her Husband and the occupation or profit of the whole Tenement untill the Heir come to the age of 16 years and then be it man or woman to enter to the one half of the said Tenement and the other half to remain to the widdow during her pure Widdowhood and if she commit fornication or otherwise miscarry contrary to the Custome of the said Mannor then she to forfeit her widdowright and the heirs to enter into the whole Tenement.[12]

Women as Constables

Though women are never found as jurors in the manor courts, they had some standing in local government. Among the tenants who went to law to protect their tenant rights in Silverdale was a woman; Jennet Bisbrowne representing an infant, Marie Bisbrowne, as her *Procheinamy*.[13] Constables were chosen from householders, the duty falling on the house rather than the owner. If the householder was a woman she was still liable - at any rate arguably so - though probably only liable to pay for a substitute rather than to act in *propria persona*. In 1651 Isabel Nicholson of Carnforth pleaded that she was old and poor and it was not right that her son Richard Lucas, constable, was trying to make her 'beare a parte of the Cunstableshippe with him'.[14] In 1683 Isabell Mason and Alice Hadwen refused to pay their proporcionable shares...towards the serving of the office of constable'.[15] In 1685 Agnes Waithman of Silverdale complained to the Justices of the Peace that her neighbours were trying to 'put the office of the Constable upon mee' although it was the Custom that 'widdowes are Freed of that Service'.[16]

Country woman, early to mid 17th Century

Childbirth

There can be no escaping some of the terrible aspects of any woman's life in the seventeenth century. Childbirth was a constant peril. It is hardly bearable even to read certain accounts of obstructed labour with the helpless mother suffering days of agonising and useless pain till she died of exhaustion. Within a week of an apparently normal birth a happy mother might be struck by puerperal fever and go on to almost inevitable death. Then there was the dreadful death rate among children.

There is a school of thought which argues that, because infant deaths were so common, mothers did not mourn the death of a baby as we do to-day. One wonders. However, whatever the women of Warton parish had to put up with, they were certainly no patient Griseldas. The Manor Court records of Warton contain very many records of fines for 'flytings, hubbleshows and bloodwipes' (that is to say quarrels, disturbances and bloodshed). Women were to the fore in flyting, mostly among themselves, but also with the men. Less often they were involved in hubbleshows (and note they could be fined in their own right in the Manor Court, even if they had a husband who, in common law, would have been responsible for them). They could stand up aggressively to men. In 1635 Mary Townson of Priest Hutton was summoned to court for 'her abuse offered and donne to Francis Turner constable...in throwing hott water at him...'[17]

Women of courage

On a more serious note it was not only Quaker women who were prepared to stand up for their beliefs. There was Mrs Walker who went up to Leighton Hall to 'demand' money owed to her husband. Sir George Middleton asked her by what authority she did so, and she replied 'by the power and Authority of the parliament & States'. Sir George had no retort but to say that they were 'a Company of idle Fellowes,' who had nothing to do with him. Admittedly this was during the Commonwealth when Sir George, as a royalist, would have had least authority. Nevertheless he had, at the time of her visit, collected a group of armed royalist rebels about him, who had already wounded one townsman. It does suggest that one ordinary townswoman was not lacking in personal courage.[18] Moreover, as has been mentioned before (see Chapter 9), when Sir George's men attacked some of the townsmen in the fields they were only beaten off when the women came out to rescue their menfolk.[19]

Not all women, of course, were either brave or virtuous and any fall from grace on their part tends to be particularly well documented because of what has come to be termed a double standard when judging men and women. The records of the Ecclesiastical Courts are a usual source of information for such affairs, but the ones so far studied have not been particularly informative for Warton parish. The church seems to have been too bothered about the amount of recusancy and dissent to spend time on mere fornicators. However scattered among the various returns recording those not attending church, either as papists or Quakers, or not paying their assessments, or resorting to conventicles are a few references to those with irregular private lives. There are complaints of fornication against both men and women, but mostly for living together *ante matrimonium*. It is true that when William Bisbrowne of Kendal was let off for fornication with Mary Dickinson of Silverdale she was not, but then it was her fourth appearance for the same fault.[20]

Bastardy

It is perhaps evidence of a present day 'double standard' to consider bastardy here, in a chapter purporting to deal especially with women. Yet it seems natural to do so because it was likely to be the woman who was left to care for the baby. However, not all seducers were villains. It is true that Edward Allanby fled the parish when the daughter of the house where he had been living was found to be pregnant. However after she was delivered he came back, and before the constable could arrest the two of them they were 'both gone and wee know not whither'.[21] The bearing of bastards was disapproved of both morally and because of the likelihood that mother and child would fall on the poor rates. Nevertheless it was possible for women to have bastard children and live it down, perhaps because of a general realisation that a bastard might be not so much the result of unusual immorality as of a more generally practised pre-marital intercourse followed by some break down in the marriage arrangements. There are wills where 'base born' children are included in the legacies. For instance in 1611 Agnes Ward, a widow of Warton township left to her 'base son' William not only a chest, two silver spoons and sixteen shillings, but also arranged for half of her unbequeathed goods to be shared equally between her brother and William.

The main evidence for illegitimacy comes from the parish registers. If to all the baptisms said to be of illegitimate children (by whatever title; *spurius, nothus* or plain English bastard) are added those where no father's name is given (or in three cases of undoubted bastardy only the father's), then the total for the whole century is only 49, or 1.78 per cent of baptisms.[22] Only two cases of a woman having more than one bastard child occur in the registers. On March 17th, 1644 there is an entry in the register *Isabella filia Eliz: Kenie de Lindeth spurius cum Thom: Crofte de Poulton base born'*. Whoever made the entry seems to have felt strongly since not only the Latin *'spurius'*, but also the English 'base born' are used, though owing to a possible confusion over Latin genders it is not quite clear to which of the three the derogatory terms apply. In 1652 the same Elizabeth Kenie appears as the mother of William and John 'base begot childeren'. The baptism of a base begot child of Jenet Hadwen of Silverdale was recorded on March 29th, 1645. On December 17th 1647 the baptism of 'Tho: fillius Jenet Hadwen de Silverdall' is recorded. It is not stated that Thomas was base begot, but the absence of the father's name makes it likely. On the whole Warton seems to conform to the general pattern that 'Illegitimacy was not a significant factor in regional history before 1750. This does not mean that pre-marital conceptions were not common'.[23]

Children and Death

Children in seventeenth century England were very numerous, but had a very frail hold on life. To-day only about 2½ per cent of deaths occur under the age of ten years. It has been reckoned that in pre-industrial England up to a third of all children would be dead by the age of ten, an estimate confirmed by a particular survey of eight representative English parishes in the late sixteenth and early seventeenth centuries.[24] Yet, because the birth rate was high, as many as four persons in every ten in a community were likely to be children under ten years of age.

This forty per cent of the population has been less studied than its numbers deserve. There has been a school of thought that claims that children of the past were by and large ill-used and underprivileged. '...the history of childhood is a nightmare from which we have only recently begun to awaken'.[25] Followers of this school argue that children were viewed as sinful and imperfect little adults who must be beaten into conformity; because they were not seen as having rights of their own they were vulnerable to abuse from parents and masters; because they died so frequently they were seen as expendable and parents had no warmth for them. Also infanticide was regularly practised. If the implication of such writers is that now at last we understand and cherish children, then the recent revelations of what can go on in our caring society must make us rather less smug. Regretfully one must assume that, if there can be such wide spread child abuse in a culture with built in legislation to protect children, it is more than likely that child abuse went on in the past, when they had not even paper protection. How wide spread such abuse was is another matter. In the 1650s Adam Martindale, Presbyterian minister of Rotherstone (Rostherne), south of Manchester, learnt that the six year old daughter of one of his flock had been sexually abused by an old man living in the neighbourhood. Martindale dealt with the matter with a calm good sense which suggests that, however much he disapproved, he did not view such a happening as a totally shocking novelty. After the old man was apprehended it came out that he had abused a number of other children as well, but that their story had either not been told or not believed.[26] All very like today, in fact.

Child Abuse

There is evidence of cruelty from recorded court cases and inquests. We know that there were practices which amounted to infanticide in the abandonment of children. Dr. Phaire, a sixteenth century practitioner who wrote a book on child care, casually describes a stiffness of limbs in children '...as when a chylde is found in the frost, or in the strete, cast away by a wycked mother...'.[27] But though Phaire noted the fact he did not condone the practice in any way. The apprentice system, whereby young people went to live and work in the houses of strangers, must have been open to abuse.

Young serving girls were notoriously at risk of sexual harassment. In a study of illegitimacy in Lancashire 14 per cent of the identified fathers were masters of the girl, and 8 per cent were fellow servants.[28] Yet, as to-day, we tend to know about abuses because in the end neighbours and relations finally said 'enough is enough' and made the abuse public. Deliberate cruelty was nowhere condoned by seventeenth century society, though a degree of physical punishment we should think wrong was. The idea that children should not be led to better ways by punishing them for their faults was not one that appealed to the seventeenth century mind.

Boy's doublet and breeches 1649-50

Working Children

Yet there were many parents willing to put much effort into the care and maintenance of their children. At a time when the cost (to the Poor Law) of maintaining a child was £2 a year parents with annual incomes of £10-15 or less must have been hard pressed to maintain a family of any size.[29] It is not surprising that children were expected to contribute very early to the family income. Probably most children were earning something by seven years old or before.[30] John Locke, the philospher, would have said this was rather late. He thought that the children of the poor should be working, for some part of the day, by the time they were three years old.[31] In an agricultural community a child could make a useful contribution quite early. William Stout of Lancaster, after describing his withdrawal from school to work on the farm added with satisfaction '...two of us at 13 or 14 years of age being equal to one man shearer'.[32]

Child-care

Little is known of how children were reared. Much of what we do know derives from child manuals, written by doctors and other authorities, rather than from records of actual practice. These manuals recommended breast-feeding, swaddling for the first month or two at least, and weaning at anything between one and three years. Almost nothing is said about toilet-training. How much of all this was put into practice is not known. Breast-feeding was almost certainly more wide-spread than to-day, for artificial feeding was not a practical proposition. With no rubber teats, no knowledge of the need for sterilisation or for modifying cow's milk such attempts as might be made were likely to be quickly fatal. For a mother who could not or did not wish to feed her child herself the only alternative was breast-feeding at second-hand by a wet-nurse. It was a common practice for those who could afford it, and universally condemned by moralists and physicians alike. The early weaning of the wet nurse's own child may have made some contribution to infant mortality, and writers at the time certainly suspected that a baby sent away from home to be wet-nursed was at risk of neglect and even worse. However the great majority of child deaths would have been due, not to neglect or crime, but to ignorance of basic hygiene, to infections for which there was no treatment and above all to poverty and the resulting undernourishment in an age when even adults could starve.

Direct information from Warton parish on any of the aspects of child care discussed above is extremely limited. Wet-nursing probably was employed in Warton, but we have no evidence one way or the other. We know of at least one apprentice wrongfully used by his master - but not abused. His master, a weaver, absconded and left the boy without maintenance, but still bound apprentice so that he could not go elsewhere to work. The big men of the parish, the vicar, the churchwardens, the overseers of the poor and others, got together to petition the justices. As a result the boy was given leave to work within Warton till the case came up at the next session.[33] We know of one illegitimate child, Peter Hubberstie,

Boy-child with skirts and sword c.1600

Swaddled baby, 1605. Wormington, Glouc.

in whose case 'dyvers of the Inhabitants of Yelland' got together to complain to the Justices because of the 'evil education' given him by his father and uncle. The inhabitants did not act out of pity for a neglected child, but because 'through want of due chastisement and maintenance' Peter had become 'verie troublesome...to all his neighbours and doth usualy wronge and abuse their children, and other great damages'.[34]

School Boys

Almost nothing is known of how Warton children spent their time, what their amusements were, or how roughly or kindly they were treated. Lucas gives an account of the play of the boys at the grammar school which suggests that they, at least, had not had their spirit broken.[35] In the new year they divided into two teams and played football, watched by their 'parents and the Chief Inhabitants'. Afterwards the captains of the two sides 'take each his party to an Ale-house and give them Refreshment'. On Shrove Tuesday the boys took part in cock-fighting and 'kailing', or throwing things at a cock to see who could knock it down. If there was a wedding the school boys made fast the church door and would not let the groom out till he had given them money. Then later they paraded under the couple's window and demanded drink money. When school broke up for Christmas they brought the master gifts, called *'Nicholas Pennies'*, out of which he gave them a 'Potation'.

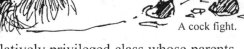

A cock fight.

Schoolboys, however, were a relatively privileged class whose parents could afford to spare them to be educated. Other children would be more likely to be at work, helping their parents eke out the family living, acting as a farm hand if they were big enough, or helping in minor ways if they were smaller; scaring crows, gleaning, tending cows and sheep on the common and *'wool-gathering'*, that is collecting shed wool for spinning like the 'childringe' of John Cansfelde and Anthony Howsman. Both the parents were fined 6d in 1602 by the Manor Court for this. The practice had apparently became a nuisance because after recording the fines the Manor Court went on to forbid wool-gathering anywhere except on the sands, and then only 'before six of the cloke in the afor nowne or after thre of the cloke in the after nowne'.[36] Which, incidentally, raises one more of the many, many problems waiting to be solved. How did the children know what o'clock it was? Lucas says that it was a neighbourhood '...where Clocks till of late were very scarce...'[37] However it was the practice at Leighton Hall, he adds, to ring a large bell hung in the tower 'to give Notice to the Servants to begin and end their Work'. There was also, Lucas implies though does not state, a clock in the church. It seems that Warton may already have begun to rely on something other than the sun's height to judge time.

Four Acres and a Cow

Throughout England in the seventeenth century, many farming families were finding it difficult to feed themselves adequately and needed secondary employments to keep themselves alive. In the uplands of Lancashire there was, for various reasons, a surplus of the landless or nearly landless, who had particular reason to need such 'by-employments' as they have been termed, and it was to textile work in particular that they turned.[1] Over the course of the seventeenth century what had once been a by-employment became for many families the sole source of income, and the beginnings of a landless workforce was created. Over the eighteenth and nineteenth centuries this pool of men and women entirely dependent on non-agricultural work became the basis on which Lancashire grew into the leading industrial producer of the world.

In the part of Lancashire in which Warton parish lay the move from by-employment to industrial production was never so dramatic. There were cotton mills in Lancaster and a small silk weaving factory developed in Galgate, but the surrounding countryside was not drawn in as it was in east Lancashire. It is only appropriate here to consider the factors in the seventeenth century which led to the opening stages of the textile trade, though it might be interesting at a later stage to study the conditions that aborted the progress to industry and left Warton, in the eighteenth century, as an almost totally agricultural area. It is true that a small flax mill was built in Yealand Conyers in 1825, but it was never large and had closed by 1851. The heckling shed, and some weavers' cottages can still be traced in the domestic buildings near the present Catholic church.[2]

The Need for By-Employments

As in the rest of Lancashire in the seventeenth century there were two factors in particular which made it difficult for the inhabitants of Warton parish to earn an adequate living by agriculture alone, and hence encouraged the growth of by-employments. These were a deterioration in the climate, and an increase in the population which had taken place over the sixteenth century and the first years of the seventeenth which made it difficult for all to have a share in the land. It seems that the population of Warton parish remained fairly stable throughout the seventeenth century as a whole, declining if anything towards the end of the century. It was a stability possibly bought at the cost of outmigration (see Chapter 8). It may be this, rather than an increasing dependence on by-employment that was Warton's solution to the problem of keeping up some sort of standard of living.

The deterioration in climate is thought to have cut the growing season by as much as five weeks in the last decades of the seventeenth century (see Chapter 3). This together with the low productivity of farmland by twentieth century standards could only to a limited extent be compensated for by taking more land into cultivation. The best land had long before been claimed, and it was the less tractable areas such as peat-mosses and the upland fringe that remained. Warton parish had little upland waste, and much of the low ground was extremely rocky or thin soiled. The peat-mosses seem to have been still valued as sources of fuel, rather than seen as potential arable land to be drained.

The Landless

In a time when food shortages threatened so frequently, every household must have cherished the aim of self-sufficiency in food, but it must have been hard to achieve for many families. We know from the study of probate inventories,[3] and from scattered information on land holdings, that while a large proportion of the population had some land, many had very little, and some had no land at all. An estimate of the number who were without any land can be made from the returns for the Hearth Tax Act of 1662.[4] Certain people were exempt from payment mainly, though not entirely, on the grounds of poverty. The lists compiled locally from the collection of the Hearth Tax were supposed to include the names of all exempt householders, though they do not always do so. It has been suggested that most people returned as 'non-chargeable' would have been labourers.[5] The lists for the Warton townships for Lady Day 1664 are among those that do list the non-chargeable. These form 38 per cent of the whole, suggesting that about this proportion may have been without land. The figure for Warton township is particularly high, with 57 per cent exempt from the tax. Towns throughout England had higher numbers of the non-chargeable and perhaps the high proportion in Warton merely reflects the fact that it was the largest of the townships and the nearest to being urban in Warton parish. For the other townships those exempt formed 25-30 per cent of the total, suggesting that some 70-75 per cent of the households outside Warton township held some land.

The Distribution of Landholdings

To say that such and such a percentage of households held land does not help in estimating how many households needed the support of by-employments unless the size of holdings is known. To determine how much land was held on average by each household we also need to know how much arable land there was in the parish. In our present state of knowledge this is difficult to estimate for the whole parish, particularly as there are complications in considering the Middleton and Bindloss family estates. It is easier for the present to consider one township, Silverdale, for which we have reasonably reliable information. The likely total of arable land available in Silverdale can be estimated by considering present potential land-use and the areas of customary cultivation. Effectively this means including all those parts where there are reasonable areas of ground where the rock is more than a few inches below ground surface, or which were not too swampy to be used. For Silverdale there were probably about 260 statute acres of potential arable land.

An estimate of the seventeenth century population of Silverdale as being in the region of 30 households was given in Chapter 8. That population estimate is derived from the Parish Registers. Some other sources suggest that the figure may be too low, but no detailed analysis of this extra information has yet been made, and there is no guarantee that such an analysis would produce a more accurate figure. Assuming that there were in fact 30 households in Silverdale, the Hearth Tax data for Silverdale suggests that 26 per cent of the households were landless. This leaves 22 households with some land. If the potential arable land (260 acres) were to be divided evenly between all the households this would give each of the 22 households 12 acres.

Inventories

But of course the land was not divided equally. There are three sources of information that can give us an idea of the actual distribution of land at that time. Probably the most helpful of these sources lies in the probate inventories. Though the inventories do not give landholdings, the wealth of individuals at that time was so closely related to landholdings that the total inventory wealth can be taken as a rough guide to the size of landholding. Only a small proportion of inventories has survived, and these do not include the poorest in the population, but the available information does give a reasonable picture of wealth distribution, though no doubt more refined studies would improve the accuracy. For Silverdale the poorest 70 per cent of individuals who left inventories shared 32 per cent of the wealth, while the richest 30 per cent of individuals shared 68 per cent of the wealth. If this information from inventories is applied to the distribution of the 260 acres of arable land in Silverdale, it suggests that the poorest 70 per cent of households shared 32 per cent of the land (83 acres), which would give them 5.5 acres each on average. The wealthiest 30 per cent would share 177 acres, giving them 25 acres each on average.

Tithe Book

The second source of information on the distribution of farming wealth is the 'Tithe Book of Warton Parish (Wool and Lamb) 1631' which records the tithe of the fleeces collected in the parish of Warton in that year.[6] From this the number of sheep owned by the listed individuals can be calculated (and this is found to accord quite closely with information from inventories). In Silverdale 23 people owned a total of about 740 sheep. The wealthiest five owners had 480 sheep between them, and the poorest 18 shared the remaining 260 sheep. If this wealth distribution is applied to Silverdale's 260 acres of arable land we find that the poorest 78 per cent would average 5 acres each, while the wealthiest 22 per cent would average 34 acres each. However, the fleece data are likely to produce a somewhat distorted picture of land ownership, owing to the very wide range of flock sizes. At the lower end very many people had a few sheep, while at the upper end farmers with access to extensive sea-marsh had very large flocks.

A page of the 'Tithe Book of Warton Parish (Wool and Lambs)' 1631 (Ref. DDTo/H/4).
Reproduced by kind permission of the County Archivist, Lancashire Record Office.

1563 Survey

The third source of information on distribution of landholdings comes from the previous century. A 1563 survey of part of Silverdale lists the landholdings of 21 tenants.[7] They held a total of about 90 statute acres of land. It is not a survey of all Silverdale households, and we must assume that some large landholders were not covered if the total of arable land was 260 acres at that time. This sample seems therefore biased to the poorer households. Taken straight from the document, the acreages given vary from about 2.5 to 5 customary acres (apart from a few holdings which are very small and are really just gardens). Evidence from the Silverdale Manor Court records shows that a customary acre in Silverdale was equivalent to about 1.5 statutory acres. This gives figures for 1563 landholdings in the range 4 to 7.5 statute acres.

Despite the imperfections in the above three sources of information there is a reasonable convergence in the resulting figures for the average landholdings, especially for the less well-off. The three sources suggest that the poorer landholders held an average of some 4 to 7.5 acres each, while the wealthiest 20 to 30 per cent of families averaged 25 to 35 acres each. It is probable that even this overestimates the holdings of the poorest tenants, including those called Cottagers.

Four Acre Rule

On all manors even these, the poorest of the tenants, were supposed to own at least four acres. This was laid down by a general Act of 1589 and was reinforced by manor regulations. In Warton Manor it was ordered that tenants selling land had to leave unsold 'a messuage-house, and four acres of land belonging to the same'.[8] The reason given was that this still left a tenant able to serve 'all offices within the township' i.e. to fill such posts as barleyman, pinder and constable. A deeper reason, the ever present fear that landless people might get a foothold in the parish and become a burden on the poor rates has been discussed previously (see Chapter 10).

It is probable that the four acre rule was being evaded, as it was on other manors. It has been estimated that in Yorkshire and Lancashire only 9 per cent of labourers held as much as four acres and 31 per cent had no more than a garden attached to the cottage.[9] For Warton parish only one piece of direct information has been found. In the 1563 survey of Silverdale already quoted, five of the twenty-one tenants listed were described as cottagers. Three of these had half an acre and two had an acre. One of the latter also had a rood of land described as an 'incroachment'. One of those with only half an acre also had, listed separately, 4 acres of arable land.[10]

Landholdings and Self-Sufficiency

But how much land did a family need to feed itself? It has been suggested that for medieval farming a landholding of 10-15 acres of average quality arable land would provide enough income after heavy manorial payments to feed a family of five just enough to keep them alive and able to work.[11] Most of the households in Silverdale had much less land than this and would need to find other sources of income. It is clear that many families supplemented the produce of their arable acres by grazing livestock on the manorial common, a right available to all tenants. But the lambs and wool produced by a small flock of sheep would not make up for lack of a decent acreage of arable land.

Just as less than 10 to 15 acres was too little to support a family so it has been estimated that, before mechanisation, a landholding of 30 acres or more would have been too large for most families to farm by their own labour.[12] The large landowner needed a source of labour within walking-distance of his holdings, and this could be supplied by those who were without land or who could not feed themselves from their small landholdings. Evidence from the Warton Parish Registers for the 1720s (comparable information is not available for the seventeenth century) shows that about 15 per cent of the adult male population at that time were day-labourers, and we have already seen that many more had only small landholdings. There is ample evidence, therefore, that many in the parish would be looking for other employment to supplement their farming livelihood. While some would be satisfied with labouring work on the larger landholdings of the wealthier parishioners, others would seek to be more independent and pursue occupations that were perhaps more reliable. We have already discussed the trading of farm surpluses in the farming chapters. The alternative of taking up by-employments is considered in the next chapter.

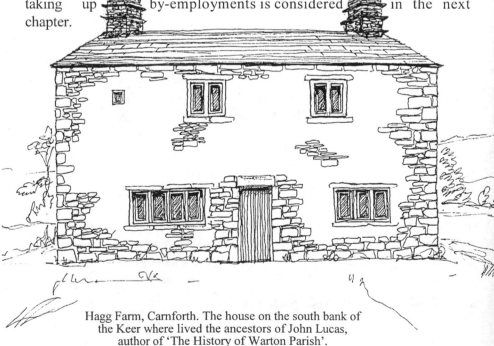

Hagg Farm, Carnforth. The house on the south bank of
the Keer where lived the ancestors of John Lucas,
author of 'The History of Warton Parish'.

HOW IT WAS
Making Ends Meet

There were many ways in which those with inadequate holdings of land could earn extra income. The following pages present the evidence garnered from the surviving wills, inventories, Manor Court records and other sources for the whole of the seventeenth century. Even when all these are put together we have information on less than one quarter of the adult male population. There is better information, by chance, for the early years of the eighteenth century, and this has been used as an addendum to the chapter to fill out the picture.

Fishing

The parish's six-mile long coastline along the eastern shore of Morecambe Bay gave it two important assets not available to inland parishes - fish and sea-salt. Fishing and the collection of shellfish were especially important by-employments in Silverdale and Lindeth though some species of fish were reserved for the Lord of the Manor. Daniel Defoe, in describing the adjoining area of Westmorland commented that:-

> *the south parts of this county are pretty well furnished with sea-fish, caught near the Kent and Leven sands, and other places upon the sea-coast, which formerly were brought weekly to Kendal market, where there have been sometimes five and thirty different sorts of fish; but since the great improvement of the town and port of Lancaster, the market for fish is considerably drawn that way.[1]*

The inventories show only one person actually describing himself as a fisherman. William Clarke of Silverdale (1666) died worth some £35, of which £23 was in animals and crops. He had 'nettes' and various types of basket, a nag and a mare, carts and ropes. But there are no fewer than thirteen Silverdale inventories which include nets, and five Warton inventories, four of which are for residents of Lindeth. These testators called themselves husbandmen, presumably seeing this as their primary occupation. The concentration of men owning nets along the estuary is in itself evidence of an important by-employment. More detailed examination of the inventories suggests that the fishing methods were similar to those practised at the beginning of the twentieth century and described by Eddie Sands. [2] It is very likely that the three main fish crops mentioned by Eddie Sands, flukes, cockles and shrimps, were also the most important in the seventeenth century. The usual way to catch flukes (a type of flatfish) was to place nets between stakes across the channels of the River Kent. Lucas explains that fishermen had to reach the nets 'so soon as the Tide ebbs from them, otherwise the Herring-Gull, and other Sea Fowls would quickly devour a great many of them'. On the darkest nights, he says, they had to use wind-direction to keep their orientation.

...the most experienced sets his Face...directly towards the Nets., and observing on what part of his Body the Wind beats, sets forward, keeping the Wind on exactly the same Point, and the rest follow in a Row with the deepest silence. When they have fished their Nets which they can see to do by the shining of the Fish, they return in the same Manner. (3)

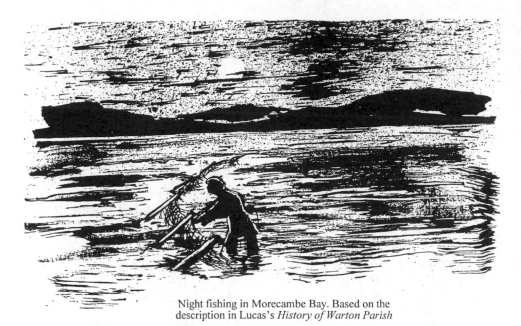

Night fishing in Morecambe Bay. Based on the description in Lucas's *History of Warton Parish*

One of the Silverdale fishermen had 'trammel nettes' - a type of trawl net which could be pulled along the Kent channels at low tide by men, or more usually by horses. Such nets may have been used to catch shrimps, which are at their largest and best in the deeper channels, where it can even be necessary for a horse to swim to pull the net along. Other fishing techniques, such as the construction of wickerwork traps along the edges of the channels may have been used, but they would not be reflected in the inventories. The concentration of hemp-growing in an area where string was needed for net-making must be more than mere coincidence. Fishermen could grow hemp, process it and spin it into string for net-making. Much of this work could be done in the winter months when there was less farming work and less daylight.

The collection of shellfish from the sands, especially cockles, must also have been an important by-employment. The inventories of John Wilson of Silverdale (1692) and William Brown of Warton (1632) include cockle pans, and others include other elements of the very basic equipment needed for cockling - rakes and sieves. The only other item needed for cockling would be the 'jumbo board', a handled heavy board which was still in use in the 1980s,[4] to pound the surface of the sand to loosen the cockles and make them easy to rake out.

Fish markets

While some of the fish would be eaten locally (and must have been an important source of food in hard times), it could also be marketed at Kendal and Lancaster. Lucas notes that a large flat stone slab near the maypole in Warton was formerly used for the fish market there.[5] He also comments that cockles were traded up to 70 or 80 miles east of Warton being '...so excellent in their kind, and so much preferable to those on the East Shore of England...'.[6] Perhaps the West Riding towns, with which there were good communications through the textile trade, were providing an outlet. Dame Anne Middleton's account book for 1675 records two purchases of cockles, both in February.[7] The fishermen's intimate knowledge of the ever-changing pattern of river channels in the estuary may have enabled them also to carry out some unofficial guiding on the cross-Bay routes.

Sea-Salt

The source of that most important commodity, salt, in the first three-quarters of the seventeenth century, was evaporation of sea-water over peat fuelled fires. The trade, called saltwelling, was carried out at several places around Morecambe Bay, one of which was near Carnforth. Lucas refers to Salt Cotes in that town '...a place on the Edge of the Sands, upon the West Side of *Gallihaw,* so called from the little Houses formerly standing there for the making of salt...'[8] The skill of the operation was in the careful collection of the saltiest sand from the estuary, followed by leaching processes, so that the final phase of evaporation was carried out on an already fairly concentrated brine, so economising on fuel. The brine was usually boiled in lead pans heated by burning peat from local mosses. The local saltwellers, including Richard Abram who was working in Warton in 1702, have been listed.[9] There is no evidence of seventeenth century saltwellers in the inventory information.

Until towards the end of the seventeenth century the local sand-salt would have had little competition. The main European producers were in western France and Portugal, where much of the evaporation process could be left to the hot sun. The war between England and France, which started in 1689, put a stop to imports from France, but salt was then imported from Spain and Portugal.[10] At about the same time rock-salt was found in Cheshire and this was carried by sea to all parts of England and Ireland. The rock-salt was refined at Liverpool and traded on, and this eventually put the local saltworks out of business.

There was in the seventeenth century a piece of land called 'Salt coate Parrocke' in Lindeth, strong evidence for the existence at some time of another coastal saltworks in the parish. Perhaps this was sited in the inlet of the bay near Leighton Moss with its supply of peat fuel. There is no evidence that this saltworks was active in the seventeenth century.

Mineral Resources

There was probably little scope for by-employment in the exploitation of local mineral resources. No evidence has been found for the mining of the local thin veins of haematite and copper ore in the seventeenth century, but it is possible that small amounts of haematite were dug from the deposits on Warton Crag to make ruddle for marking sheep as it undoubtedly was later.[11]

Wood for Charcoal

Much of the rocky and thin-soiled limestone ground in the parish is of little value for farming, but produces a thick natural woodland cover if browsing animals can be kept away. The coppicing of such woodland for charcoal-making could only be practised by large landowners. In Warton it was Sir George Middleton of Leighton Hall who was able to guarantee the production of 600 cords [12] of wood a year to make charcoal as his contribution to his shared ownership of a forge at Milnthorpe.[13] It may well be that the plantations he fenced off for coppicing were those about the edges of the Leighton estate that were noted as still producing wood for charcoal in 1760.[14] While this was business on a large scale, there were opportunities for local labour to assist with the coppicing and the woodland management. In 1675 Dame Anne Middleton, Sir George's widow, recorded payment to two men for 'cuttinge and cordinge'.[15] The highly skilled work of charcoal burning was probably carried out by itinerant workers.

By-Employment in textiles

Nearly a quarter of the parish inventories for the seventeenth century refer to spinning wheels. Evidently spinning was widely practised, and even more yarn may have been produced with spindles, items which are too small to be recorded in inventories. It was a skill that could be readily learned within the family. But what was being spun? Was it hemp, flax or wool, or all three?

Hemp

It has already been suggested that some of the locally-grown hemp was spun into string and rope and used for making fishing nets. Nearly half of the Silverdale inventories mention hemp, and over a third of the Yealand inventories. The husbandry of the crop can be traced through inventory entries. Description of hemp as 'sowen' or 'on the earth' occur between April and August. From the end of August the references are to seed or harvested hemp. The parish was noted for its good crops of hemp and the seed fetched a good market price.[16] Hemp was harvested by pulling it up by hand to get the longest fibre possible. It then had to be soaked in water (retted) for eight to ten days. As this made the water foul, retting was forbidden by an Act of 1542 anywhere where animals were watered. In Warton parish a convenient place to carry out the retting was on the peat mosses. Lucas notes the 1542 act and comments 'This Law they here still observe, and water them in their Moss Pits'.[17] Silverdale Manor Court ordered that no-one should ret their hemp or flax 'in any person or persons Mossdale in Silverdale Mosses excepting in their own without first asking liberty to do so of the owner...'[18] The encouragement of ponding in the peat mosses to make retting pools would be an autumn activity and so would not interfere with peat-cutting (when good drainage was needed) which took place in the spring.

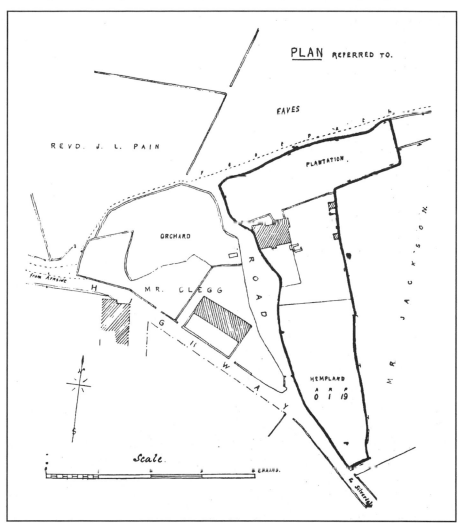

A hempland near Cove Road, Silverdale, referred to on a deed of 1912

Bacteria in the water partially rotted the woody stem of the hemp, and the fibre could be freed from the unwanted stem by drying and beating (or scutching) the hemp, which knocked away the woody parts. Locally the drying and scutching processes were known as 'baking' and 'breaking'. Warton Manor Court ordered that no-one should bake or break hemp '...within any part of their fyer howses' i.e in a domestic oven.[19] There was a danger that drying the hemp over the house fire might lead to a conflagration.

145

The final stage of preparation of hemp fibre was heckling, in which the fibres were straightened by a special comb. It will be seen that hemp growing was a long and labour intensive task, but it produced a very versatile fibre. It could be used to make string and hence nets for fishing, but it could also be spun into a fibre that the local weavers could make up into a very tough material for working clothes called 'harden' and for making sacks.

Flax and Wool

Flax is mentioned in only three per cent of surviving inventories and seems not to have been grown as an important textile fibre in the immediate locality, though it may have been valued for the linseed oil obtained from the seeds. One use of linseed oil was to oil fleeces before spinning. It is likely that growing flax was not commercially viable in the face of the considerable quantities of linen and linen yarn that were being imported from Ireland and the Baltic. Linen was certainly used locally, even if it was not grown. Fifteen per cent of inventories refer to ownership of linen or linen cloth.

Hemp. A male plant

Wool was certainly being spun and woven locally in the seventeenth century, but there is no evidence that the parish was involved in working for such textile concerns as Kendal was well known for. In other parts of the north-west the 'putting out' system was well developed by this time. Middlemen or 'badgers' acted as intermediaries, selling yarn to local households and later calling back to buy the woven cloth. Where this trade was taking place large stocks of yarn or cloth are recorded in the local inventories. In Warton parish there is no evidence of stocks of yarn or cloth on this scale. Eight inventories mention looms, but there is little to suggest that the owners were supplying more than a service to people in the immediate neighbourhood. Looms were not particularly expensive, being valued at well under a pound, but they did take up a considerable amount of space. There are a few references in the inventories to suggest that while most people did their own spinning the yarn was then sent to near-by websters to be made into cloth. The inventory of Peter Bainbridge of Carnforth (1683) lists 'Cloth at webster 10s', and the inventory of Elizabeth Swainson of Warton (1632) refers to a 'canvass webb of 7 yardes att workinge with the webster'. Perhaps a greater use of the wool yarn was for knitting into socks and other garments. Knitting may well have been an important by-employment during long winter evenings, but it is an activity that leaves no trace in inventories.

Of the eight persons whose inventories mention looms only three described themselves as websters (Anthony Hadwen of Carnforth [1630], George Corleis of Silverdale [1589] and John Lucas of Warton [1676]), and of these John Lucas specifies 'woolen webster'. All three were also involved in farming. Anthony Hadwen had cows, sheep and hay. George

Corleis had sown corn worth £3 and John Lucas left 10 ½ acres of land to his wife in his will. The only textile worker who may have been entirely dependent on his trade for his income was Christopher Walker of Silverdale, who is described in his will in 1691 as a shearman (one who shears the nap of cloth smooth), a particularly skilled job. He had a workshop at Carnforth where he kept his shears and spinning wheel. This is the only record of anyone working away from home. Even Christopher Walker owned 'a little heifer'.

Woodworking

Woodworking skills were in great demand and provided by-employment for many who acquired the tools (often through inheritance) and the training. Joiners made furniture and household fittings and their valued tools were often kept in a special chest. John Smith of Yealand, husbandman, left his son 'One Joynerworke Cheste' in his will of 1699. In 1696 John Nicholson, husbandman of Carnforth, left property in his will to his brother Thomas Nicholson, also of Carnforth, whom he describes as a 'joyner'. William Mansergh of Borwick, yeoman (1699), left 'one Joyner work Chist ...together with the Moyety or one half part of all the Cooper timber & boards about the same [the house]' to his son John. Another cooper, Robert Burrow, is mentioned in Warton Manor Court records for 30 March 1668. These Warton coopers were perhaps more likely to be engaged in white-coopering (making pails, butter churns, wash-tubs and so on, for household use) or dry-coopering (casks for flour and other dry goods) rather than the more specialised wet-coopering (casks for liquids).

More substantial woodworking, especially for building, was carried out by carpenters. Only one carpenter is named as such in the documentary evidence. He is John Wilson of Warton,[20] but Gervase Hubbersty of Yealand Conyers, in his will of 1610, left 'unto Thomas my sonn All the greate Timber which I boughte for him which belongs to his occupation'.

Ship building

The end of the seventeenth century saw the beginning of Warton's ship-building industry, which reached its peak in the eighteenth century.[21] The site of the shipyard cannot be located precisely, but it is known that it was in Lindeth, and probably near Leighton Moss. Vessels such as the 'Content' (1697) and 'Imployment' (1698) were built in Lindeth, the latter being intended for the Virginia trade. William Stout had a financial interest in the 'Imployment' which was of 70 tons and did in fact make the Atlantic crossing a number of times,[22] but many of the ships built at Warton may have been destined for the humbler duties of carrying iron ore from Furness across Morecambe Bay and south to Bristol and the Wye valley.

Building

Building provided other opportunities for by-employment. The building materials for small houses and farm buildings were in abundant supply in the

147

parish - stone, wood, clay for walls and bracken and sods for primitive roofing. No doubt many of the poorer people put up their own shelters. The tenants' rights to wood and timber for building have already been mentioned (see Chapter 3). They also had the right to take stone from the common. Sand and clay could be dug so long as 'everye one where hee gette any claye or Sande shall even the pytt or hole againe...'[23] Clay would be used for the daub of wattle and daub. For the more substantial buildings the services of a carpenter must have been required, and perhaps specialist wall-builders. Dame Anne Middleton's Account Book for 1675 refers to payments to two men, John Crofte and John Crosier, for building or repairing walls.[24] The inventory of James Addison of Borwick (1637) refers to him as a Roughmason. Among his modest possessions were his work-tools valued at £10, and four sheep. While it was permissible for tenants to take stone from the common it was not to be traded outside the manor. Thomas Robinson of Yealand Conyers was fined by Warton Manor Court for 'gettinge and leadinge stones oute of Warton Liberties contrary to the custom of the Manor'.[25]

Limeburning

Lime, which could be produced locally from the limestone, was commonly used with sand to make a mortar for building walls. The Warton Manor Court records refer to a wall being laid 'in lime and sand'.[26] Simple early kilns to burn limestone to make lime would be made from sods and the most likely fuel would be charcoal. Tenants had the right to get stones and sods for kilns for their own use, but the lime was not to be traded outside the parish. This evidently still applied at the end of the eighteenth century, when Richard Garth of Warton was fined by the Manor Court for 'digging up the Common in Warton aforesaid for sods for making a Limekiln and for getting limestones upon the same Common and when burnt into Lime there carrying the same Lime out of this Manor and disposing of the same out of the same Manor...'.[27] The burnt lime, before slaking with water, could be hazardous. John Rowson was ordered to 'keepe a Couer for his lymepytes in his garthe and keepe them soe covered'.[28]

Other Trades

There is documentary evidence for tanners, maltsters and blacksmiths in Warton parish in the seventeenth century. All these trades would require special working premises. The occupation requiring the most sophisticated siting and premises - milling - has been dealt with earlier (see Chapter 6).

Tanning

Three men, all from Priest Hutton, are referred to as tanners in their inventories. Richard Gibson (1667) left 'the woodtroughes and Implements to the barkehouse' to his two sons. John Gibson (possibly one of these sons) died in 1681. His inventory includes unwrought leather 'in barkes' and 'ledder drowne and undrowne'. The third tanner, Thomas Proctor, died in 1685. The references to barkhouse and bark show that these men were using the still-familiar oak-bark process for preserving leather. The necessary oak-bark or oak-galls would be available from local woodlands, and the process involved soaking the skins with oak-bark in a pit or a vat for periods of up to 15 months. For softening or stretching the skins infusions of poultry or pigeon dung could be used, or a warm infusion of dog-dung. This vegetable process is especially suitable for cattle hide leather.[29] Hair was probably removed from the skins with lime - another use for this locally available product. The lime also helps to plump the skins for tanning. In the early part of the eighteenth century Warton Manor Court ordered that no skinner should wash or dress sheep skins or other skins within ten yards of St.Oswald's Well.[30]

The only other evidence of anyone working in the leather trade is the occasional mention of skins or sheepskins. For example the will of Thomas Cancefield of Warton (1610) includes the item 'William Johnson owes me 20s. and a dozen of calf skynns'. Perhaps the leather trade of Kendal supplied the parish with most of its needs, especially in such specialised work as saddlery and shoemaking. Shoe repairing, however, would no doubt have been a local by-employment in the parish. The 'accompte' added by the executors to the inventory of Thomas Turner of Priest Hutton (1633) includes the item 'to James Warde for soleing a pair of shoe 11d'.

Maltsters

Nearly half of the inventories list small quantities of malt, indicating that many households brewed their own beer. But the production of the malt from barley appears to have been carried out by a few specialist maltsters in Carnforth. They must have had the requisite vessels for steeping the barley and allowing germination, and the kilns for drying it. Thomas Nicholson, yeoman (1641), was carrying out malting on a large scale. His inventory lists £22-worth of malt and '195 bushells of Barley bought by the deceased some whereof is now in his kilne & some untaken upp £68-5s'. He also had debts owing for malt from fourteen people. Another Thomas Nicholson of Carnforth (1663) has an inventory item of £10-worth of malt, plus 'sackes and poakes', and nine people owed him sums up to £1-8s for malt. Another who may have been engaged in malting was Richard Mason, also of Carnforth (1675), who had fourteen bushells of barley and eighteen bushels of malt and meal. Another maltster, Thos. Clarkson, is mentioned in Dame Anne Middleton's Account Book in 1675. He was paid 24s for two bushels of malt.[31]

Blacksmiths

The trade of blacksmith required special skills as well as specialised equipment and supplies. Among their many jobs would be the making and repair of farm tools and some kitchen equipment, and the shoeing of horses and oxen. Oxen had to be shod, 'The Ground of this Parish being stony...they shoe their Oxen against Plowtime...'[32] Supplies of iron would be available from local forges such as Sir George's bloomery at Milnthorpe which was set up in the mid-seventeenth century.[33] Thomas Houseman of Warton left a will dated 1635, in which he is named as a blacksmith, but there is no accompanying inventory. John Cockerham of Borwick, whose 1611 inventory includes '1 Pair belles with a stiddye, a vise, hammers, fyles & other smithe toole £2-10s', is named as a smith. His inventory shows that Cockerham was also fully involved in husbandry. James Waithman of Carnforth (1613) wills that his 'son Jarvice to have the end of the house next to the yeate that I builded for a Smithye...' Warton Manor Court records mention two other blacksmiths - Robert Sander [34] and another Thomas Houseman of Warton.[35] There was also a smithy at Leighton Hall.

Silverdale pottery

The very large quantities of broken earthenware found in Silverdale in the area north of Cove Road has led to the conclusion that this area was the site of a pottery.[36] It is thought the pots were being produced in late medieval times. The likely source of the clay was from the diggings at the north end of Haweswater, the Clayholes. The fragments found seem all to be parts of jugs and bowls, some of the bowls having an applied 'pie-crust' frill round the rim. The clay is smooth and many of the sherds are glazed in colours 'varying from chestnut to sage-green, but always with a tendency to brownish'.[37] Fragments thought to be Silverdale pottery have been found at Cockersands Abbey and at Eskdale, suggesting it was quite widely traded. It is not clear whether the Silverdale pottery survived into the seventeenth century. There is no documentary evidence for its existence, and no mention of potters or potting equipment in the inventories. In 1674 James Hadwen of Silverdale left 'Pottes and pipes' to the value of £13 in his will. We can only speculate on whether this large stock was the result of running a pottery, the residue of stock from the Silverdale pottery, or stock bought in from another pottery.

Other Employments

Various other employments are mentioned in casual references in Manor Court records and elsewhere. There are several references to alehouse keepers, one of whose obligations was to 'sell a quart of the best ale for 1d, to every house keeper within the manor that shall send for it'.[38] John Wilson of Silverdale seems to have been a butcher. His will and inventory (1692) reveal that he had a slaughter house and held a stock of hair worth a shilling. Butchers are also mentioned in Warton Manor Court records when a somewhat involved order was made that '..No Butchere bringinge ther flesh to the marketes must let summ part of the skyne growe to the fleshe...'[39] Presumably the import of the order was clearer at the time. There is also in the Warton Manor Court Book one mention of a tailor, and one of a cook at Leighton Hall. In Dame Anne Middleton's Account Book

Ox shoes

for 1675 [40] it is recorded that 4d was paid to John Cooper 'for dyinge my Ladies stockins', and 3s to Lawrence Parkinson for 'wrighte worke'. The inventory of James Wilson, husbandman of Borwick (1627) includes 'Weaver reedes 2s.6d.' A reed was a frame fitted with split reeds, used on looms. They are now made of wire. It is not clear from the inventory whether James Wilson had a stock of wild reeds, or, more likely, finished frames. It is even possible that he had a stock of wire reeds.

Additional information from the eighteenth century

The previous pages describe only those occupations for which there is documentary evidence. Any numerical examination of by-employments and trades in seventeenth century Warton is restricted by the lack of comprehensive information. Wills and inventories give only limited coverage of the population and are biased to the wealthier inhabitants. Many categories of employment, such as shoemaker and day-labourer, are not represented, and there is a very human tendency for the named occupations to be upgraded to give more status. Fortunately we have a much more comprehensive source of information on occupations in Warton parish for a period of ten years after the close of the seventeenth century. From 1718-1728 the parish registers add the occupation of almost all the adult males who were married, buried or presented a child for baptism. In this short period an estimated 50-60 per cent of occupations of all the adult males in the parish were recorded. This figure compares with a probable 15 per cent or so from wills and inventories for the seventeenth century, and only slightly more when other sources for the seventeenth century are included. Not only is the coverage in the parish registers far superior, but also the occupation designations, presumably given by the vicar, are apparently much more objective and accurate.

This ten-year period occurring only a couple of decades after the close of the seventeenth century must be relevant to the earlier period. Here are the 'missing' occupations pursued by the humbler parishioners who did not leave wills or inventories. We have evidence of four shoemakers, seven tailors, a butcher, seven almsmen and no fewer than twenty-six day-labourers. The sample size (178 occupations out of an estimated total of 310 adult males in the parish) means that we can be reasonably confident about scaling up the data to give likely totals of adult males in each occupation. These figures are presented in Table 14.1, alongside the information from the seventeenth century sources. The listing of day-labourers and almsmen in the eighteenth century data helps in estimating the proportion of the population who had very little or no land. Other occupations, such as blacksmith and weaver, seem to be well represented in the seventeenth century data, since the numbers are comparable with those recorded in the parish registers of later date.

Workman 1650's

151

Table 14.1 Occupations in Warton parish.

Occupation	1600 - 1700		1718 - 1728		
	wills & inventories	plus other sources	in parish register	est. total in parish	% age of total
Yeoman	52	52	12	21	7
Husbandmen	45	45	70	123	39
Farmers	-	-	6	10	3
Webster	4	8	14	24	8
Shearer	1	1	-	-	-
Blacksmith	2	5	4	7	2
Miller	1	4	6	10	3
Tanner	3	3	-	-	-
Maltster	-	5	2	3	1
Carpenter					
House	-	2	3	5	2
Ship	-	-	3	5	2
Joiner	-	3	-	-	-
Cooper	-	2	4	7	2
Mason	1	-	5	9	3
Roughmason	1	1	-	-	-
Fisherman	-	18	-	-	-
Shoemaker	-	-	4	7	2
Tailor	-	1	7	12	4
Butcher	-	-	1	2	1
Innkeeper	-	-	1	2	1
Sailor	-	-	2	3	1
Waller	-	2	1	2	1
Saltweller	-	1	-	-	-
Almsman	-	-	7	12	4
Day labourer	-	-	26	46	14
				310	100
(A) TOTAL in all known occupations	110	153 [43]	178		
(B) Est. Total adult males in period	725 [42]	725	310		
Percentage of (B) with known occupations	15	21	57		

The fact that no-one in the eighteenth century parish registers was designated as a fisherman suggests very strongly that this occupation was still a true by-employment, taken up by husbandmen when the more demanding work of cultivation of the land permitted. Fish and shellfish were always available for harvesting, but crops on land required a strict routine of seasonal work. Other occupations not recorded in the parish registers are spinning and knitting. Both fairly obviously could be fitted into spare time when work on the land permitted.

There are, of course, some changes in occupation apparent in the eighteenth century information. Ship-building brought in ship's carpenters, and there are the first records of sailors in the parish. Tanning seems to have gone - perhaps moved to other nearby parishes, and there are fewer maltsters. The eighteenth century parish register information allows us to fill in many of the details missing from the imperfect seventeenth century data. We can say with confidence that, at least in the latter part of the seventeenth century, there were shoemakers, tailors, masons and butchers working in the parish. It was already clear from inventory information that the parishioners needed tradesmen with special skills or equipment - the blacksmiths, coopers, millers and websters. But the additional information from parish registers makes it obvious that many people were no longer making their own shoes or clogs, making their own clothes, or butchering their own animals. Increasingly they were prepared to pay others to do these jobs for them. And if people were spending money on tradesmen within the parish they would also be spending money outside the parish and particularly at the local market centres at Burton, Lancaster and Kendal, so contributing to the growth and prosperity of those places.

In conclusion it can be said that, in the seventeenth century, even though almost half of the adult male population were occupied for some or all of their time in some sort of trade, a majority still owned land for cultivation by themselves or their families. The parish was still mainly concerned with agriculture and was to continue so into the next century.

CHAPTER FIFTEEN

HOW IT WAS
Faith and Religion
From Reformation to Restoration

If we seek to discover what was the nature of the religious life of a parish like Warton in the seventeenth century we are limited by the nature of the evidence available. A remote country parish was not likely to produce writers and thinkers to describe the doctrinal framework or the kind of piety in which people lived. The evidence is far more likely to come from the statistics of the parish registers and visitation returns, from the legal documents resulting from arguments and from quarrels, and fragmentary notes appearing in manor or quarter session records. These will indeed provide a body of facts of a rather external nature, but it will be hard to find what their faith really meant to the inhabitants. Perhaps we should start from the wider picture of the nation as a whole, the movements of religion, thought and ecclesiastical life, and then see how the fragmentary information we can collect about the parish fits this broader picture.

Reformation in England

As the seventeenth century dawned the people of England had hardly emerged from the cataclysm of the Reformation. The fairly settled medieval pattern of belief and church order was shaken by the rejection of Papal authority, by the doctrine of Grace associated with Luther, by the theocratic image of Calvin's Geneva, with its emphasis on Predestination, and by attempts to 'purify' churches from superstition. The Reformation in England was very largely a political one, controlled by law, and retaining in many ways the structure of the Catholic Church. There was continuity of episcopal government and parish structure. The church buildings were 'cleansed' from idolatry and superstition by the removal of images of various kinds; the liturgy was translated into the common tongue and simplified; but the church buildings remained and most of the clergy continued under the new regime.

The Elizabethan settlement

After the reforming laws of King Edward VI's government and the Papal reaction under Queen Mary, Queen Elizabeth and her ministers and bishops set out for a settlement which would reform abuses criticised by the Reformers, maintain an English liturgy and an English Bible, devise a doctrinal position which married old and new, and maintain an episcopal ministry while rejecting Papacy. The aim was to find a *via media* which would hold together conservatives and reformers, and to enforce this with the power of the law. In fact it never came off. The spectrum of religious outlook stretched from those who had experienced Genevan polity and wanted nothing less, to those whom only a submission to the Pope would satisfy. The former came to be called Puritans, the latter Recusants, but neither aimed at creating denominations. What they all wanted was a Church of England based on their own views.

155

Calvinist and Laudian

Probably the predominant movement was Calvinist. This stressed the election of the faithful by God to salvation. It also aimed at a much more thorough-going purging of catholic elements in the liturgy, in the contents of churches and in devotion to Mary and the saints. Those who followed this way also aimed at a new Church order, Presbyterian or Independent, and the rejection of episcopacy. In opposition to this was a movement which, while retaining the Reformation, wished to keep the Church of England close to its catholic tradition of episcopacy and the Book of Common Prayer, and to restore the symbolism, order and art in church buildings. This movement rejected the Calvinist emphasis on predestination and election and it was dubbed 'Arminian' after a Dutch theologian. Its leaders were men like Lancelot Andrewes, Bishop of Winchester and William Laud, Archbishop of Canterbury. The piety of the poet, George Herbert, the ordered devotion of Nicholas Ferrar, the founder of the quasi-monastic family community at Little Gidding, and the prayers composed by Lancelot Andrewes provided a form of religion later styled 'Anglican'. Theological differences ran parallel with political ones and the first four decades of the century saw a struggle which culminated in the Civil War.

Papists and Recusants

In the early part of the century the situation was very fluid. People had lived through years of rapid change and there can have been little certainty as to what the future ecclesiastical order would be. Already there were appearing groups which would later develop into 'denominations', seeking to maintain alternative ways of worship to those established by law, but they did this in the face of Acts of Uniformity which made such activities punishable. In general officialdom was more sensitive, more fearful, of catholics or 'papists', than of protestant non-conformists, partly because the former might be associated with Spanish or French subversion, even invasion. Officially Mass was prohibited, attendance at the established church was compulsory. It was a felony to assist or harbour a Catholic priest, let alone be a priest; the penalty for that, if caught, was death.

Many papistical worshippers looked back with nostalgia to the Medieval Church and wished to retain Papal supremacy. Despite the excommunication of Queen Elizabeth and the Gunpowder Plot most of these had no treasonable intent. They simply wanted freedom to worship in the time-honoured way. Many were prepared, whatever their private beliefs, to fulfil the minimum required church observances, and they are sometimes called 'Church Papists' to distinguish them from 'Recusants', who refused to conform at all. As the threat of Spanish dominance was increasingly felt, punishments for recusancy increased.

156

Recusants in Lancashire

In fact the various Acts against recusancy were never consistently pushed in their full rigour. This was particularly the case in Lancashire, where for reasons that are still under discussion, catholic sympathies were wide-spread. There was laxness, or even corruption, in the Diocesan centres of Chester and Richmond. The gentry, acting as Justices of the Peace, were reluctant to punish, few having sympathy for the new liturgy themselves. Defendants and witnesses could avoid appearance in court, and excommunication was widely disregarded. Since the number of recorded recusants was dependent on the effort put into finding them it is not easy to estimate their true numbers. It is generally agreed, however, that in Lancashire the proportion of catholics in the population was high. John Bossy, in his detailed study of the English catholic community gives his opinion that '...it was certainly true in the eighteenth century, and would probably have been true in 1600, that there were more Catholics in this relatively small area than in the rest of the North put together'.[1] The area he is talking of is not the whole of Lancashire, but the agrarian plain which lay west of the emerging textile districts about Manchester, but did not extend 'much beyond Lancaster'. Bossy, that is, was excluding Westmorland, Cumberland and Lancaster over the Sands. His definition places Warton parish as a border area.

A body of priests who had withdrawn from the reformed church was able to provide an alternative form of worship clandestinely from the start. These were followed, after 1574, by trained missionary priests from the English College at Douai, by the launch of a Jesuit mission to England from Rome, and then by a Benedictine mission in 1600. Predictably they bickered with each other. One hundred and forty-five priests worked in the North during Elizabeth's reign, though only 42 were arrested.[2] There was, it seems, a lack of zeal in rooting them out in a region where catholic leanings were so common. Attempts to quell the 'papists' remained erratic into the seventeenth century. There were periods under James I and Charles I when the risk of fines and sequestration declined, there was even temporary suspension. At other times there was firmness, as when the Catholic JPs were purged later in the 1620s and 1630s. The period from 1640 to the outbreak of the civil war, a period which included the long-foretold Irish rebellion, was a time of a very determined drive against recusants. In 1641, the year of the rebellion, nine thousand recusants were convicted in Lancashire.[3] Between 1584 and 1646 eleven priests, including Jesuit, Dominican, Franciscan and Benedictine priests, and four laymen were executed at Lancaster castle.[4]

Reformation in Warton parish

The large parish of Warton consisted of seven townships, but the one parish church served the whole, though from Pre-Reformation days there seems to have been a chapel at Silverdale. Its chequered career is discussed in Chapter 17. We do not seem to have any record of how the Reformation changes had been carried out in this large parish. When John Lucas came to write his *History of Warton Parish* in the early years of the eighteenth century he apparently knew little if anything about how the Reformation had affected local life, and his dramatic passage describing the loss to the church of Altar ornaments, '...chalices, Patins, Crosses, &c of Silver...and other ornaments... embezled and made away...'[5] is only speculation, though very reasonable speculation.

Lancaster Castle

The Rector at the start of the Reformation was John Stringer who, like many of his predecessors, was a prominent churchman, with other appointments, and may hardly ever have been seen locally. He appears to have purchased the advowson (right of presentation) and presented himself. By 1548 he seems to have sold or otherwise passed on the 'lease of the parsonage' to Gervase Middleton.[6] There were many disputes and in 1547 the Crown assumed the right of presentation and gave it to the Dean and Chapter of Worcester. Only five years earlier the Cathedral Priory had been suppressed and replaced by a 'secular' Cathedral of the new foundation with Dean and Chapter in place of the Benedictine monastery. They became titular rectors of Warton and when Stringer died in 1553 they appointed Thomas Lynsey as the first vicar. At the end of the century the vicar was William Owborne M.A. who was also vicar of Bolton-le-Sands.

Puritanism in Warton parish

On the death of Owborne in 1613 Worcester appointed Anthony Bugg who remained for nineteen years. He would seem to have been a protégé of Matthew Hutton, the local boy who had become Archbishop of York, for when the latter died in 1606 his will described Bugg as 'a scholar in Cambridge', Hutton's own university, and he left him a sum of money and 'such of my books as are fytt for him' to the value of £4-6-8.[7]. Hutton's own theological opinions placed him among the church leaders who leaned more towards the Puritan position (see Appendix 4). This seems to suggest that the local leadership during these vital years was of a Puritan rather than a Laudian kind. The wills of the time usually express pious ideas and in a few cases hopes of being numbered among the elect. This may suggest similar views, but this is not conclusive. Anthony Bugg's books and the phraseology of wills are discussed in more detail in Appendix 3. Bugg's successor, James Smorthwaite B.A., was instituted in 1632, but little seems to be known about him. From the fact that he had ceased to be vicar in 1646 it seems likely that he was deprived of his living when, as is discussed below, a Presbyterian church order was established in Lancashire. This would suggest that he held to the Prayer Book and episcopacy.

Triumph of Parliament

The triumph of the Parliamentary party in the Civil War led to the establishment of a Puritan order in religion. Episcopacy and the Book of Common Prayer were abolished, but there was some conflict between those who held to the Presbyterian order and Independents who formed the backbone of Cromwell's army and stood for the autonomy of each local church. In fact Presbyterian, Independent and Baptist ministers held the livings of the ejected churchmen. During the short period of the Commonwealth there was a degree of toleration, which fitted well with Cromwell's personal view, but Papists and Episcopalians were proscribed. It was during this time that a variety of sectarian movements appeared, Levellers, Fifth Monarchy men, Seekers, Diggers, all with radical and even communistic ideas, but by far the most significant of these sects, and the longest lasting, was the Society of Friends, who followed George Fox and came to be known as Quakers.

Classis

Where the Presbyterian order prevailed it took the form of a local *'classis'* which seems to have been the equivalent of a presbytery in the Calvinistic hierarchy of church courts, or of the diocese in the Church of

England. Lancashire had nine of these *'classes'* of which the eighth was centred on Lancaster. They more or less repeated the hundreds. In the Lancaster *classis* there were the parishes of Lancaster, Cockerham, Claughton, Melling, Tatham, Tunstall, Whittington, Warton, Bolton, Halton and Heysham. The *classis* had nine ministers, one of whom was Richard Walker of Warton, and eighteen elders, all of them gentlemen or yeomen. Three of the elders came from the near-by township of Kellet, but none from Warton. Whether James Smorthwaite had been ejected is uncertain, but Richard Walker, already a member of the *classis,* was instituted as vicar by order of the House of Lords in 1647 and remained until 1654. In that year, or the following one, presumably on his death, Francis Jackson M.A., who had previously been schoolmaster at Kirkby Lonsdale, was presented by Oliver, Lord Protector. The presentation by Cromwell indicates that he must have held Puritan opinions.

Catholicism in Warton parish

Not everyone in the parish, however, had been able to accept even the changes in the church brought about by the Reformation. In the pre-restoration years the main dissenting group was catholic. Catholicism in Lancashire in the seventeenth century is sometimes described as 'seigneurial' because it often depended on gentry protection. In Warton the catholic community was not large, but fairly stable and was dependent on the Middletons of Leighton Hall, who had remained in the old faith from the beginning. Thomas Middleton was the squire in the early part of the seventeenth century. At first he seems to have been prepared to conform at least outwardly. A certificate of his conformity to the Church of England was signed by the vicar, the nine churchwardens and nine sworn men of the parish on September 1st, 1605.[8] In 1629, however he was considered a recusant and had to compound for his sequestered estates by an annual fine of £100.[9] This catholic community survived through the interregnum, and its history in the post-restoration years is considered in the next chapter.

Faith and Religion
The Post-Restoration Years

CHAPTER SIXTEEN

Act of Uniformity 1662

The restoration of the monarchy in 1660 provides a watershed in the religious life as well as the political life of the century. Before accepting the throne Charles issued the Declaration of Breda, to smooth his coronation. This promised 'liberty to tender consciences' in matters of religion 'not affecting the peace of the realm'. But the Cavalier Parliament consisted largely of country gentry, many of whom had suffered under the Commonwealth. They were intensely anti-Puritan and determined to restore more than the monarchy. They felt an alliance with the ejected Anglican clergy and aimed at restoring the church of Hooker, Laud and Andrewes. To fulfil his promise Charles called the Savoy conference in 1661, consisting of bishops and Presbyterian divines, to review the Book of Common Prayer. The latter produced a list of 'Exceptions' to the Book, but most of these were rejected by the bishops. The Convocations began a revision of the Prayer Book, but this made few concessions to the radical Puritan demands, and when it was completed the Act of Uniformity of 1662 required that all ministers should publicly assent to the revised Prayer Book and ordered its exclusive use. As a result some 2,000 ministers refused and were ejected from their livings.

Toleration Act 1689

The king was very sympathetic to the Roman Catholic church and his brother was a bigoted catholic, but the feeling of the country was against any return to catholicism, or even any toleration of it. It was already clear that there were three or more forms of religion in existence in the country and that 'uniformity' must give way to 'toleration', but it was a long time before this was accepted. In 1689, by the Toleration Act, freedom of worship was granted to protestant dissenters, but not to Catholics or Unitarians, and disabilities remained for all. The penal laws against Catholics remained particularly severe. It is striking to consider that for some eight centuries there had been one church in Warton, even if its character had changed from time to time, yet in the same area to-day, on a rough count, there are eight denominations and some sixteen places of worship. Of course, the united nature of Christianity in earlier centuries is something of an illusion. Heresy, the conflict of Religious Orders and the tensions of church and state were manifestations of deep divisions, but they never took institutional form, largely because the politics of the time required unity and sanctioned coercion to achieve it. From the late seventeenth century there developed institutional expressions of various religious points of view.

The Catholics

In Warton Catholicism remained the faith of an important minority after the restoration as it had before, still under the protection of the Middletons of Leighton Hall it seems. When the openly recusant Thomas Middleton died in 1640 he had been succeeded by his son George Middleton, whose name never appeared in the recusancy rolls. The estates were again sequestered, but this time because he was considered as 'malignant', that is an active royalist. Sir George (he was knighted by the king in 1642, unlike his father who had been fined £13-6s-8d in 1631 for refusing the honour [1]), kept enough conformity to avoid punishment on religious grounds. He maintained an interest in the parish church, retaining a large pew there with '8 Escocheons very well cut in Bass Relieve',[2] and he is commemorated by a memorial there. His initials, together with those of Sir Robert Bindloss of Borwick, appear on the refurbished font. He also kept the farming of the tithes, for though he temporarily lost this when his estate was sequestered in 1646, he was again the farmer after 1649 when he compounded. That Sir George's conformity was only outward seems to have been an open secret. George Fox, the Quaker, was brought before the justices of the peace in 1663, among whom was Sir George. Fox's account of the meeting appears in his Journal.[3]

> *Then said George Middleton, "You deny God, and the church, and the faith." I replied, "Nay, I own God, and the true church, and the true faith. But what church dost thou own?"*

Escutcheons formerly in Sir George Middleton's private family pew and now set in one of the front pews in Warton Church, close to his burial-place.

Fox seems to have struck home for Middleton had no reply but to call him 'rebel and traitor', to bluster and to say 'Did you ever hear the like?' It was often the case in Catholic families that it was the wife who avowed their true religion while the husband conformed to avoid the social and political drawbacks of recusancy. Sir George's second wife, Lady Anne was an open recusant. She was the daughter of George Preston of Holker, the devout restorer of Cartmel Priory, who was described as at first a 'Church papist' and finally as an avowed Roman Catholic.[4] Lady Anne's name repeatedly appears in lists of known recusants. It seems probable that, even under Sir George, the catholic community could look to Leighton Hall for support.

Catholicism in Warton parish

At any rate a small but persistent community of catholics lived in Warton parish, and their presence was duly recorded by the churchwardens.[5] Between 1665 and 1686 the numbers returned lie in the range of 14 to 27, a number which does not seem to have included young family members. Where this small community worshipped and who ministered to them is not known. All through the years when catholicism was prohibited there were priests working everywhere in England. They did not proclaim their profession and wore no clerical dress, but there they were. In 1616 the Jesuits made a general survey of the mission work in England. 'This divided the missioners into three sorts: those who lived in the large households of magnates, and were more or less immune from interference; those who...lived a concealed, restricted and rather lonely existence in gentry houses...and those who circulated'.[6] Peripatetic priests, travelling from one safe house to the next with no fixed abode, were probably the most numerous in the early decades of the seventeenth century and continued in existence, particularly in the north and in upland areas, till at least the beginning of the next century.

Leighton Hall

Unless further evidence is found all that can be said of the catholics of Warton parish is that they were probably served by priests living at, or based on, Leighton Hall. The records are scanty; Mr Beesley a Douai trained priest was recorded as living at Leighton round about 1588. A Mr. Peter Gooden, trained at the English College in Lisbon, was at Leighton as chaplain to the widowed Lady Anne Middleton and apparently stayed there till 1680 when, at the time of the persecutions following the discovery of the 'Oates Plot', he left Leighton and took refuge at Aldcliffe Hall with the seven devout catholic ladies who lived there. Another Lisbon trained priest is thought to have been at Leighton in 1697.[7] Whether mass was said and confessions heard at Leighton itself is not known. Sir George at least, as a conforming Anglican, must have been chary of allowing it. No chapel is known of till 1782 when the Towneleys, who had inherited the Hall, arranged for a house for a priest with an adjoining chapel in Yealand where now the presbytery attached to the 1852 church stands.[8]

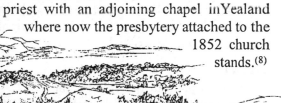

Leighton Hall, as it must have appeared after rebuilding in the eighteenth century.

Confirmation at Leighton

Leighton did, however, see one large scale catholic ceremony. In 1687, during the time of toleration under James II, eighty-four people were confirmed in the catholic faith at Leighton. It was part of a breath-taking journey through England undertaken by Bishop John Leyburn, the first catholic bishop to work in England since the reign of Queen Mary. During two summer months he is said to have confirmed 20,859 people, presumably a fair proportion of those who had grown up unable to be confirmed because of the lack of a bishop in England.[9] It is not clear from how wide an area the eighty-four people confirmed at Leighton came, but they must have been relatively local, for the bishop was working his way south and had already held confirmations at Sizergh and Witherslack just over into Westmorland and the next day moved on to confirm 157 people at Aldcliffe and 158 at Thurnham just south of Lancaster.

Dr Richard Sherlock

There were rumours that towards the end of the century there was a papistical centre at Borwick Hall, perhaps involving the Bindlosses themselves, but centred on Sir Robert Bindloss's chaplain, Dr Richard Sherlock. He was said to be 'so zealous a man for the Church of England that he was accounted, by precise persons, Popishly affected and a papist in masquerade'.[10] In the seventeenth century the word 'precise', used in a religious context, bore a rather special meaning. It was used to describe the more exacting Puritans, men who were perhaps over-ready to see all Laudians as crypto-catholics. Within the parish no-one seems to have thought of the Bindlosses as popishly inclined. The Sir Robert Bindloss who died in 1630 had provided in his will for a salary of £20 a year for a 'preaching minister' in the chapel at Borwick.[11] The later Sir Robert, Sherlock's patron, 'was a person who had a just esteem for the Church and her Ministers' according to Lucas.[12] After his death the protestant tradition was kept up by his widow. She arranged for the vicar of Warton to read divine service in the chapel once or twice a year, though she herself preferred to attend the parish church.[13] However, Sir Robert had permitted his daughter and heiress to marry a catholic. In 1718 the churchwardens reported that 'Tis supposed that att Leighton Hall & att Borwick Hall papists resort to Masse'.[14]

Dissenters

In most parts of the country the 1662 Act of Uniformity, by trying to impose on all acceptance of episcopacy and the Book of Common Prayer, led to the establishment of various different dissenting groups which, when toleration was granted, built their own meeting houses. The main dissenting threat to orthodox Anglicanism in Warton parish in the seventeenth century came from Quakers. Lancashire Quarter Session records for the period[15] mention seven houses in the parish as places where 'conventicles' were held; the houses of John Cumming, Robert Hubbersty, William Hugginson, Richard Lancaster, William Waithman and of two men of the name of John Backhouse. After the Toleration Act of 1689 Robert Hubbersty's house was formally registered as a dissenting meeting house. Six of these houses were in the Yealands, and all the names are well known in other Quaker contexts, confirming that Quakerism was the main form of dissent. In 1703 a 'new building called Stablesteads' in Carnforth was registered as a dissenting meeting house.[16] It is not known for what sect it was erected, but in 1715 it was recorded in the Warton Parish Register Book that 'There is a Meeting house, of Presbiterians in the Parish which is licensed according to Law...'.[17]

The Quakers

Many of the 'Separatists' who left the church found satisfaction in one or other of the many religious sects which sprang up in the second half of the seventeenth century. Yet many serious-minded people could still find no spiritual home. They continued to seek Truth for themselves, sometimes alone and sometimes in organised groups of like-minded 'Seekers'. The Westmorland Seekers, based on Preston Patrick, were a well organised group of Separatists who waited and hoped for God to send them a leader. They believed they had found one when, in 1652, George Fox arrived in the district. He had left his Midland home in 1646 and made his way slowly north, via Derby, where the judges who imprisoned him called him in derision 'a Quaker', because he told the court to 'tremble at the word of God'. He continued through Lincolnshire and Yorkshire and turned west to Pendle Hill. Atop of the hill Fox became convinced that to the north there lay 'a great people to be gathered'[18] and his vision was fulfilled in his meeting with the Westmorland Seekers.

Fox at Swarthmoor

Having preached and worshipped with them in the Sedbergh area, on the Sunday morning, he went with them to the little chapel on Firbank fell and although he did not join their worship in the chapel he announced his intention of speaking on the fell-side that afternoon. As a plaque on the Pulpit Rock states 'Here or near this rock George Fox preached to one thousand Seekers for three hours on Sunday, 13th June 1652'. Great power inspired his message, and the meeting proved of the first importance in gathering the Society of Friends, known as Quakers. Fox travelled on via Kendal to Ulverston where, at Swarthmoor Hall, the home of Judge Thomas Fell and his wife Margaret, he was accorded a sympathetic hearing, and there, with the help of Margaret Fell and the leaders of the Seekers, an organising base for the new movement was established.

Yealand Meeting

Under Fox's leadership the movement grew rapidly, its newly inspired adherents preaching a vigorous message that challenged the authority of the established church and led inevitably to conflict and persecution. From 1652 we have the names of eight local men who, probably with their families, met and formed Yealand Meeting; Withers or Widders, Hubberthorne, Leaper, Stout, Bisbrowne, Fleming, Hugginson and Chorley. Meetings were held in members' houses or in barns, and from the first they were persecuted for holding such meetings. In 1733 a Quaker, Joseph Besse, made a compilation of all the records of persecution of Quakers, which he entitled *The Sufferings of the People called Quakers*. Among his entries for Lancashire is found 'Richard Hubberthorne and others were bound Hand and Foot and so carried and laid out in the open fields in a cold Winter Night, to the Hazard of their lives'.[19] Fox recalls in his Journal that in 1652:-

Puritan dress

I went to Yelland. In the evening came a priest to the house, with a pistol in his hand, under pretence to light a pipe of tobacco. The maid of the house, seeing the pistol, told her master who thereupon, clapping his hands on both the doorposts told him, He should not come in there. While he stood there, keeping the doorway, he looked up and spied over the wall a company of men coming, some armed with staves, and one with a musket. But the Lord prevented their bloody design, so that seeing themselves discoverd, they went their way, and did no harm.[20]

Non-payment of tithes

Just as Fox was convinced that no place was holier than any other, so was he convinced that no person, however well educated, was more accessible than anyone else to the will of God. Since many people shared these beliefs it followed that they refused to support the church and the clergy by paying tithes. The records of Yealand Meeting and Besse's *Sufferings*, show that by 1678 sixty-eight members of Yealand Meeting (presumably all the male members) had written testimonies to having refused to pay tithes. In that year Robert Withers of Over Kellet had goods worth £98-1s-1d taken from him, including twelve cows, five horses and eighty-seven sheep in respect of the tithe demanded. The next year Thomas Leaper of Over Kellet had goods worth £41-16s taken, which included not only animals but furniture, tools and household articles. In 1685 a demand for £16-2s was made of John Backhouse for the non-payment of tithes for three years, and three cows, two young heifers and a yoke of oxen worth £21 were taken from him. From Richard Lancaster of Yealand Conyers four cows, four heifers and a steer, plus his horse were taken, worth in all £26 in payment for a fine of £18-6s-6d.

Fines for Meetings

Twenty pounds seems to have been the standard fine for holding a meeting. William Waithman of Lindeth, John Backhouse of Yealand Redmayne and Richard Lancaster of Yealand Conyers were all fined this amount. A man who attended meeting was fined 10s with a further 5s if his wife or mother attended too. Most of these fines for women were taken in goods - oats, malt or beans. Margaret Lucas of Over Kellet was fined 5s, for which one of her sheep, worth 6s, was taken. Between 1678 and 1700 fifty-six local Quakers are recorded as having had goods seized for non-payment of tithes or for holding or attending meetings. Of these, twenty came from the Yealands, suggesting that either membership there was greater than elsewhere or, as may well have been the case, persecution was more vigorous there. During the same years Quakers are recorded as coming from Warton, Silverdale, Arnside, Carnforth, Priest Hutton, Over Kellet, Hale, Burton, Capernwray, Lindeth and Melling.

Oaths

Then, as now, Quakers refused to take an oath, both because Christ taught 'Swear not at all' and because to do so implied a double standard of truthfulness, whereas sincerity and truth should be practised at all times. In this too, therefore, Quakers were again vulnerable to persecution. The Minutes of the Yealand Meeting record that in 1652 George Hodgson of Yealand:-

> *... one of the tennants of that Manner, being called Quaker, and being called to be a Jewery man, was required to lay his hand on the Book to be sworn, the said George Hodgson for Conscience sake, could not answer their request, whereupon Robert Bindloss, the Cheife Stuard, said fine him, which he did, in 5s for which fine James Crofft, Bayliffe, upon 21st day of the first month made distraint of four sheepe worth 20s and nothing returned.*[21]

Friends had no objection to taking part in government apart from the necessity of taking an oath. Richard Hubberthorne, the Yealand Quaker whose life is touched on below, assured Charles II that Friends would assist in government 'in righteousness and civil things'[22], but still the oath-taking stood in the way. Between 1660 and 1740 thirteen Lancashire Friends were prosecuted for not swearing when summoned to civil office, nine as jurymen, one as a constable, one as a churchwarden and two to unspecified posts.[23] Warton Manor Court records show two incidents where there was trouble with Quakers summoned to be jurymen. In 1668 William Waithman was fined twelve pence by the Warton Manor Court 'for Denying to take his oath to execute the office of a Jury-man'.[24] In 1672 Hugh Cornthwaite was 'presented' by the same court, but no fine mentioned 'for refusing to resaife the oth of a Juryman'.[25] No other cases are recorded. Since no Quaker could have taken an oath and remained in the Society it seems probable that care was taken on the whole not to call them to serve. There are instances of Friends serving as constable, one in Swarthmoor in 1678 and one in Caton in 1707, but the constableship was a much disliked office and perhaps, if a Quaker was prepared to take it on, his neighbours might be willing to overlook the matter of the oath.[26]

Lancaster Castle

In 1660, on 13th January, twenty-six people were taken from a meeting at Yealand by a constable with a party of armed soldiers. They were kept under guard till the following day when they were taken to Lancaster Castle. On 20th January a similar thing happened, but this time the people were taken to a neighbouring justice who sent one man, twelve women and a boy to prison. Besse records that by the end of 1660 there were two hundred and seventy Quakers in prison in Lancaster Castle, mostly for refusing to take the Oath of Allegiance, which as Besse says was 'a snare which few escaped, because by their constant and publick Manner of assembling for Worship, they stood always exposed to the Malice of those who sought occasion against them'.

The following letter was written on behalf of over fifty Quakers imprisoned without trial in Lancaster Castle in 1661:-.

> *To the Justices in Commission for the peace...or to any others whom this may concern to read and mind with the spirit of meekness Sheweth*
>
> *That we, with others our fellow prisoners, were... apprehended and sent to prison, where we have innocently and patiently suffered bonds for the space of fourteen weeks (and some more) this winter season, although nothing can justly be laid to our charge as a matter of fact deserving such imprisonment, both to the prejudice of our health, the ruin of our estates and the expense of our time in a separation from our wives, children and families, and from our labour in our lawful callings in the creation, whereby we might be in a capacity to help others and not be burdensome to any, being (as you well know) husbandmen and tradesmen upon whose diligence and daily labour the subsistence of our families as to the outward consists, the neglect whereof may in all likelihood impoverish them and us; and so bring an unnecessary charge and burden upon others, which if it should be incurred upon this account and by this imprisonment could not be laid to the charge of the oppressed, whose sufferings is but upon suspicion and not for any actual transgression but only for conscience sake...and we desire nothing from you but that we may live quietly and peaceably in our own houses, eat our own bread and follow our own callings in the fear of God, for the good of all; and to meet together to serve and worship our God according as he requireth of us. And if you will not grant these things unto us, then shall we lie down in the peace of our God and patiently suffer under you...* [27]

Richard Hubberthorne

One member of Yeland Meeting who died for his faith was the Richard Hubberthorne of Yealand Redmayne already mentioned above. A yeoman farmer who had served as a captain of cavalry in the Civil War, he was converted to Quakerism at the meeting of Westmorland Seekers addressed by George Fox. He became a Quaker missionary, travelling in the ministry in many parts of England and Wales. When George Fox was imprisoned in terrible conditions in Launceston, Richard Hubberthorne was one of three Quakers who offered to change places with him. When Oliver Cromwell heard of their offer he turned to his Council and asked, 'Which of you would do so much for me if I were in the same condition?'.[28] At the Restoration of the monarchy in 1660 Richard Hubberthorne went to see the king and talked with him about the views of the Quakers and their sufferings in the cause of Truth. With George Fox, Richard Hubberthorne drew up a declaration designed to make clear the position of Quakers regarding plots and fighting. 'All bloody practices we do utterly deny with all outward wars and strife and fightings with outward weapons, for any end or under any pretence whatsoever'.[29] In 1662 the Quaker Act was passed, making it a criminal offence to attend a Quaker Meeting or to refuse to take an oath. Many Quakers were committed to prison under the Act and Richard Hubberthorne among them. He was confined in Newgate prison. It was an unusually hot summer, making the usual bad prison conditions still worse and he shortly died. George Fox said of him that he had laid down his life for the truth, and in it 'he liveth and resteth'.

Hilderstone burial ground

In those early years Friends met for worship in their own houses, or in some available barn or even in the open air: there was no immediate need for buildings in which to worship. The urgent need was for graveyards. The Church, for its part, would not allow parish churchyards to be used for the interment of unbaptised Dissenters and, on the other hand, Quakers would certainly not wish their dead to be buried in so-called consecrated ground. Small parcels of land were therefore obtained for use as Quaker burial grounds. Yealand Meeting had one at Hilderstone, which can still be seen beside the road south of Holme; not far from it is the graveyard of the Cummings and Backhouse families; on Birkrigg Common, near Ulverston, is the burial ground of Sunbreck where many early friends, including Margaret Fell, lie in unmarked graves; and many similar sites remain scattered throughout the country. Headstones were not in general use with Friends until the mid-nineteenth century.

Yealand Meeting-house

Several meeting houses were built in the 1670s and 1680s although many of them had to be rebuilt during the next century. Early meeting houses in the north-west were Brigflatts (1675), Lancaster (1677) and Kendal (1687). When in 1689 the Toleration Act brought some relaxation of the restrictions to which Friends had been subjected there was an immediate increase in Quaker building, so that by 1700 meeting-houses were on average no more than eight miles apart through the north. The meeting-house at Yealand Conyers was built in 1692, by which time the Great Rebuilding was reaching the area and it was built in stone, whereas

The Quaker Meeting House, Yealand, built in 1692. The thatch
has now been replaced with a slate roof and the windows altered

some of the earlier ones had been less well constructed. Its roof, however,
was of thatch. This was destroyed by fire in 1737 and replaced by slates.
The fact that Yealand meeting-house is aligned east and west is not
significant, being as likely as not related merely to the contours of the site.
As in their dress, Quakers preferred dignified plainness in their buildings,
rejecting unnecessary elaboration and ornament. Yealand Meeting-house
remains a simple rectangular room, furnished with benches for the
worshippers. A screen dividing the room made it possible for the men and
women to conduct their separate business meetings simultaneously.
Although they had different areas of responsibility, men and women were
from the first equal in every way within the Society. Until the end of the
eighteenth century the Friends Meeting-house was the only place of worship
in the Yealands and it remains the only meeting-house in the ancient parish
of Warton.

The Post-Restoration Parish

Warton was not among the parishes with Presbyterian ministers who
refused to conform. Francis Jackson had been the minister since 1655 when
he had been presented by Cromwell, but he accepted the new order and was
duly re-instituted on March 29th 1661 on the presentation of the Dean and
Chapter of Worcester. The reason given for the vacancy was the death of
Smorthwaite, the vicar apparently deprived in 1646, thus maintaining a
fiction that no Puritan ministry had existed. Of Thomas Atkinson, who was
vicar from 1670 to 1681 we know nothing, though from Lucas's description
of the reforms of his successor, it may well be assumed that he was lax.

On Atkinson's death in 1681 Thomas Lawson became vicar, it was said through the influence of his father-in-law who farmed the tithes. In the Victoria County History he is described as a 'literate' of Glasgow College[30], a word which, according to the Oxford English Dictionary came to be applied in the Church of England to one admitted to Holy Orders without having obtained a university degree. However Lucas, who must have known him in his youth, repeatedly describes him, as in the quotation below, as Master of Arts. To Lucas he was something of a hero and a reformer. Finding practices:-

> ...offencive both to God and all good Men, the pious vicar, Mr Thomas Lawson A.M. set himself seriously about a Reformation thereof; and when he found that his publick and private Admonitions, though very pathetic, would not prevail...he took care to have such Church Wardens and other Officers made Choise of in the Parish, as he knew to be Men of Integrity, and would not look upon their Oaths as a Thing of Course and Form...(31)

These men he was able to rely on to bring to punishment those who were obstinate in their irreligious courses. Lucas then describes the effect as little short of miraculous.

> Though at first they did meet with some Opposition, and opprobious language from the Patrons of vain Sports, yet they presently drave them out of the Church-Yard (their general Randezvouze) and by finding out, and pursuing them to their more distant and private Haunts, did frequently break up their unlawfull Assemblies, and brought them in a little Time, to be more frequent in their Attendance on the publick Worship of God; some of them, I hope, out of a due Sense of their former Neglect and Miscarriages, and others out of a Fear of being presented..

Psalm-singing

Lucas, in the same passage, tells how Lawson:-

> ...promoted the Singing of Psalms with Notes, himself paying a Master for teaching some that were willing and apt to learn but not able to defray the Charges thereof. This brought great Numbers to the Church; some out of Devotion, and others out of Curiosity, who being through the Mercy and Grace of God made sensible that there was much more solid Pleasure in the Performance of their Duty, than in the vain Exercises they had been used to, became for the future far more constant at their publick Devotions.

Lawson's churchwardens, in making their routine presentment to the bishop stated that 'Our Minister is a man of Sober chast and Just life, and unblameable (to the best of our observation) as to the Inquiries in this Article'.[32] They further said, in the presentment, that he read Common Prayer on Sundays and Holy Days, instructed in the Catechism, celebrated the Lord's Supper (but with no mention of frequency), had no curate and visited the sick. They mention that he had no other benefice 'but is constantly resident among us'. Lawson comes out less attractively in the controversy over the upgrading of Silverdale as a chapel of ease which is discussed in detail in the next chapter.

Aylmer and Sherlock

After two very short incumbencies at the start of the new century, Warton came under the influence and care of a rather remarkable clergyman, William Aylmer. As a student at Oxford he was converted to Rome and went to Douai where he eventually became Professor of Divinity. He later returned to the Church of England, preached a 'Recantation Sermon' before the Bishop and Mayor of Oxford in 1713 and the following year was presented by the Dean and Chapter of Worcester to be vicar of Warton.[33] His services to the parish as a doctor, for he was doubly qualified, have already been mentioned (see Chapter 9).

There was another clergyman active in the parish for a time about whom Lucas gives much information. This was the Dr. Richard Sherlock, already mentioned as being suspected of leaning towards catholicism. The details of his life, as given by Lucas and in the pages of the *Dictionary of National Biography* do not support the suspicion. He was an episcopalian who had had to leave his living in Ireland at the time of the troubles in 1641. He was then, in turn, evicted from a chaplaincy in Oxford and a curacy in Woodstock for his beliefs. In 1656 Sir Robert Bindloss offered him a position as chaplain in the chapel at Borwick which had been endowed by his grandfather.

> *Sr Robert was a Person who had a very just Esteem for the Church and her Ministers, both then under a Cloud; and being every way what they call an accomplished Gentleman, it was no wonder that very many were fond of the Honour of conversing with him: which had this unhappy Effect, that it made him in Love with (some of it wicked) Company, and many of the Evils that attended it (which proved the Ruine of his vast Estate), and too many of the Family followed his Example...The good Chaplain saw this with Grief, and therefore after general Discourses and Intimations had had little or no Effect, he applied to his Patron more closely, and in a Letter he wrote him, laid down this and the Vices of the Family, in Terms so home and serious, and yet so mannerly, that one could not imagine a Mind so void of Goodness, as to be offended with his holy Freedom....he earnestly pressed either to be harkened to in this Matter, or to be immediately discharged from his Office.[34]*

If Lucas is to be believed the result was a curious one, for Bindloss heard him with submission and ever after honoured him as his friend. Nothing is said about any reformation of life, and Bindloss is known to have recommended him to the Earl of Derby, whose domestic chaplain he became. After the Restoration Sherlock was appointed by the Crown to the rich living of Winwick in Lancashire, the proceeds of which he largely spent on the training of young curates and on charity. He was a prolific author, crossing swords with Hubberthorne and Fox. His nephew Thomas Wilson, the famous Bishop of Sodor and Man, gave a new edition to his devotional work *The Practical Christian* prefixed by an account of his life.

Non-Christian Alternatives

Warton was still, after the Restoration, not only the parish church of a parish of over 11,000 acres, but the only place of worship, apart from a few semi secret dissenting meeting-houses and the chapel at Silverdale. The story of the latter is of sufficient interest to be given a chapter of its own. We have examined the life and work of the Parish Church, Anglican or Presbyterian, and of dissenters, Catholic, Protestant and Quaker, but have said nothing about those who rejected Christianity altogether. This is because we have no record of them. When Lucas tells us that Vicar Lawson and his wardens brought to punishment those who were obstinate in their irreligious courses he suggests merely neglect of religious practice and scandalous behaviour, not atheism or an alternative non-Christian religion. In the atmosphere of the time, to follow such alternatives was a dangerous matter, but how many in their heart of hearts rejected all forms of Christianity we do not know. In the next century, when non-Christian views could be expressed more openly, Thomas Hest, vicar of Warton from 1775 to 1789, certainly told his bishop that 'We have alas many who have no Regard for Religion, who commonly absent themselves from the public worship of God...' Since he blamed the wicked and profane parents of the rising generation for the bad example they had set, he presumably thought the problem was a long standing one, but even here it is not clear what exactly he meant in speaking of people who had 'no Regard for Religion'. He blames their non-attendance on weaknesses of human nature; indolence or a desire to be thought 'witty' by ridiculing the scriptures.[35]

Witchcraft

The one form of alternative practice of which there is evidence in the seventeenth century is witchcraft. It was a period when this erupted everywhere, the Devils of Loudun in Catholic France in 1634, the Salem witch trials in 1692 in Puritan New England and the trial of the so-called Lancashire Witches in 1612. King James VI of Scotland was fascinated by witchcraft and published *Daemonology* in 1597. In 1486 Dominican Inquisitors had published *Malleus Malificarum*, an encyclopaedia of demonology endorsed by a Papal Bull, and in 1608 a Puritan divine, William

Perkins, had published *A Discovery of the Damned Art of Witchcraft*. Jonathan Lumby's recent book on witches in Lancashire[36] shows how wide-spread was the belief in witches in the north of England, so one might expect to find some evidence of it in Warton parish. We have found none. The only reference to a witch that has come to our notice seems merely to have been a term of abuse. When John Browne and his wife called Richard Helme a 'theefe', Helme reciprocated by claiming that they were both witches by whom he had suffered much loss.[37]

A Formative Century

Great changes had occurred during the century, marked by controversy, persecution and war. It started with the single parish aiming to comprehend all Christians on the basis of the Bible, the episcopal order and a reformed Catholicism, expressed through a requirement of uniformity, all enforced by law. It ended with an established Anglican institution, flanked by deeply held Roman Catholicism on the one hand, and Quakerism and other Protestant Non-Conformity on the other. The parish church had once been the undoubted centre of a community (society, group, call it what you want) of people with like minded religious beliefs. Maybe not everyone held the beliefs very deeply, maybe that people with a difficult living to earn, people living remote from the church and people who preferred idling and drinking did not always trouble to attend, but if they wanted to express any religious need there was only the church. It was there they were baptised, married and buried. It was there they asked for good harvest weather and protection from disease and war. For these same people the parish church was also a parochial centre in a different sense. It was the only really large gathering place (other than the chancy open air). It was where they met those who lived at a distance; it was there that information that came down from the central government was promulgated. The church was also the centre of most of the festivities, a matter which is taken up in Chapter 18. Inevitably Catholics, Quakers and all dissenters were seen as not only theologically wrong, but also as breaking up an old homogeneity. Refusal to pay tithes was a compounding of this breaking up of an old communal conformity. Toleration was still only in its infancy, but the end of the seventeenth century saw the end of the integrated Christian society, and the beginning of an attitude which saw one's religious activities as a matter of personal preference. However, the charter for Pennsylvania issued in 1701 for William Penn's colony was much before its time in asserting that no one was 'at any time to be compelled to frequent or maintain any religious worship, place or ministry whatever contrary to his or her mind'.

CHAPTER SEVENTEEN

HOW IT WAS

The Silverdale Chapel

The chapel at Silverdale may well antedate the Reformation. It has been suggested that it began as a chantry, established for the saying of masses for the souls of the founders. It then probably went out of use at the Reformation,[1] but was apparently revived as a chapel of ease. In 1650 its existence was noted in a survey of Warton Church. It was said to have no maintenance so that the 'poor inhabitants are forced to hire a poor minister for 20 nobles per annum',[2] that is to say £6-13s-4d a year accepting that the usual value of a noble was 6s-8d. The inhabitants hoped for a settled maintenance for 'a preaching minister', that desideratum of all good churchmen of more Puritan views. In 1657 a Mr Samuel Harrison 'preacher of the Gospel' was settled curate at the chapel at Silverdale by order of the Parliamentary committee variously known as the 'Committee for Plundered Ministers', or the 'Committee for Preaching Ministers', a sort of board of Ecclesiastical Commissioners set up under the Commonwealth to manage the affairs of the reorganised church.[3] The salary granted, a later curate told Lucas, was £40 a year,[4] It was paid out of the suppressed rectory and will have ceased at the Restoration. An after career for a pre-reformation chantry as a semi-dependent chapel of the parish church was known elsewhere.[5]

James Atkinson Schoolmaster

In 1679 Silverdale chapel was re-built on the old foundation,[6] but this hopeful move foundered for a while on all too human misunderstandings and feuds. The story can be collected from a series of letters between the participants which have, fortunately, survived.[7] A schoolmaster, James Atkinson, had been appointed and was later ordained deacon. There seems to be no record of his salary except that at some point £3-3s-4d was given to him by the vicar and others for reading prayers every Sunday afternoon. Then in 1687 a dispute broke out which continued for at least eight years. It is not easy to sort out the rights and wrongs of it, but it appears that James Atkinson, with the approval of the Silverdale inhabitants, wanted to be licensed as curate and to officiate at Silverdale as the local minister and, apparently with the consent of Lawson, the vicar of Warton, the Bishop of Chester did so license him.

Then Lawson wanted the license withdrawn. He stood upon what he claimed was an earlier understanding that Silverdale chapel was not a consecrated church and existed merely to hold afternoon worship, mainly for the infirm, for whom the journey to Warton was impossible, and to discourage the spread of non-conformity. He clearly thought that Atkinson was aiming at dividing the parish and he did not want the Silverdale inhabitants to abandon attendance at morning worship at Warton. Several other factors seem to have aggravated the situation. There was supposed to be a salary of £5 per annum paid to Atkinson, but there was disagreement about who should pay it, the Dean and Chapter of Worcester as holders of the rectorial estate, or the vicar out of his stipend.

Another factor was the personality of the two clergymen involved. Both wrote very pathetic letters to the Bishop of Chester, Nicholas Stratford. Atkinson seems not to have received any payment over long periods though one supposes he received some remuneration from his school. Lawson's official salary of £80 per annum seemed a princely one compared with Mr Atkinson's five pounds, even if that had been paid. Nevertheless Lawson was, he said 'much in debt & my charge is Great'. He had nine children, one of whom was handicapped in some way and had to be boarded out. Moreover from his letters we learn that Lawson was 'often but ill & sore troubled with hypochondriac Mellancholly'. Perhaps he had chronic bouts of depression and this affected his attitude and his suspicion that Atkinson was plotting against him. The incumbents of Halton, Poulton and Tunstall certified that he was a 'person of orthodox & Loyall principle, Dilligent in his Function and exemplary in his Conversacion', and Dr. W. Hopkins, the spokesman for the Dean and Chapter of Worcester assured the Bishop that Lawson was an 'honest and laborious man upon that cure'. Certainly Lucas regarded him as 'a pious and diligent Vicar', but he also admired Atkinson, 'the pious Curate', who had officiated at Silverdale for over 40 years.[8]

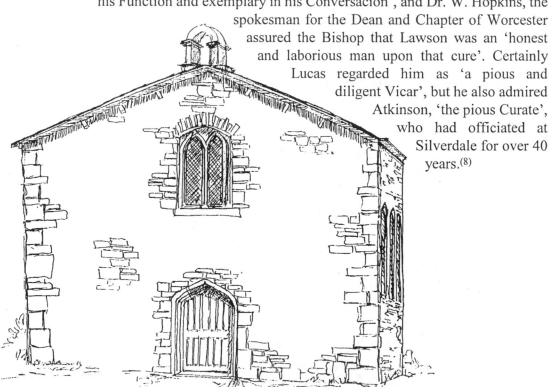

Silverdale Chapel of Ease as it would have appeared before modern alterations

When one considers the distance people had to walk to reach the church from Silverdale it is no wonder that the argument also brought up the difficulties of the journey. When the Silverdale inhabitants petitioned the Worcester chapter for a salary for the curate they wrote:

> ...for as much as wee are bound up by the sea on the one hand & Mosses on the other soe that at some times we cannot with conveniency travell to the Mother Church at Warton beeing in a very obscure & remote place & consisting of nere Three score families amongst which are very many aged & Decrepit people abounding alsoe (till of late that by the p[ro]curement of the Vicar of Warton wee had an honest orthodox & painefull Schoolm[r] & Curate) with many schismaticks & Quakers...wee humbly beseech your wor[shi]ps fav[or]ably to...vouchsafe by some small pension out of the Rectory of Warton to bee yearly p[ai]d to our Curate.

It appears that the Chapter increased the vicar's stipend and required him to pay £5 to maintain some kind of service at Silverdale 'to keep out dissenters from entering upon the said chapel'. Lawson seems to have grudged this payment and preached himself there once a month. He claimed the church at Warton was not 'farre remote...and the way very goode', though accepting that the chapel served a purpose for the use of the elderly and infirm and to keep out dissenters.

In 1692 the Chapter asked the Bishop to arbitrate and he sent James Fenton, Vicar of Lancaster, to visit and report. He found that the distance from Warton to Silverdale was four miles and:-

> open to all the severity of the weather seawards. In the midst lies a deep Mosse, where I thought we must have left our horses, & were once in despair of making our way, till Mr Lawson's clerk broke down a hedge, & conducted us thro mens grounds, who might have indicted us for trespasse. We got with much difficulty to Silverdale chapel...

Whether or not the inhabitants had taken pains to lead Mr Fenton by the worst possible route he was, on arrival at the chapel, impressed by their demeanour. He and his party found thirty of 'the chiefe ancient Inhabitants' waiting for them, who expressed a very earnest desire of having constant prayers at the chapel throughout the year.

...since there had been Constant Service there not one in the dale had turned Quaker, nor had any loitered & played among the hills on Sundays as their practice had been before, but their children and the younger sort were very much reclaimed by Mr Atkinson's constant cathechising. The more understanding men feard that (if their chapell was shut up for any time) they would relapse into their former looseness on the Lord's-day & a great part of them be made a prey to the Quakers. In reference to the vicar & church of Warton they freely owned their subjection & declard that on every sacram[en]t-day at Warton their chapell should not be open, but that they would repair with their Curate to Warton to receive. Mr Atkinson shewd great humility & respect to Mr Lawson...

Mr Fenton's recommendation was that a speedy determination be made of a difference which had raised scandal and 'great heats'. He stressed the great distance and the badness of the way and the good done among the inhabitants by a pious man and the harm that would come if the chapel were closed. He concluded by saying that 'The Quakers are pleased with the difference & stand expecting & wishing it. My Lord I beseech your Lordship to write to Worcester to satisfy them and obtain the continuance of the five pounds.' Three years later the dispute about the salary still grumbled on and Worcester arranged that their agent should pay Atkinson his £5 direct and deduct it from the vicar's £80. Lawson continued to urge his poverty. The death of Lawson in 1710 did not, however, improve Atkinson's position. His complaint to Lucas was that in the four years after Lawson's death he only received £2-10s-0d in all.[9] Atkinson was still alive in 1725, but it was only in 1756 that a curate was licensed to the augmented chapel.[10]

Funerals, Feasts and The Church

CHAPTER EIGHTEEN

Saint Oswald's Church

John Lucas, the historian of Warton parish, gives a detailed description of St Oswald's, the Parish Church, as he knew it at the end of the seventeenth and the beginning of the eighteenth century. The building cannot have changed much in its general outward appearance since he wrote, or indeed since the early seventeenth century. Its fabric is largely fifteenth and sixteenth century with part of the south wall a little earlier. Lucas recorded that it is dedicated to St. Oswald, King of Northumbria, as it is to-day, though it seems at some periods to have been given a Holy Trinity dedication. Oswald's feast was then observed on the Sunday nearest to August 1st. Lucas also believed that the name Senset Well for the once important watering place beyond the east end of Well Lane is a contraction of Sentussus Well, itself a contraction of St. Oswald's Well. He gives no reason for this derivation.[1]

The Church Building

Lucas describes the church walls as strong and roughcast with lime and very small, blue pebbles from the seashore, and the roof as entirely covered with lead. In his time a change of river course had revealed a quarry (of freestone) near Cotestones at the mouth of the Keer, from which the stone was believed to have come. Although basically the building was as it is to-day it must have made a rather different impact on the appearance of the village for Lucas adds that whenever the roughcast was renewed the church 'looks very white, so that the Church may be seen Eastward at the distance of many Miles, though it stands at the Foot of a high Hill'.[2]

But if the outward appearance has changed little, the interior must be very different. Lucas tells us that the windows were 'very proportionate and agreeable to the exact Cimmetry of the whole Fabrick' and that they contained 'small Fragments of painted Glass which are in everyone of them, but more especially in the large one at the East End, and yet not one Figure or Inscription entire or so much of them left that Conjecture can be made what they have been'.[3] He would like to see them taken down and the whole new glazed. No doubt he meant with clear glass, and this indeed happened. It was in the nineteenth century that changing fashion dictated their replacement with stained glass.

When he comes to describe the choir he notes that the chancel is maintained by the impropriators, the Dean and Chapter of Worcester. He says that before the Reformation no seats were allowed in the church nor:-

...any different Appartment assigned to any distinct Person; (the Patron only excepted, who was admitted within the Bars or Partitions of the Chancel...and there the Farmer of the Impropriate Tithes of this Parish has his seat to this Day), but the whole of the Body of the Church was Common, the whole Assembly in the more becoming Postures of Kneeling or Standing were promiscuous and intermixed. I suppose this Church was furnished with Seats soon after it had been divested of it's superstitious Ornaments: for on a Pew near the little South Door the following Characters are very neatly cut in the Wood, I.B. 1571, which Pew when I was a Boy was possessed by James Backhouse of Borwick and is still by the same Family. The Seats for the Men (a few Pews excepted) have only a Board or Plank at the Back, but those for the Women are but one single Plank without anything at the Back, and are therefore certainly the properest Sort to prevent Lolling or other indecent Postures in the Church. [4]

Clearly segregation of the sexes was practised. Both the local magnates, Middleton and Bindloss, had large private pews. The rood loft remained, but in poor condition with its paintings largely defaced. In many churches no font survived the Commonwealth period, so Warton is typical in having a font dated 1661, though the font itself seems to be much more ancient and to have been refurbished then. Lucas's description of the altar arrangements is as follows:-

In the time of our happy Reformation King Edw.VI appointed that one decent Table should be provided for every Parish to be set in the Body of the Church, where they remained until Archbishop Laud's time when it was removed to the east end of the Choir and enclosed with Rails, but the factious Party soon after prevailing they broke the Rails down and levelled the place with the rest of the Church, at the Restoration 1660 the Altar Table was set in its place again, and the Rails set up within my remembrance.

The Communion Table in this Church stands upon an Eminence (ascended by three Steps) that takes up the entire Breadth of the Quire, and was secured according to ancient Custom from the rude Approach of Dogs &c. by decent Rails and Banisters about the year 1699. It is covered wth green cloth, and at the Celebration of the Holy Eucharist with fine linen... [5]

Washington family

Lucas records the existence of the Arms of Washington '(Arg. 2 Bars Gul. in Chief 3 Mullets of the 2d.) well cut in the Stone, with a Crescent for Difference, which is a plain Indication that this Family, ancient and yet credible in the Town...have been large Contributors towards the Building of this Fabrick'.[6] It is interesting in these days when this object, now placed in the interior of the tower, is a place of pilgrimage for citizens of the United States of America, that Lucas wrote this before the birth of the first President of the USA.

Bells

Lucas records that there were three bells, one dated 1578, and notes that they were rung every Sunday morning at seven o'clock to give parishioners notice to prepare themselves by prayer for 'the Publick Offices of the Church'. The largest was tolled at the death of a Parishioner.[7]

One can assume that, except when the church formed part of a Presbyterian *classis* in the Interregnum, the services followed the Book of Common Prayer exactly and that on Sunday morning there was Morning Prayer, followed by the Litany, followed by the first part of the Communion Service. The sacrament would be celebrated only a few times a year. There was no organ in Lucas's time, but a tradition that there had been one led him to suggest that it had been destroyed along with the Rood, images, paintings etc. c.1570. There would probably be a group of instrumentalists and the metrical psalms were probably precented by the Parish Clerk who, at the time Lucas wrote, doubled as usher at the Free School.

Saint Oswald's Feast day

One day was naturally important, the Feast Day of the patron saint.

> *...the Feast of the Dedication...is now annually observed on the Sunday nearest to the first Day of August: and the vain Custom of Dancing, excessive Drinking &c. on that Day being, many years since, laid aside, the Inhabitants and Strangers spend that Day in duely attending the Service of the Church and making good Cheer, within the Rules of Sobriety, in private Houses, and the next in several Kinds of Diversions...*[8]

A rush-bearing ceremony of the type formerly practised at Warton. The location of this one is not specified (from 'Rush-bearing' by Alfred Burton, 1891).

Two of the activities of the church are described by Lucas. The first is rush-bearing in connection with the feast of dedication: on that day there was:-

> *...usually a Rush-bearing, which is on this Manner. They cut hard Rushes from the Marsh, which they make up into long Bundles, and then dress them in fine Linen, Silk, Ribbands, Flowers &c. Afterwards the Young Women of the Village which performs the Ceremony that Year, take up the Burdens erect upon their Heads, and begin the Procession...which is attended not only with Multitudes of People, but with Musick, Drums, Ringing of Bells, and all other Demonstrations of Joy they are able to express. When they arrive at the Church, they go in at the West End (the only publick use that ever I saw that door put to), and setting down their Burdens in the Church, strip them of their Ornaments, and strow the Rushes in the Seats leaving the Heads or Crowns of them deck'd with Flowers, cut Paper,&c. in some Part of the Church, generally over the Cancelli. Then the Company return to the Town from whence they came, and chearfully partake of a plentifull Collation provided for that Purpose; and spend the remaining Part of the Day and frequently a great Part of the Night also, in Dancing (if the Weather permits) about a May-Pole, adorned with Greens, Flowers &c. or else in some other convenient place.*[9]

Funeral customs

The second activity described by Lucas is the observance of funerals.[10] First he mentions the great entertainment of all who come to a funeral.

> *The Heir of the Deceased plentifully furnishes One, two or more Tables, according to his Ability, of which the whole Company partake, every one according to his liking. And afterwards there is distributed to every one a Penny Wheaten loaf, and a large Shive of Cheese (which they take away with them) and also a Drink of Ale. If the Heir be poor he has no Feast, and I think I have heard that of late Years, some have omitted the Cheese.*

But 'the whole company' definitely did not include everyone in the parish for Lucas goes on to say:-

> *Nor, while the Guests are thus feasted, are the Poor forgotten, but that all that come (and great Numbers I have seen upon this Occasion, many whereof would rather go 7 or 8 Miles to a Penny-Dole, than earn Six Pence in the Time by a more laudable Industry) are put into some large Barn or Yard, and as they come out receive every one a Penny or more according to the Charity or Circumstances of the Giver...*

In a further slightly inconsistent account of funerals, Lucas suggests another mode of dividing up the guests. The clerk, he says, gave notice that:-

..the Friends and Relations are desired to go to the Alehouse in the Town (which he names) and the Neighbours and Acquaintance to another, where every one has a Penny Loaf & Ale allowed, according to the Ability of the Deceased; and this they call an Arval.[11]

The word Arval is a borrowing from the Norse according to the Oxford English Dictionary, and comes from words meaning 'inheritance' and 'ale', that is to say a Funeral Feast. The use of the words 'Arval'and 'arval bread' are not peculiar to Warton but were widely used in the north.[12] William Stout who, among other activities, kept a grocer's shop in Lancaster recorded in his autobiography that:-

At this time [1693] we sould much cheese to funeralls in the country from therty to one hundred pound weight as the deceased was of ability, which was shived into 2 or 3 [slices] in the pound, and one, with a penny manchet, given to all the attendants.[13]

Lucas tells how, when the funeral party arrives, they enter by the gate on the north side of the Church, go round the east end and carry the corpse beyond a thorn bush, where formerly a yew tree stood and then enter by the porch.[14] The corpse is then placed in the choir while the vicar reads the funeral office '...and if the Deceased was the Master of a Family, and of Moderate Circumstances, he usually preaches a Funeral Sermon'. After the service 'Relations and dear Friends' carry the dead to the grave and there 'throw in the laurels, Rosemary &c. they have in their Hands', evergreens being, Lucas says, 'an emblem of the Soul's Immortality, and the Resurrection of the Body'. He also comments on a change in customs that had taken place in his life time.

... Most of the Householders of this Parish were furnished with a finely wrought Coverlet which was used to be thrown over the Bier, when the Corps of any of the Family was carried to the Church, but of late they, the richer Sort especially, have made use of a black Pall...[15]

The Bride's Chair and Harvest Customs

Lucas has other stories of village amusements, shooting at the butts on the crag, cock-fighting, bonfires on midsummer's day, merriment at weddings including, for brides from Silverdale and Lindeth the ceremony of sitting on 'the Bride Chair' on the way back from church. It was, and is, a worn stone overlooking Morecambe Bay by Barrow Scout, but Lucas does not even hazard a guess as to the origin and meaning of this custom.[16] His fullest description is of the Harvest festivities.[17] He allows that the custom is wide spread but gives a particular description of it as he knew it in Carnforth. First he describes how the work was got through:-

In this part of the Country each Village commonly hires a Fiddler which, during the Time of Harvest, goes from one Field to another, and plays to the Reapers: at which Times I have seen the young People whose Backs had been bowed down with hard Labour, in the hot Sun for several Hours, dance as briskly in the Stubble as if they had been on a Theatre; and then their Strength being renew'd by the Muscles of their Bodies having been put into different Motions, and their spirits revived by the Harmony of the Musick, fall to their Labour again with redoubled Vigour and Activity...

Then he describes the actual Harvest Home:-

When Harvest is over they have a Merry Night as they call it, against which each Family of the better sort contributes, some Time before, it's Quota of Malt, which is brewed into Ale, of which, and of a plentifull Entertainment provided at the joynt Expences of the Masters of Families, the whole Village are Partakers. The Old People after Supper smoak their Pipes, and with great Pleasure & Delight behold the younger spending the Evening in Singing, Dancing, &c....the Youth of this Town, upon this Occasion, usually dance sub dio *(if the weather permits) on the lower Part of a little Hill near Hellbank.*

The Hellbank was in Carnforth and, Lucas says, was '...about the middle of the town near the Meeting of Four Wayes...'. Since the seventeenth century town lay along North Road one possible site is outside the Shovel Inn (or an older inn on the site, since the present building only dates from 1750), a convenient place for the old people to sit. The touch about the weather is pleasing, because otherwise the whole account is almost too idyllic.

Gambling

Elsewhere Lucas speaks of those 'the younger sort especially' who engage in 'idle sports and pastimes'.[18] One would like to know more about these. Judging by the number of 'hubbleshows', that is commotions or hubbubs, for which the inhabitants were fined by the Manor Court, drinking was one of the amusements. There is one mention, in Warton Manor Court records of unlawful games for money 'quit-shotes, lightinges or bybeites',[19] but no description of how these were played.

Pipers and Actors

Two other tiny facts are known about amusements in Warton, or perhaps one and a half facts. The parish seems to have had, at one time, its own piper. At any rate in 1593 'John Johnson pip[er]' and his wife were fined by Warton Manor Court for slander and 'flyting', that is disputing.[20] Secondly on January 2nd 1676 Leighton Hall paid out five shillings 'to the Actors for the play'.[21] Strolling players from outside? Or, since it was within the twelve days of Christmas, mummers from the village come to entertain the household? Who knows?

Making One's Mark

CHAPTER NINETEEN

Archbishop Hutton's School

There had been a Grammar School in Warton since the end of the sixteenth century. It was founded in 1594 by Matthew Hutton of Priest Hutton, after he became Bishop of Durham. By the next year, when he obtained a formal charter for the school from Queen Elizabeth, he had become Archbishop of York, whence the present title of Warton's school, 'Archbishop Hutton's School'. Hutton had himself climbed up the educational ladder[1] but, though one may guess at the influence this had on him, there is only the wording of the charter as guide to his actual motives in founding a school in the parish of his birth. The charter says that he 'greatly desires to erect and found a certain free school and hospital or alms house in the town of Warton...in the parish of which town the same Archbishop was born, to the glory of God, the promotion of good learning and the support and relief of the poor'.[2]

Whatever his motives, Archbishop Hutton was following a trend of the time. 'Few periods of English History can boast such a conspicuous enthusiasm for the benefits of education'.[3] There was increased provision for education at all levels from the Universities and the Inns of Court down to 'petty schools' set up in villages and towns by single teachers. Grammar Schools were founded in many places as part of this movement. Archbishop Hutton made himself responsible for a salary of £20 p.a. for the school master and of £6-13s-4d for an usher, which was reasonably generous by contemporary standards. They were to be 'prudent and honest persons', but what they were to teach, and to whom, can only be inferred from what is known of other contemporary schools. Queen Elizabeth's Charter gave the Archbishop power to make 'suitable and beneficial statutes', but if he did they have not survived. There were to be six governors responsible both for the school and for the alms house, the Hospital of Jesus, that went with it. Hutton made specific arrangements in his will for the endowment of the school to be continued by his heirs.

Early Problems

At least twice in the seventeenth century these arrangements faltered, though only briefly. In 1637, because no Governors had been appointed for an unspecified length of time, the Archbishop's grandson, another Matthew Hutton, appointed five gentlemen from the locality together with the incumbent of Warton to be the six Governors. The allowance was to be continued and he and his heirs were to have the nomination of the Governors, the Master, the Usher, the Warden of the Almshouse and also of the poor people admitted to the latter. Governors were allowed to make rules, but only 'with the advisement and consent' of the Archbishop of York.[4]

It was probably during this turmoil that a regrettable incident took place. William Curwen, an apparently self-styled curate in Bolton-le-Sands, who had already been in trouble there, had an adulterous meeting with a beggar woman in Warton schoolhouse. The woman later bore a child.[5]

Sometime thereafter another hiatus occurred. The inhabitants of Warton had to petition the heir again. Mr Curwen, the Master who had been appointed in the 1637 crisis (presumably no connection of the adulterous William Curwen) had moved on to another preferment, two of the governors were dead and one had moved elsewhere. Moreover 'the revenues belonginge to the Free schole and hospitall are not disposed of accordinge to theire firste and full intentions, as evidently may be made to appeare, but converted to private and sinister uses'.[6] After that the Huttons continued to pay the allowance to Master and usher throughout the century, even in the Commonwealth years when, as royalists, they had to compound for their sequestered estate.[7] Fortunately, Parliament had decreed that money paid out for charitable and educational purposes was to be respected when estates were sequestered.

The Curriculum

Lucas gives a description of the school building as it was when he was a pupil there at the end of the seventeenth century.[8] It stood just above the town on the side of the crag and was approached up some broken stone steps. Above the entry was an inscription cut in stone *Anno Domi 1594 Deo et bonis literis Matt: Hutton Epvs: Dvnelm* [In the year of our Lord 1594. To God and good learning. Matthew Hutton Bishop of Durham]. The stone still exists having followed the school through its various homes to its present site in Back Lane where, at the time of writing, the stone awaits funds to allow it to be displayed. The floor of the school house was 'overlaid with oaken Boards'. One end of the building, which Lucas refers to as 'the usher's end', was single storied and open to the roofbeams. The other end had a second story consisting of two 'chambers', one 'neatly plastered and has a chimney in it'. Beside them was the library. Over the door at the foot of the stairway was a Greek inscription on the plaster, but it was already too worn in Lucas's time to be read.

Warton schoolhouse

An inscription in Greek served to mark the school's status. From its foundation it was rated as a Grammar School. Almost certainly some degree of literacy was needed as a prerequisite to admission. Grammar schools were founded to teach Latin and Greek rather than basic reading and writing. Some did take in younger children to teach them reading, though often charging for this instruction. At St Bees, for instance, it was the Usher's job, according to the statutes, 'to teach children to read and write English and to say by heart the catechism in English...'[9] It might be thought that the invaluable Lucas, having been himself a pupil at the school, would offer some enlightenment on what was the practice at Warton, but though he gives lively descriptions of the boys' amusements he does not mention lessons. It is perhaps of relevance that when Archbishop Hutton's School was re-opened in 1833, after the foundation had been allowed to lapse for some years, it was laid down that no child was to be admitted till competent 'to read in a Common Spelling Book' and spell words of two syllables.[10]

The Teaching of Writing

At the upper levels one may assume that Latin and Greek were taught. William Stout, a pupil at the nearby Heversham Grammar School, was fourteen in 1679 and by that time had 'made some progress in the Lattin there, and was entring into the Greek grammar...'[11] What else might have been taught is not known. Science did not really enter into the curriculum of grammar schools. Arithmetic might be taught. A school in Chigwell, Essex, appointed a second master who was to be 'skilful in cyphering and casting of accounts and teach his scholars the same faculty...'[12] William Stout, the same who by fourteen was learning Greek, had to be sent to 'a scrivener' after he left school to learn 'to arethmatick'.[13]

Writing was taught separately from reading, and only after reading had been mastered. It often had to be paid for separately. William Stout finishes the above description of his schooling by saying '...and the writing master coming...mostly in winter, wee got what writing we had in winter'. At the beginning of the eighteenth century the teaching of writing in Warton Grammar School seems to have been considered inadequate. In 1718 James Jackson, Churchwarden, made complaint to the consistory court that a certain John Harris was teaching scholars to write in the church 'without any lawfull Authority to the great prejudice of the Seats of the s^d church which are often pulled up to make writing tables...'[14]

The Cost of Education

The effect of the school on the general level of literacy in the parish is even harder to gauge. Judging by information from elsewhere only a minority of children would have attended school at all. It was not necessarily the fee which kept children out, for it was a 'Free School'. It has been argued that this meant it was exempt from ecclesiastical control rather than non-fee-paying, but the latter is perhaps the more usually accepted meaning. There were some customary payments to the schoolmaster to be made, but these were not compulsory. Every Shrove Tuesday, on the occasion of the annual cock-fight, there were gifts to the master called 'Cock-pennies'. The pupils paid 'every one according to the Ability or Generosity of their Parents'. There were also 'Nicholas Pennies' to be paid on the day school broke up for Christmas.[15]

There were however many hidden costs. There was the question of keep. Lucas says:-

> The Boys which come to this School out of the circumjacent villages bring their Victuals along with them every Morning; and at Noon (either in the School, or on some scar on the Crag in Summer, or by a good Fire in some of the Townsmen's Houses in Winter) do cheerfully feed thereon...[16]

It would all have added to the cost. Boarding out would have been even more prohibitive. William Stout's parents had to pay the considerable sum of £4 a year to board him in Heversham.[17] Most financially deterrent of all would have been the loss of children's earning power and the help they could give with work at home. Children's work has been discussed earlier (Chapter 12), but it is of interest that even comparatively well-to-do children were kept off school when they were needed on the farm. William Stout gave this account of his interrupted schooling.

> As we attained to the age of ten or twelve years, we were very much taken off the schoole, espetialy in the spring and summer season, plow time, turfe time and harvest, in looking after sheep, helping at plough, goeing to the moss with carts, making hay and shearing in harvest...so that we made smal progress in Latin, for what we got in winter we forgot in summer...[18]

Yet William Stout says that his parents were very careful to get him learning. It seems probable that many less careful parents, even among those who could have afforded to send their children to school, simply did not do so. It was a natural problem in a rural school. Even after education became compulsory in the nineteenth century the log-book of Archbishop Hutton's school contains complaints of children kept off for hay-making or for hoeing turnips.[19] Grammar Schools were often founded with the poor in mind, but even in the sixteenth century they were being taken over by the better-to-do. Moreover it went without saying at the time that half the children of the parish would not be attending. Archbishop Hutton's foundation was for boys only. Girls were not admitted until 1836.[20]

Almost nothing is known of what other possibilities for learning there might have been. It would certainly have been difficult for children from 'the circumjacent villages', to use Lucas's phrase, to trek each day to the school which might be over four miles away. There is one suggestion that local arrangements may have been made. In the 1680s, when the inhabitants of Silverdale were petitioning for payment for their curate, they described him as 'an honest orthodox schoolmaster'.[21]

Jurymen's signatures and marks made at Warton Manor Court on the 14th April 1613 (DDTo/0/2). Reproduced by kind permission of the County Archivist, Lancashire Record Office.

Literacy

It is always difficult to know how literate a given community was in the past. The usual method is to examine contemporary documents and see how many of the signatories could sign their name and how many made their mark. It is true that, to speak strictly, the ability to sign a name is proof of no more than exactly that. However signing probably has some correlation with ability to read, certainly in the seventeenth century when writing was taught after reading. Such studies as have been done suggest that literacy was increasing over the seventeenth century. For instance, of the men who made depositions for the Northern Circuit 65 per cent made their mark in 1640, but only 41 per cent in 1690. The figures for women are 93 per cent in 1640 and 86 per cent in 1690.[22] Literacy levels tended to be lower in the countryside than in towns, though rural parishes could vary enormously among themselves.[23]

Research for Warton still needs to be done and it is possible that the evidence simply does not exist. A very rough estimate of the change in ability to sign a name over the century can be made for Warton township from the Manor Court records. Some, but by no means all, of the records have the signatures or marks of the jurymen appended. In each year between 1608 and 1613 in which such lists of signatures appear well over half the jurors made their mark rather than signing. In fact the average for all the lists was 82 per cent not signing. (In three cases the 'mark' made was the man's initials.) In each year between 1668-1677 in which lists appear less than half the jurors were unable to sign. Over this later period the average number having to make a mark was only 33 per cent. The proportion of those unable to sign is less than in the quoted work of Houston, but one cannot conclude that Warton was particularly well-educated. Jurors might well be among the better educated men in the manor, whereas men making depositions for a court would come from all walks of life.

Even if only some inhabitants could read it must have helped spread the idea that the written word had something to say and have opened up possibilities and broken down boundaries which had hitherto tied village ideas to very local matters. The increasing desire of people, after the Reformation, to be able to read the Bible for themselves is often instanced as one of the causes of increasing literacy over the sixteenth and seventeenth centuries. It is not to be forgotten, however, that there was much other reading matter appearing, some of it learned, much of more popular appeal. There were the 'almanacs' which appeared each year. These were more than calendars, they gave information on a great variety of matters, including sensational news, scientific and historical facts, astrological predictions, information on fairs and roads etc. By the 1660s some 400,000 were being sold each year 'enough to provide a copy each to two-fifths of the households in the kingdom'.[24]

Books in Warton Parish

There were books to be had in and about Warton. James Backhouse of Kirkby Lonsdale, who has been mentioned in an earlier chapter as a general dealer in clothes and grocery, also had a fair stock of books. In the inventory drawn up of his possessions in 1578 there were various psalm-books and bibles, fourteen or more untitled books, as well as *'Esopes fabulls'*, Tullyes *Offices*, 'Catoes and an Englishe boocke', 'Terrencis *Dyalogues'*, 'Virgills', as well as accidences, grammars, primers and *Puriles* (sc. elementary reading books) and *ABsis* (ABCs). There were also a score of pairs of pens and ink-horns and a ream of paper.[25] (These holdings raise the question, of course, of what, educationally, was going on in Kirkby Lonsdale at that period.)

Christopher Harrison of Abbot Hall, as well as dealing in a big way in knitted stockings (see Chapter 7) had a number of books. It seems to have been a more serious collection than Backhouse's. It included, apart from bibles, prayer-books, anonymous treatises and testaments, such titles as *Smith's Sermons, Napier on the Revelation, 'Baker's Lectures', Dod upon the Commandments, Brunston's Treatisse, John Dennistons worke, Gifford upon the Revelation, Commentaries on the Proverbbes, Satanns Sophistries* and a book on husbandry.[26]

There are two wills from Warton parish itself which refer to sizeable collections of books. The first is that of Anthony Bugg, vicar of Warton from 1613 to 1632. His book list is of such interest in connection with religious beliefs in the parish that it is dealt with in more detail in Appendix 3. Francis Jackson, a later vicar who died in 1670, left books to the value of £6-13s-4d, but no titles are given. It is only known that he left a further £2 worth of 'mathematical books' and instruments. He had been a schoolmaster in Kirkby Lonsdale before being appointed to Warton as vicar.

There are also books in the will of Francis Jackson's father, Richard Jackson. He was the rector of Whittington (about eight miles from Warton), and outlived his son by ten years, dying in 1680. He was the son of a rich mercer and seems to have had a very large family, three sons and three daughters by his second marriage and an unknown number by his first. It is possible, though, that his penultimate daughter Vigessima ('Twentieth'), who married the next vicar, may have been named after a church date rather than the number of his children. He is known to have been a member of the presbyterian classis in 1646 [27], but in the absence of any titles in his inventory it is not possible to know if his library reflected his religious opinion. His will contains the following bequest.

> *I give unto my Sonne Leonard Jackson all my Library of Bookes whatsoever as well printed Bookes as Manuscripts w[hi]ch are in my Studie, desireing hee will keep them for his owne onely use and not part w[i]th them to any, for they are all of them precious and profitable Bookes; And I give him alsoe the Deske w[i]th the Seaven boxes in it, w[hi]ch lyeth on my Study Table, it was made in the yeare of our Lord 1604 as is Engraven upon it and the Key thereof w[hi]ch is upon the Ring I keep in my pockett, (haveing other Keyes and my Signet Seale hanging w[i]th it)[28].*

The library is valued at £40 in the inventory. Jackson seems to have been something of an antiquary for he enumerated various coins he had; a Roman penny of Tiberius, another of Vespasian, and coins of Edward VI, Elizabeth, King Charles 'with this Inscription for ye protestant Religion ye privilege of parliament, and ye Libertie of ye Subject, with this Motto in Ring or Edges of it (viz) Exurgat Deus et disipentur Inimici'; and a Crown penny of the King of Sweden and a silver one of the city of Ments [Mainz?].

The Bible

There is no other surviving will from Warton parish itself which could indicate that anyone else aspired to this sort of learning. There were, however, a fair number of people who had one or two books. Even in the first half of the century 6 per cent of inventories mention books. By the second half the figure had risen to 14 per cent. Even that may be an underestimate since there are wills which mention books though none are listed in the relevant inventory. Just over half of these entries specify a bible, either alone or with 'other books', but only one title of a book is given. It was a 'great book' called *The Mirror or Looking Glass for Saints and Sinners* which John Bayleman of Yealand Redmayne left in his will in 1696. More ephemeral reading matter, such as almanacs, news-sheets and popular ballads may have been known in Warton parish, but none appear in the inventories, and only one mention has been found in any other source. In December 1675, Dame Anne Middleton of Leighton Hall paid out sixpence for 'an almanacke',[29] a cost which would have made most people in the parish think twice. As well as these privately owned books the library at the Grammar School was 'furnished with a good Store of Classick Authors (if not imbezled) for the Use of the Masters and Scholars'.[30] One would like to know who the remark 'if not imbezled' was aimed at.

Postscript

Research is a continuous process and, in finding the answer to one problem, several related questions are brought to mind, the answers to which may then throw doubt on the original conclusion. There is a temptation to go on and on in search of an impossible completeness. There came a point when the group of Mourholme Society members who wrote these chapters felt they must try for publication however many gaps were left. If not there was a danger that their work, and moreover the work of those who had gone before, might merely remain as an archive gathering dust.

As it is we hope that the book, with all its gaps, may stimulate others to carry on the work. There are plenty of as yet untapped sources in record offices and elsewhere. For example the Mourholme Society archives contain a photocopy of the complete Warton Manor Court Book. It covers the period from 1688 to the present century, is a mine of information and, since the original is in private hands is not otherwise easily available.

Then too, though we have striven to avoid the trap, there is the danger common to all local historians of being so carried away by the interest of their chosen subject that the wider setting, both in place and time is underplayed. More work is needed on such points as how far Warton's relatively sheltered position in a deteriorating climate differentiated it significantly from neighbouring parishes. Was it unusual in having so many sheep? Were the tenants who fought for their rights in touch with those engaged in a similar battle near-by or did they fight alone? What went before and after our arbitrarily chosen beginning and end points?

And, moving away from written sources, there has only been a beginning in field-work and the possibilities here are great; surveys of existing buildings such as the farm buildings so rapidly being disguised as dwelling houses; field-patterns, surviving field-walls, and abandoned sites such as the now lost mills of the parish.

The Mourholme Society already has its eyes on the nineteenth century, another arbitrarily chosen period, but the field is wide.

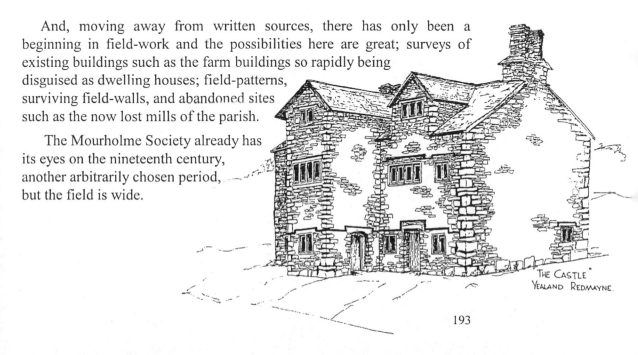

THE CASTLE
YEALAND REDMAYNE

193

HOW IT WAS
Wills and Inventories

In the course of preparing this book much recourse was had to the wills drawn up by the inhabitants of Warton parish in the seventeenth century. Wills had long been made by members of the upper stratum of society, but from about the middle of the sixteenth century they began also to be made by farmers and better to-do craftsmen.

After the testator died an inventory, a list of personal goods, credits and debts was compiled, under oath, by friends and neighbours - the Appraisers as they were called. The inventory was a central part of proving the will and so had to be drawn up.

Inventories have been found a most valuable source of information to the local historian, but they must be used with caution and with knowledge of how they were drawn up. They include much detail of household and farm goods, tools and material of industry, stores of food, crops (gathered in or still standing in the field) and personal possessions such as clothes and ornaments. They did not include land, whether freehold or copyhold, or the dwelling house, outhouses and barns etc.

The pitfalls in using inventories as evidence have been well summarised by Dr J.D. Marshall.[1] In particular, as he points out, wills and inventories cover only a part of the male population of any district. (Wills of women are comparatively rare for, though spinsters and widows had testamentary capacity, wives did not.) It is probable that, in general, fewer than 40 per cent of the adult male population, and sometimes far less will have traceable death records of this kind. It is usually assumed, moreover, that the 40 per cent who made wills, and so had inventories made of their goods, contained a statistically biased proportion of the better to-do. Why after all go to the trouble and expense of proving a will unless there was property to be argued over?

Until 1852 wills were proved, and administration granted, in the Church courts; for Warton parish this meant primarily the Archdeaconry of Richmond. These wills are now kept in the Lancashire Record Office at Preston. Two hundred and twenty two wills made by the inhabitants of Warton parish between 1600 and 1699 were studied along with 157 inventories (not all wills had a surviving inventory attached and, contrariwise, some inventories were without wills). There are known to be also a further nine wills proved in the Prerogative Court of Canterbury and three proved at York. These have not been studied.

It seems that somewhere over the centuries there has been a considerable loss of death documents. Gaps of two years with no wills or inventories occur, and it may be that genuinely no-one of the 'will-making classes' died in those years, but there is a suspicious gap of six years between 1655 and 1660 during which no wills and no inventories have been traced for anyone in the parish. In the small township of Borwick nothing at all has survived from 1638 till 1670, and for Priest Hutton only one inventory between 1642 and 1661. For the biggest township of all, Warton itself, there is only one inventory and two wills for the years between 1651 and 1669.

As some sort of check on what proportion of people made wills another line of approach has been taken. The recorded names of jurors in the Warton Manor Court Book between 1607 and 1613 were matched against wills and inventories. There are 34 names of jurors, but for only eight of the names can an inventory be found, and for three more a will alone (and this is on the generous assumption that any man of the same name dying within the next fifty years was identical with the juror). This means that at the most a third of the jurors have left surviving wills and for only a quarter are there surviving inventories. Yet these jurors are the very men one would suppose most likely to have made wills being, on the whole, men of standing in the community. To know just how serious the gaps in documentation are, one would need to find out, at the very least, how exceptional Warton was in its loss of death records among the seven townships of the parish.

Throughout the book an attempt has been made to work always within the limits of the evidence; to accept that the information is incomplete and to acknowledge that the poor are under-represented. Nevertheless the inventories supply much qualitative information and can, cautiously, be used to draw quantitative conclusions.

Incidentally, here and throughout the book, no attempt has been made to convert the prices given in the inventories into modern terms. It would be an enterprise beyond the scope of a very local history like this because of the vast changes both in the purchasing power of a pound and in the relative cost of different goods. Seventeenth century prices have therefore been given unchanged. Fortunately still older coins, groats, nobles etc. were not used in the inventories so it has been possible merely to assume that readers know that, till 1970, there were twenty shillings in a pound and twelve pence in a shilling. And incidentally that the sign for a shilling was 's' and for a penny 'd'.

HOW IT WAS
The Hearth Tax

In 1662 an Act of Parliament allowed the raising of money by a tax of two shillings a year on every hearth. It was a much disliked tax and was discontinued after 1689. The records engendered by the collection of the tax during the years it was in force have been of considerable value to local historians. In order to collect the tax it had been necessary to know how many hearths there were in the kingdom. Parish constables were given the task of drawing up lists of hearths. These lists were, basically, to contain the names of every householder and how many hearths he had. Certain categories of people were exempt, most noticeably on the grounds of poverty. The result, from the point of view of the historian, was some very useful statistics in the form of lists giving the names of all householders and the number of hearths in every town, village, hamlet and settlement. Just as importantly the lists provided the names of those thought by their contemporaries to be in a state of poverty.

The lists would be of greater value if it were not for some inherent weaknesses in the method of collection. In the first place they were collected by local constables without training and subject to local pressures. There were the self-interested, desirous of tax-evasion if not downright tax-avoidance. There was a general tendency not to trouble with listing the exempt. There was the complication that the reasons for exemption were mixed. It was not only the hearths of the poor that were exempt, so too were industrial hearths such as kilns and also hearths in small charitable institutions. Poverty itself was variously defined. It usually meant those too poor to pay Church or Poor Rates, but might mean those with property and income below a certain rather confusedly expressed level, though then only if their poverty was certified by parson and overseers, which must in itself have added to local variability. There was probably also a general wish to lighten the burden of a tax which was not going to be spent locally. In 1688 William Fleming, a Cumbrian gentleman, wrote to his brother 'Tell the constable the same Hearth-man is coming again. Tell him to be as kind as his conscience will permit to his neighbours'.[2]

Some Hearth Tax returns for all the townships of Warton parish have survived for certain years between 1664 and 1673 and can be seen on microfiche in the Lancashire Record Office. Only the returns for Lady Day 1664 include non-chargeable hearths. The detailed basis on which they were collected in the Warton townships is not known. It is unlikely that industrial hearths made a significant contribution to the number of exempt hearths in Warton, and though Archbishop Hutton's school and almshouse were, presumably, exempt, that too would be of minimal importance.

HOW IT WAS
Books, Wills and Beliefs

The beliefs of the Church of England had taken shape in Edward VI's reign in the form of forty-two articles - later, under Elizabeth, the 'thirty-nine articles'. It has been noted that these include a substantial injection of Calvinist beliefs; in particular, an assertion of 'predestination', even as built into the fabric of the universe, and accompanied by an 'election' of the redeemed. This was related to the puritan strand in English religious thought in the middle sixteenth century, and this puritan tradition was strong in Matthew Hutton of Priest Hutton, Archbishop of York from 1595 to 1606 (see Appendix 4).

Matthew Hutton

Matthew Hutton made his will in 1605. He left a score of named books to relatives and friends. His chaplain (whom he had supported through Cambridge) was given his choice of books up to the value of £6-8s-4d. Anthony Bugg, 'scholler in Cambridge', was given a sum of money, and 'such of my books as are fytt for him', to the value of £4-6s-8d.[3] In 1613 Bugg became vicar of Warton.

The name Bugg was rare in northern counties and, though the names Bugg and Bugge can be found now, they are not known to have been current locally in Anthony Bugg's day. (The Victoria County History gives him as Buggs; this seems to be a misreading; it is not used in Hutton's will.) The name may have been more frequent in East Anglia. Francis Bugg (1640-1724), the renegade Quaker, for instance, was from Mildenhall in Suffolk. Anthony Bugg was installed at Warton in April 1613 and stayed until his death in 1632.

The present interest in Bugg derives from the inventory of over eighty books drawn up when he died and from the implications of some of them for the religious outlook in the Warton area in the seventeenth century.

The money value put on the whole list was between £9 and £9-10s in 1631, twice the value of the books left him by Hutton in 1605 - though the alteration in book values over the period is not known. There are still some problems of transcription, and it is clear that the compiler of the inventory list was not competent beyond English. Not all authors and titles have been identified, but some main groups can be seen.

There were some classical works, presumably from Bugg's Cambridge days: Virgil's *Eclogues*, Sallust, Cicero's letters (in J. Sturm's edition), his speeches and his *De Officiis*, *Greek Isocrates* and *Cesar's Comentaryes*. There were reference works like Thomas Tomatius's dictionary and a 'poetical dixtionary'. Sir Thomas Elyot's *Castle of Health*, of the mid-sixteenth century was of general interest. There were copies of Marcus Aurelius and Aristotle's *Ethics*.

The religious works included traditional writers like Jerome (*'Hieroms homilies'*), Cassiodorus (a fifth century litterateur who founded a monastery), Anselm, archbishop of Canterbury around 1100, and numerous commentaries on the scriptures. There were two books (*upon Thavangelist* and *upon Paul's epistels*) by Nicholas de Lyra, a fourteenth century lecturer in Paris, famous for his Postillae, or commentaries, and for his insistence on literal rather than allegorical meanings. Collections of sermons included Smyth's *Sermons*, Anamcles[?] *Sermons upon the Festivall*s and *Culman upon the Festivalls*. There was also John Napier's *upon the revelacion,* which he published in 1593, long before his logarithms.

The first work in the list is one *Geneva bible*. This (the puritan bible) was a translation published in 1560. Next is a *Synopsis*, not further explained but worth eighteen shillings, more than any other single book in the list.

The third entry is less clear. The first three letters are 'Buc', followed by what may be, from the thick flat top stroke, an ordinary backward 'e', or an 'o'. The last letter is apparently an 'r', though it is not the usual final 'r' met in this list. It is presumed that the name was probably 'Bucer' (Butser); no book title is given.

Martin Bucer (1491-1551) was a leading Reformation theologian in Strassbourg. Like others, he had to flee after failing to sign the 'Interim' of the emperor Charles V in 1548, an attempt to find some religious *modus vivendi* between protestant and catholic among Charles' German subjects. Bucer came to England at the invitation of Cranmer and stayed with him in 1549. He collaborated with Cranmer in his book upon the sacraments. Bucer is credited with providing the intellectual side of this collaboration and, since both were always ready to settle differences, the result could be called a typical English compromise.

Edward VI made Bucer the Lecturer in Theology at Cambridge. Bucer also acted as tutor to Edward VI - who even helped him to get a German stove when he was cold and ill, and granted him an annuity. The Duchess of Suffolk aided him, too, and two of her sons were Bucer's students. There are letters from her family, including an appreciative one from Jane Dudley (Lady Jane Grey), aged fourteen. He remained in Cambridge till his death in 1551. In the reign of Mary I his remains were exhumed and burnt. He had known Erasmus (1466-1536), a humanist forerunner of the Reformation. Bugg had Erasmus's *Addiges* (Adages). (If it was the 1615 edition, it must have been Bugg's own copy, not one inherited from Hutton.) Bucer also knew Luther and Bugg had among his books *Luther on the Galatians*.

The local connection here is that Matthew Hutton began his degree at Cambridge in 1546 and finished in 1551, the years of Bucer's stay in Cambridge. There is no doubt that he was part of Bucer's circle which included Edward Grindal who was Archbishop of York before Hutton, and a friend and a profound influence on Hutton's thinking.

Continuing the book-list, we come to *Brintius upon thavangelist.* Johann Brenz (1499-1570) is variously spelt. In Latin he was Brentius or Brencius. He was a mayor's son from Swabia, who supported Luther and organised a church on Lutheran lines. After vicissitudes and escaping to Basle, he settled in Halle. He was considered a main influence in the Reformation, helping to write the Wurttemberg Confession of Faith, and his work became known in England. Richard Shirrye translated part of his scriptural work, 'A verye fruitfull Exposicion upon the syxte Chapter of Saynte Iohn' (1550). Many of the reformers wrote on John as having a directer theological approach.

Stappleton promptuariu[m] appears in the list. Thomas Stapleton (1535-1598) left Oxford to follow his parents to Louvain when Elizabeth came to the throne. He had an erratic temperament: he left a chair at Douai for a Jesuit novitiate, and abandoned that, amid recriminations, before taking a chair of theology at Louvain and being considered as a possible cardinal. He expressed doubts about the extent of papal authority over princes, and denied that the pope had any right to dethrone them for purely civil reasons. He attacked English divines, but also wrote of Becket and Thomas More in his 'Tres Thomae' (1588) and translated Bede. It is not certain that Bugg had this work since his *Bede's ecclesiastic history of England* has a different title from Stapleton's work.

Bugg had '*Bunnyes resolution* & two ould sermon books'. The two sermon books are probably to be regarded as miscellaneous items rather than by Bunney. There were two brothers called Bunney, from a Yorkshire family. Francis, the younger (1543-1617) wrote three tracts against Bellarmin, a major Catholic controversialist; and Bugg had a hostile tract against him *(Piscator contra Bellarmin de iustificacione)*. Francis became connected with the north-east of England and was a popular preacher. His elder brother, Edmund (1540-1618), became a preacher also. He travelled much in the north, and preached extempore; he was also considered 'forward and meddling' because of this. Both were admirers of Calvin, and Edmund published an *Abridgment of Calvin's Institutions* (1580). Bugg had a copy of Calvin's *Institutions,* but the edition is not known. Edmund is probably the brother referred to in Bugg's list. For he was chaplain to Archbishop Grindal, Hutton's puritan predecessor, and sub-dean of York for nine years. Moreover one of his publications was entitled *A book of Christian Exercise*, appertaining to Resolution. Edmund Bunney was also part of the Grindal/Hutton circle and his monument can be seen in York Minster.

John Argall, another English divine, was a noted disputant at Oxford. He performed in a play when Elizabeth paid a visit in 1566. His chief work was *De vera poenitentia*, which appears in Bugg's list.

There are three works by Musculus in the list, probably from Archbishop Hutton's own library since Phylip Foorde, another recipient of Hutton's books, was left other works of Musculus. This was the name by which Wolfgang Moesel (1497-1563) chose to be known - there was a scholarly fashion for latinising your name. He was a poor lad taken into a monastery, where he preached and read Luther avidly. Leaving his abbey to marry he was reduced to penury. He went to Strassbourg, Augsburg and Wittenberg, where in 1536 he became a delegate to Worms. He eventually moved to a chair in theology at Berne. Bugg had his works *upon Matthew* (1541) and *upon John* (1548) and his book *upon coman places of the scripture* (Loci communes, 1554).

'Ferus pestles' hides a work by Johann Wild (late fifteenth century - 1554) on the Epistles (pestles). Ferus (=wild) was a Latin form of the name. His works included commentaries on Matthew and on John, as well as on the Epistles. He had much learning and oratorical power. In religious terms he was a middle of the road man. He was attached to Rome, but he didn't scruple to condemn the abuses, attacks on which had brought Luther into such disfavour. His supporters said that the hostile passages in his writings were written by Protestants.

Aretius Theo: problemes is in the list. Benedictus Aretius, who came from Berne, was a preacher of the reformed church, at Marburg, and a popular theological teacher, who died in 1574. The work here is probably his large *Examen theologicum* which was reprinted many times. But his lasting reputation was for Alpine botanical knowledge, and his association with Conrad Gessner, 'the Pliny of Germany'. (Though Aretius Felinus was also a name under which Martin Bucer wrote.)

The four volumes of the works of Osorius in the list recall a minor incident of Elizabeth's time. Osorio was a weighty Portuguese divine, who wrote an exhortation to the queen, urging her to turn papist. He was answered by Walter Haddon, the master of requests to the queen; but he sensibly stayed in Portugal.

Another book which was certainly Bugg's own, not inherited from Hutton, was *Withers Motto*. The Motto, 'a curious self-confession' was not published till 1618. George Wither had been imprisoned for his first verses (1613) and freed after writing the king a satire. (Elizabeth of Bohemia, the king's sister, was an early patron.) His main work was *Fair Virtue* (1622). He became puritan, a decade after Bugg's death. He was 'a fiery puritan' and sold his property to raise a troop of cavalry. He was captured, but Sir John Denham intervened on his behalf on the ground that while Wither lived, he (Denham) would not be accounted the worst poet in England. Wither lost much after the Restoration, and his poetry was forgotten. Southey and Lamb revived interest and his *A Collection of Emblemes* has a modern edition. Cromwell had employed him on the administration of royalist estates in Surrey, and he is sometimes said to have been made a major-general there.

Warton's greatest churchman, Archbishop Hutton (1548- 1606) was undoubtedly of very firm protestant beliefs. He has even been called a 'puritan bishop'.[4] There is too little biographical detail about Warton's vicars to assess how far this firm Protestantism continued influential in the parish. It can be said, though, that a scrutiny of Anthony Bugg's book list does suggest that the puritan tradition exemplified by Matthew Hutton was being maintained in the early seventeenth century in Warton. Bugg's reading was wide ranging, but there seems to be a reforming bias. There are no other book lists known for the parish for comparison. Francis Jackson, a later vicar of Warton who died in 1680 left books worth £6-13s-4d as well as mathematical books worth £2, but their titles are not known. There is so far no direct biographical information on Bugg to judge his impact on Warton, and his will is missing. However, there is a collection of local wills of these years which can be studied. In the preamble to wills of the period there was often a religious formula used which can throw some light on the testator's beliefs.

The 222 wills found for Warton parish from 1600-1699[5] were studied (there are many more death records but the rest were either inventories without wills or purely administrative papers). Twenty two of these wills contained no religious statement in the preamble. Most, but not all of these were nuncupative wills, which were often made in extremis and dealt only with practical matters on the disposal of the testator's estate. This left 200 which could be studied for their religious content.

Wills, religious preambles

It was found that the religious attitudes in the preambles to these could be divided between seven categories. These were:-

1. Unconditional commending of the soul into the hands of 'Almightie god'.
2. A hope for a pleasant after-life, only.
3. An expectation of the remission of sins, only.
4. A hope for the remission of sins and a pleasant after-life.
5. A hope for the remission of sins, and the company of the elect.
6. A hope for the company of the elect, only.
0. No religious preamble. (These have not been included in Table A.1.)

Examples are:
1. I commende my soule into the handes of Almightie god.
   I commit my soule into the mercifull hands of Jesus my Saviour.
2. I Commend my soule into the hands of Almightie god...steadfastly beleiveinge the salvation of my soule and body.
   I Commend my soule into the mercifull handes of Almightie god..steadfasly beleivinge...to attain unto life everlasting.

3. I Commend my sinfull soule into the mercifull hands of
   Almighty god...trusteinge...to have free Remission of
   all my sinnes.
   Trusting...to have full and free Remission & forgivenes
   of all my sinnes and Transgressions...
4. ...trusting...to have remission of all my sinnes & a joyfull
   resurrection at the Judgment Day.
   ...remission of all my sinnes & my soule to enjoy the bliss
   of eternall happiness.
5. ...J.C. my Gratious Remissioner...after this lieff to have
   the joyfull fruition & possession of Eternal Joye amongst
   the Ellected Children of god.
6. ...trustinge...ye peaceable & ioyfull fruition & possession
   of eternal ioyes amongst the elected children of god.
   ...trusting to have the peaceable fruition & possession of
   everlasting joy amongst the elect Children of God.

Table A.1 PREAMBLE: WARTON WILLS 1600-1699		
Cat*	1600 - 1649	1650 - 1699
1	28	15
2	20	15
3	42	27
4	14	15
subtotal	104	72
5	7	4
6	12	1
subtotal	19	5
total	123	77

* for definition of categories see text on page 202

(Such phrases as 'among the children of God' or 'among the saints and angels', though very possibly equivalent to 'among the elect' were not certainly so and are treated here as only indicating a hope for an afterlife. They were few in number.)

The 200 wills with preambles were assigned to one of the six categories according to the preambles. The two tables of frequency according to the first and second halves of the century are shown in Table A.1. These wills cannot be asserted to be a normal sample or answerable to standard assessments. The problems of using wills as evidence is dealt with more fully in Appendix 1. Only broad hints from inspection can be expected.

The breakdown shows that the first will to mention Categories 5 or 6, the hope for the company of the elect, was on 2nd of April 1613 (Bugg's tenure began in that month). James Waithman, yeoman of Carnforth, made his will as follows:-

> *I commend my soule to the mercifull protection of allmightie god faithfully trusting in the merrittes and sufferinges of my gratious redeemer after this lyeff to have the peaceable and joyfull fruition and possession of eternall Joye amongst the ellected children of god...*

The next will to mention election was made in 1615 when Robert Ingleton of Warton, husbandman, died.

> *...considering the certeyntie of death to me and all men, and the uncerteyntie of the tyme of death...Trusting in the merittes and sufferinges of my gracious Redeemer after this Lyeff to have the peaceable and Joyefull fruition and possession of eternal ioye amongst the ellected Childeren of god. And do hereby pray that it will please god to streighten and continew this faithe in me...*

Here certainly was the Calvinist note of election.

For the first half of the century there are 123 wills to be studied. The figures were collected separately for each township. In the first half of the century Priest Hutton and Silverdale show no wills using Categories 5 and 6, but the other five townships each show a noticeable proportion; a quarter of all wills in Borwick, almost a fifth in Warton and round about a sixth in the Yealands and Carnforth. In drawing any conclusions it should be remembered how small the actual number of instances is; only seven even in Warton, the largest township.

The wills from the second half of the century were fewer (77) but, as in the first half of the century, the most used category was still Category 3; a hope for the remission of sins. This reflected the general Protestant belief in a dispensation acquired by faith rather than by pious works (indeed one will specifically states this axiom). The hope for the company of the elect (Categories 5 and 6) was rarer but not extinguished. None in Borwick, Silverdale or the Yealands, only one even in Warton, and one for the first time in Priest Hutton. Only Carnforth still shows a small gathering (3 out of 23 wills).

Quaker wills

An interesting anomaly appeared in the Yealand wills. In the second half of the century there is an excess of wills falling into Category 0 (no religious preamble) or Category 1 (a general commendation of the soul to God only). Indeed among the 13 surviving wills no other formula is found. This is not because of an excess of nuncupative wills. The fact that a number of the testators had known Quaker names, such as Backhouse, Hubbersty and Cummings, rather suggests that it may have been Quaker influence affecting the formulation of the preamble to wills in the Yealands.

The choice of these two categories would be consistent with the Quaker attitude to formalised professions of religious faith.

In general the findings are in keeping with the other evidence that there was a particularly firm form of protestantism to be found in Warton in the first half of the century (along, that is, with a very wide range of other views). The mixture of beliefs that found shelter within an apparent adherence to the Church of England was discussed earlier in Chapter 15. In saying that among these views there were some very definitely puritan it has to be remembered that in an only partly literate society the wording of a will may have expressed the beliefs of the one or two educated men customarily used to draw up a will rather than the testator's own beliefs, particularly if the latter were not very strong or fixed. It seems probable, though, that the very exact references to a hope of being among the 'elect' found in Categories 5 and 6 would have to be shared by writer and testator.

HOW IT WAS
Matthew Hutton

Matthew Hutton, who was born in 1529 in Priest Hutton, died in 1606 in his 77th year, having been Archbishop of York since 1595. In 1594 he founded a grammar school in the parish of his birth. Warton's present primary school, the lineal descendant of the original grammar school, is still known as 'Archbishop Hutton's'. It has seemed worth while, in this book on his native parish, to collect together what is known of his life from the rather scattered sources.[3] Hutton's place in the complicated development of the Elizabethan church is only slightly touched on. For those interested, his theological position was very fully discussed by Peter Lake in 1979 under the heading 'Matthew Hutton - a Puritan Bishop?'[4]

In and around Warton it is still said that Matthew Hutton was a foundling, given the name of the township where he was born because his own name was unknown. The story seems to arise from some malicious church gossip in the eighteenth century. It was not current in Hutton's own time.[5] In fact the Archbishop had known relatives in Warton parish. One of his brothers, Robert, became Rector of Houghton-le-Spring in County Durham and a Prebendary of Durham cathedral. He was left £20 in the Archbishop's will. A third Hutton brother, Edmund, is named,[6] but nothing more is known of him unless he was the Edmund Hutton, of Priest Hutton, a husbandman who died in 1594, leaving a modest competence in his will. In the Grant of Arms issued to Matthew Hutton in 1584 he was described as descended from 'parents sufficiently famous or illustrious in the County of Lancaster' *(Ex antiqua Huttonorum familia in Lancastriensi Palatinatu nobilibus satis parentibus oriundus).*[7] That of course was the sort of thing the College of Heralds was supposed to find out for you and no names are given.

Education

Matthew Hutton's parents were, at any rate, able to see that he received a good primary education. According to Lucas he got his education at 'a private school in Warton' (about which nothing is known) and by the age of 17 years was living in the family of a Yorkshire gentleman who 'taking Notice of his fine Genius', sent him as a sizar with his son to the University of Cambridge.[8] A sizarship throws some light on the standing of the Hutton family. A sizar was an undergraduate receiving an allowance from the college to enable him to study. In the sixteenth and seventeenth centuries a sizar, according to the Oxford English Dictionary, 'performed certain duties now discharged by college servants'.

In 1546 Hutton was entered at Trinity College, Cambridge, and was soon drawn into a circle of moderately radical protestant thinkers there, grouped around Edmund Grindal, the future archbishop. It is not known whether Hutton took these protestant views up to University with him, or acquired them there. Since the north-west is usually viewed as clinging to old ways in religion it would be of interest to know if there was a strongly protestant family in Warton parish as early as the 1540s. Hutton remained at Cambridge for the next twenty years. His graduate and early post-graduate years were spent in the protestant reign of Edward VI, but in 1554 Mary I came to the throne and in the next three and a half years 'nearly 300 people high, low, rich and poor, were burnt as Protestant heretics'.[9] Other prominent protestants escaped death by taking refuge abroad. Hutton stayed on in Cambridge. He was not yet important enough to be sought out and, presumably, simply kept his head down. In Cambridge, with its strong protestant tradition, there would be many colleagues doing the same.

University Career

The advent of the protestant Elizabeth to the throne naturally made a great difference to Hutton's prospects. He rose steadily in the university. He took his B.A. in 1551, his M.A. in 1555, B.D. in 1562 and D.D. in 1565. In 1561 he was made Lady Margaret Professor of Divinity and the next year Regius Professor. All in all it could be said of him that '...he was established as one of the soundest scholars and most eloquent preachers in the University'.[10] His fame was spreading outside University circles. In 1565 the Earl of Leicester wrote to him to say that his '...knowledge and zeal towards the truth', had come to the Queen's attention.[11] Then in 1567 he was appointed Dean of York. He resigned the Regius professorship, the Mastership of Pembroke College and the canonries of Westminster and Ely which he had acquired (though he kept for another nine years the lucrative living of Boxworth in Cambridgeshire to which he had been instituted as rector in 1563). For the rest of his life he was to live and work in the north of England.

The move seems a complete break in his career, but in many ways it might have been anticipated. He was unalterably devoted to the Church of England. Nevertheless he believed that the church might benefit from further reform in a protestant direction. These reformist views had already brought him into minor trouble in the 'vestiarian controversy'; that is the disturbance raised by the refusal of ultra-protestant ministers to wear a surplice as enjoined by the church authorities. The surplice seemed to some an undesirable and misleading remnant of popish superstition. The University was split over the matter. Hutton put his name to a letter to Lord Burghley, the Chancellor of the University at the time; a letter which merely asked that the wearing of surplices should be waived for those who objected 'not because of anything inherently unlawful [in the practice] but to preserve the unity and peace of the church'.[12] The letter was not approved and the government still insisted on conformity. Hutton always lamented this failure to reach a compromise which he saw as the beginning of the irredeemable differences between the established church and puritan reformers, differences he felt which 'with wisdom and good policy they could have been avoided then' when it was no more 'but a cross and a surplice'.[13]

The position of moderate reformers like Hutton was a hard one. Any criticism at all of the established church was sometimes confused with disloyalty to the crown, the head of that church. The fate of Hutton's friend and patron, Edmund Grindal, was a warning of how easy it was to offend. Grindal, after he had been raised to the see of Canterbury in 1575 was anxious to supply the church with 'preachers' that is ministers sufficiently learned and well-trained to preach and expound the scriptures from the pulpit. It was a matter very dear to the heart of reformers. The Queen, on the contrary, was suspicious of extempore preachers and what they might preach. She thought it far safer for ministers to stick to reading the edifying and approved discourses in the *Books of Homilies,* which had been issued in 1563 for use in parish churches. Grindal, nevertheless, set up what he called 'Exercises', meetings to instruct ministers and help them to preach. In 1574 the Queen ordered Grindal to discontinue his Exercises. He refused and was placed under virtual house arrest in his own palace. He died nine years later, still unforgiven. Hutton had the courage to write letters of sympathy to the archbishop during his arrest.

In the north things were different. Hutton's move there may have saved him from a dilemma, for in the north the strength of recusancy made it a more obvious danger than puritanism. Even the 'Exercises', which were forbidden in the south, were encouraged in the north. In 1583 it was actually made obligatory on ministers in the Diocese of Chester (which at that time included Lancashire) to attend monthly Exercises. Only in the months from November to February were they excused, presumably as a concession to the barbarities of the northern climate. It might be noted here that in 1604 Mr Oborne, the incumbent of Warton, was described as 'a preacher'.[14]

Matthew Hutton's tomb in York Minster

Dean, Bishop and Archbishop

Hutton spent the last forty years of his life in the north; as Dean of York from 1567 to 1589, as Bishop of Durham from 1589 to 1595, and as Archbishop of York from 1595 until his death in 1606. He had married for the second time in 1567, the year of his move to York. (His first wife, a niece of the Bishop of Ely, died in 1562 very shortly after the marriage.) The second wife, Beatrix bore him eight children of whom six lived to adult life. She died in 1582, but the children were not long left motherless, for Hutton married in 1583 a widow, Frances Bowes, who survived him by many years. Nothing is known of Hutton as a family man, except that, in a life otherwise free from all scandal, it was said of him that he amassed a surprising amount of property to leave to his children. A few letters to his eldest son Timothy survive, but they are all on business matters. Only in one is there a personal note which does suggest a little fatherly anxiety. Timothy was due in York on government business, but there was much infection in the city. Hutton added at the bottom of the letter 'PS More safetie not to coome, but more present credit to come...Yf you coome you shall be welcome; yf you come not, I will not take it in evill part'.[15]

Meanwhile his reputation was growing. Until a few years before his death he was not only a vigorous ecclesiastic, but also an active member of the Council of the North under its Lord President, the Earl of Huntingdon. The latter was a most fortunate colleague for Hutton to work with. Hutton at all times upheld the necessity of accepting the lawful authority of the Queen as head of the church. In Huntingdon, her vice-regent in the north, he had a royal representative whom he could gladly work with, '...the perfect lay counterpart; a model of what a godly magistrate should be'.[16] The two men worked together to suppress recusancy and promote the godly values of their protestant faith.

Hutton, as Dean of York, was able to work well too with his Archbishop. Grindal was both a friend and a fellow thinker. It has been said of Hutton's years as Dean of York, that he '...was the only active resident dean of York for a century and a half...'.[17] In 1575 Grindal was translated to Canterbury and Hutton's relations with his successor, Edwin Sandys were less good. In fact the two men quarrelled very fiercely over a number of matters, and Hutton had ultimately to apologise publicly to Sandys and admit that he had used 'some very violent and unguarded expressions'.[18] However, it has been said that 'in the north Archbishop Sandys quarrelled with everyone that mattered...including the dean both of York and Durham',[19] so perhaps Hutton was not much to blame.

In other ways Hutton seems to have been a patient and caring man. This is shown particularly in his relationship with catholic recusants. Although Hutton saw the fight with catholicism as central to his work in the north, yet he preferred always to try persuasion with individual recusants.

His patient attempts at conversion were noted with approval by central government. '...your liff and actions ar reported very good of all your neighbours, and in sekying to reform those that ar out of the waye, the ordinary waye to reduce them which I heare you use is, by gentle instruction of them first to se and fele their palpaple errors, and so to prepare them to see the truth.'[20]

Hutton was, it seems, not without courage. Towards the end of the Queen Elizabeth's life, he was asked to preach a sermon before her. He took as his text 'The kingdoms of the earth are mine and I do give them to whom I will', and followed it up by a sermon showing that a queen, for the good of her kingdom, ought to choose a successor. This was carrying honesty to the point of fool-hardiness. No-one must ever mention to the Queen that she must die and be succeeded. Fortunately for Hutton the Queen chose to be diplomatic. At the end of the sermon, when everyone looked to see the preacher annihilated, the Queen quietly opened the window of the closet in which she sat and '...very kindly and calmly, without show of offence (as if she had but waked out of some sleepe) she gave him thanks for his very learned sermon'. But afterwards 'She sent two councellors to him with a sharp message, to which he was glad to give a patient answer.'[21]

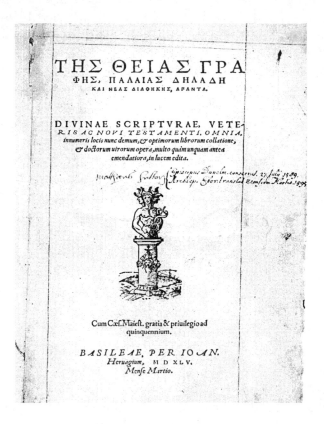

Matthew Hutton's bible. Photographed by permission of the Vicar of Warton.

Hutton died in 1606. To some extent his world was failing him by that time. Church and government were growing more and more suspicious of all non-conformity. Hutton's attempts to persuade before punishing recusants no longer received praise. In 1599 Archbishop Whitgift wrote, '...here hath bene information gyven that recusants are of late increased in that province, and that you are too milde with them. Some of your ministers doe also affirme the same to be trewe'.[22] This criticism Hutton was able to accept, but when James I came to the throne Hutton received a letter from the King's secretary not only requiring him to proceed against catholics but particularly to see 'that the puritanes be proceeded against according to the lawe, except they conforme themselves...' To a man who had spent his life fighting catholicism this seemed to be attacking the wrong enemy. It wrung from him a last testimony to his life-long views.

> *I wish with all my heart that the order were given not only to all Bishops, but to all Magistrates and Justices of the Peace, &c. to proceed against Papists and Recusants, who of late...have grown mightily in number, courage and insolencie...*
>
> *...The puritanes, whose fantasticall zeal I mislike, though they differ in ceremonies and accidents yet they agree with us in substance of religion and I thinke all or most of them love his majestie...but the papists...are opposite and contrary in substantialls of religion and cannot but wish the pope's authoritie and popish religion to be established.*[23]

Two years later he was dead.

Hutton and Warton Parish

It would be fitting in this book to give particulars of Hutton's relationship with the parish of his birth, but really there is almost nothing known. He founded a grammar school and almshouse there, it is true, but that was in the fashion of the time. His two predecessors in the see of York also founded grammar schools in the parish of their birth. Archbishop Grindal at St. Bees in 1588, and Archbishop Sandys at Hawkshead in 1585.

The charter of Archbishop Hutton's Grammar School says, in formal fashion, that he desired to erect it in the parish of his birth to the glory of God and the promotion of good learning. Of any more particular motive one can only speculate. It is not even clear how far he had kept personal touch with the parish. He left £10 'to my cosin, Robert Dawson of Warton' in his will which suggests he was at least in touch with his relations (nothing is known of this Robert Dawson unless he was the By-law-man of that name chosen by the Manor Court in 1593). Anthony Bugg, vicar of Warton from 1613 to 1632 must have been known to Hutton at Cambridge, since Hutton left him books in his will, but no evidence has been found to establish that Bugg was a Warton man by extraction (see Appendix 3).

One anecdote and one fact about Hutton remain to be told which may have relevance. The anecdote is that when Hutton was Bishop of Durham, i.e. sometime between 1589 and 1594, as he was travelling over the Cam, a stream near Ingleton, he dismounted, walked to a particular spot at some distance from the highway and there knelt in prayer. A servant ventured to ask him why he did so. He replied that '...when he was a poor boy, without shoes or stockings, travelling this cold and bleak mountain on a frosty day, he remembered that he had disturbed a red cow on that identical place, in order to warm his legs'.[24] The placing of this event at Ingleton makes it possible, but no more than possible, that Hutton at the time was on his way from Durham to Warton and, in view of the date, just possibly in connection with the founding of the Grammar School.

Finally, there is still preserved in Warton parish a Greek Bible, printed in Basle in 1545 (a re-edition of the first complete Greek Bible printed by the Aldine press in 1518) with Matthew Hutton's name inscribed on the frontispiece. The name looks very much as though it was Matthew Hutton's own signature. His titles have been added in another, though roughly contemporary hand. No-one knows the history of this bible, but it forms the only tangible link between Matthew Hutton and his place of birth.

NOTES AND REFERENCES

Abbreviations used in the notes

Lucas's History   J.Rawlinson Ford & J.A.Fuller-Maitland, John Lucas's History of Warton Parish (compiled 1710-1740), 1931.

WMCB   'Record of Court Leet and Court Barron within the Mannor or Lordship of Warton by the Sands in the County Palatine of Lancashire', 1668-1902.
(The original book is in private hands. Photocopies held by the Mourholme Local History Society by courtesy of Mr Adam Hilling, Lord of the Manor.)

SMCB   Silverdale Manor Court Book, Cumbria (Kendal) R.O., WD/D/52/17a

VCH   William Farrer & J.Brownbill, Victoria History of the County of Lancaster, Vol.8, 1914.

Introduction

1. For the carboniferous limestone foundation of these Morecambe Bay parishes, see the survey by the Institute of Geological Sciences, Natural Environment Research Council, *British Regional Geology, Northern England,* (Fourth Edition, 1971), Chap 5, p.36 and ff., and the map of the north, Plate XIII. The horseshoe of carboniferous limestone coastal parishes is very clearly shown here, and is familiar to anyone who knows the area.
2. J.D.Marshall (ed.), *The Autobiography of William Stout* (Manchester, 1967), p.286, where a chance entry in shipping records reveals that the *Content* was built at Warton in 1697, a vessel of 100 tons.
3. Lucas's History, p.44. The movements of farm servants are authoritatively discussed in Ann Kussmaul, *Servants in Husbandry in Early Modern England,* (Cambridge 1981), Chap.4 esp. pp.57-69. The data here suggests that farm servants travelled from a mean of 7-20 km. between employments, although in general they did not travel far from home. Settlement examinations (at the county record offices) give original material on movement. The distance from Warton village to Cartmel (Churchtown) was about 20 km., but the road over the sands was easily travelled in good weather.
4. B.G.Awty and C.B.Phillips, 'The Cumbrian Bloomery Forge in the Seventeenth Century', *Transactions of the Newcomen Society*, Vol.51, 1979-80, esp. pp.27-31.
5. J.D.Marshall, 'Agrarian wealth and social structure in pre-industrial Cumbria', *The Economic History Review,* 2nd series, Vol.XXXIII, No.4, 1980.
6. See our team's description of glacial deposits, in Chapter 1 of our book text.
7. J.D.Marshall, 'Agrarian wealth and social structure in pre-industrial Cumbria', *The Economic History Review*, 2nd series, Vol.XXXIII, No.4, 1980, p.516, Table 4, where the growth of inventory wealth in Cartmel and Hawkshead is shown as keeping pace with the growth of such wealth in Cumbria, 1661-1750. Cartmel, as is argued here, was a large mainly 'limestone' parish with some similarities to the Warton area.
8. Cf. E. de Selincourt (ed.), *Wordsworth's Guide to the Lakes,* (Oxford 1971 reprint), pp.62-63.
9. T.S.Willan, *The English Coasting Trade, 1600-1750,* (Manchester 1938), pp.187-8. The likelihood is that the slate trade did not really develop until the eighteenth century, an inference drawn from Professor Willan's survey. The Coniston slate quarries appear to have been in operation in the late seventeenth century, as the parish registers for that chapelry suggest by mentioning slaters in 1689 and 1693.
10. J.D.Marshall, *Furness and the Industrial Revolution* (Barrow 1958), p.12. H.L.Gray's study *English Field Systems* (London 1915), is still the standard work on the so-called Celtic Systems, although, as we show Gray could make misjudgements.
11. J.D.Marshall, *Furness and the Industrial Revolution* (Barrow 1958), p.13.
12. F.Tönnies, *Community and Society* (Gemeinschaft und Gesellschaft, Trans. C.P.Loomis), London and New York, 1955.

13. J.D.Marshall (ed.), *The Autobiography of William Stout* (Manchester, 1967), pp. 201,204,205,213, 217, entries for 1729 to 1734; it is clear that potatoes in Lancashire were already becoming the staple food of the poor. They are mentioned in West Cumberland in the previous century, but thrived on the rich soils of the Lancashire plain.

14. Parish register aggregations of the places named, by courtesy of the Cambridge Group for the Study of Population and Social Structure.

15. John K.Walton, *Lancashire, a Social History 1558-1939*, 1987, p.27-28; G.P.Jones 'The Poverty of Cumberland and Westmorland', *Transactions of the Cumberland and Westmorland Antiquarian and Archaeological Society*, New Series, LV, 1956, esp. pp.204-5.

16. John K.Walton, *Lancashire A Social History 1558-1939*, 1987, p.39.

17. M.Spufford, 'The total history of village communities', *Local Historian*, 10 (8), November 1973, pp.398-401.

18. For the unreliability of the Gregory King Table, see G.S.Holmes, 'Gregory King and the social structure of pre-industrial England', *Transactions of the Royal Historical Society*, 5th Series, Vol.27, 1977, pp.41-68.

19. M.Spufford, 'The total history of village communities', *Local Historian*, 10 (8), November 1973, p.401.

Chapter 1: The Setting

1. Robert Ashmead & David Peter, 'Warton Crag Mines', *Mourholme Magazine of Local History*, Vol.II, No.1, pp.5-9.

2. John Rawlinson Ford (ed.), *The Beetham Repository*, 1906, p.164.

3. Lucas's History, p.3.

4. *Ibid.*, pp.141,142.

5. J.D. Marshall (ed), *The Autobiography of William Stout of Lancaster 1655-1752*, 1967, p.71.

6. J.D. Marshall, *Lancashire*, 1974, p.49.

7. John K. Walton, *Lancashire, a Social History 1558-1939*, 1987, p.123.

8. David Peter, *Warton with Lindeth, A History, Part one*, 1985, p.6.

9. Lancs.R.O., 'Records of Court Leet of Warton, September 1593', DDTo/O/2.

Chapter 2: Town Fields and Enclosures

1. C.S & C.S. Orwin, *The Open Fields*, 1938, Pt.II. pp.67-194

2. E.Kerridge, *The Common Fields of England*, 1992, p.5.

3. H.L. Gray, *The English Field System*, 1915, pp.158-160.

4. *Ibid.*, p.162.

5. G.Youd, 'The Common Fields of Lancashire', *Transactions of the Historic Society of Lancashire and Cheshire*, Vol.113, 1961, p.21.

6. F.J. Singleton, 'The Influence of Geographical Factors on the Development of the Common Fields of Lancashire', *Transactions of the Historic Society of Lancashire and Cheshire*, Vol.115, 1963, p.40.

7. G.Youd, 'The Common Fields of Lancashire', *Transactions of the Historic Society of Lancashire and Cheshire*, Vol.113, 1961, pp.3-10.

8. C.E.Searle, 'Customary Tenants and the Enclosure of the Cumbrian Commons', *Northern History*, Vol.XXIX, 1993, pp. 126-153.

9. Lancs. R.O., 'Rental of the Manor of Warton, made for King Henry VIII, 1511', DDTo/H4.

10. P.H.Booth, *Warton in the Middle Ages*, published by Warton Village Society, 1976, p.4.

11. H.L. Gray, *The English Field System*, 1915, p.245.

12. P.R.O., 'Land Revenue, Miscellaneous' Book 220,ff.27 58.

13. Lancs. R.O., 'Warton Rental 1609', DDTo/L/3.

14. Lucas's History, pp. 133-134

15. *Ibid.*, p.120.

16. Lancaster Reference Library, MS. 2899.

17. G.Youd, 'The Common Fields of Lancashire', *Transactions of the Historic Society of Lancashire and Cheshire*, Vol.113, 1961, p.30.

18. *Ibid.*, p.10.

19. Lancs.R.O., 'Enclosure Award for Yealand Conyers and Yealand Redmayne', AE/5/16.

20. J. Rawlinson Ford, 'The Customary Tenant-right of the Manors of Yealand', *Transactions of the Cumberland and Westmorland Antiquarian and Archaeological Society*, Vol. 9 n.s., 1909, p.152.

21. Lancs.R.O., 'A Survey and verdict of the manor court of Warton made by Robert Toulson' (17th century), DDTo/I/2; WMCB, n.d.(bound between the records for May 1677 and October 1677).

22. G.Youd, 'The Common Fields of Lancashire', *Transactions of the Historic Society of Lancashire and Cheshire*, Vol.113, 1961, p.35.
23. WMCB, October 1673.
24. Lucas's History, p.135.
25. C.Morris (ed.), *The Journeys of Celia Fiennes*, 1947, p.190.
26. Mrs Ford, 'Sketches of Yealand', *Lancaster Guardian,* Sept.16th, 1911, p.8.
27. Lucas's History, p.5

Chapter 3: What was grown

1. VCH, p.152.
2. Joan Thirsk (ed.), T*he Agrarian History of England and Wales, Vol.IV, 1500-1640*, 1967, p.8.
3. John Fitzherbert, *Booke of Husbandrie*, 1598, (Facsimile edition), 1979, p.45.
4. For the use of inventories as evidence see Appendix 1.
5. John Findlater, 'To Everything there is a Season', *Mourholme Magazine of Local History*, 1996.1, p.14.
6. H.H. Lamb, *Climate, History and the Modern World*, 1995, p.202.
7. Lucas's History, p.135.
8. G.Youd, 'The Common Fields of Lancashire', *Transactions of the Historic Society of Lancashire and Cheshire*, Vol.113, 1961, p.30.
9. Lucas's History, p.135,136.
10. L.D.Stamp & S.H.Beaver, *The British Isles: a geographic and economic survey*, (6th edition), 1971, p.179.
11. J.C. Drummond & Anne Wilbraham, *The Englishman's Food*, 1939, p.128.
12. Alan Crosby, 'Oats in the Lancashire Diet 1780-1850', *Regional Bulletin Centre for North West Regional Studies*, N.S No.11, 1997, pp 17-23.
13. John Holt, *General View of the Agriculture of the County of Lancaster 1795*, facsimile reprint 1969, p.56.
14. Redcliffe Salaman, *The History and Social Influence of the Potato*, 1949, pp.451 & 452.
15. Mrs Ford, 'Sketches of Yealand', *Lancaster Guardian,* Sept.16th, 1911, p.8.
16. Lucas's History, p.4.
17. *Ibid.*, p.44.
18. *Ibid.*, p.127.
19. Lancs.R.O., 'Arbitration between Sir George Middleton and his Yealand Tenants 1658' , DDTo/H/2.
20. Lucas's History, p.4.
21. *Ibid.*, p.43.
22. *Ibid.*, p.5.
23. Oliver Rackham, *Trees & Woodland in the British Landscape*, 1996, p.144.
24. Cumbria R.O., 'View of the Moiety of the Manner of Silverdale 1563', WD/D (AG).
25. Lancaster Reference Library, 'A copy of the Custom of the Mannor of Warton', MS 230.
26. Lancs.R.O., 'The Award, George Middleton and his Silverdale Tenants 1671', DDTo/H/2.
27. Lancs.R.O., 'Arbitration between Sir George Middleton and his Yealand tenants 1658', DDTo/H/2.
28. Lancs.R.O., 'Account of the moss of Warton, Storrs and elsewhere 1648', DDTo/H/5.
29. Lucas's History, p.84.
30. *Ibid.*, p.137.
31. SMCB, May 1678.
32. WMCB, October 1698.
33. Lucas's History, p.54.
34. J.D. Marshall (ed.), *The Autobiography of William Stout of Lancaster 1655-1752*, 1967, p.68.
35. SMCB, July 1691.

Chapter 4: Livestock

1. J.D. Marshall, 'Agrarian wealth and social structure in pre-industrial Cumbria', *Economic History Review,* 2nd series, Vol XXXIII, 1980, p.512.
2. R.Trow-Smith, *A History of British Livestock Husbandry to 1700*, 1957, p.258.
3. Lancs.R.O., 'Records of Court Leet of Warton, September 1593', DDTo/0/2.

4. C.S and C.S. Orwin, *The Open Fields*, 1938, pp.43-45.
5. Joan Thirsk, *The Rural Economy of England*, 1984, p.136.
6. R. Cunliffe Shaw, 'The Townfields of Lancashire', *Transactions of the Historic Society of Lancashire and Cheshire*, Vol.114, 1962, p.28.
7. Lancs.R.O., 'Enclosure for benefit of Constable, Borwick', QSP/446/17.
8. WMCB, May 1677.
9. SMCB, 1679.
10. Lancs.R.O., 'Arbitration between Sir George Middleton and his Yealand Tenants 1658', DDTo/H/2.
11. C.M.L. Bouch & G.P. Jones, *A Short Economic and Social History of the Lake Counties 1500-1830*, 1961, p.102.
12. J.Bailey & G.Culley, *General View of the Agriculture of Cumberland 1794*, in 1972 reprint, p.249.
13. R.Trow-Smith, *A History of British Livestock Husbandry to 1700*, 1957, p.320.
14. John Holt, *General View of the Agriculture of the County of Lancaster 1795,* in facsimile reprint 1969, p.166.
15. Arthur Young, *Annals of Agriculture,* 20, 1793, p.6.
16. A. Pringle, *General View of the Agriculture of the County of Westmorland 1794* 1969 reprint, p.328.
17. Stephen J.G.Hull & Juliet Clutton Brock, *Two hundred Years of British Farm Livestock*, 1989,p.130.
18. R.Trow-Smith, *A History of British Livestock Husbandry to 1700*, 1957, p.226.
19. Lucas's History, p.55.
20. John Satchell, *Kendal on Tenterhooks*, 1984, p.8.
21. Lancs.R.O., 'Record of the Court Leet of Warton, September 1593', DDTo/O/2.
22. WMCB, October 1694.
23. WMCB, March 1668.
24. Lancs.R.O., 'Records of Court Leet of Warton May 1610', DDTo/O/2.
25. WMCB, October 1686.
26. J.D. Marshall (ed.), *The Autobiography of William Stout of Lancaster 1655-1752*, 1967, p.71.
27. Lancaster Reference Library, 'A copy of the Custom of the Mannor of Warton', MS230.
28. C.B. Phillips, 'Town and country: economic change in Kendal c.1550-1700' in Peter Clark (ed.) *The transformation of English Provincial Towns 1600-1800*, 1984, p.99-132.
29. M.Mullett, 'Reformation and Renewal' in Andrew White(ed.), *A History of Lancaster 1193-1993*, 1993, pp.49-90.
30. Lucas's History, p.64.
31. Lancs. R.O., 'Tithe Book of Warton Parish (Wool and Lambs) 1631', DDTo/H/4.
32. John Satchell, *Kendal on Tenterhooks*, 1984, p.8.
33. Mary Higham, oral communication, 1997.
34. Lucas's History, p.53.
35. Michael Wright, 'Thomas Middleton's Colt Park re-discovered', *Mourholme Magazine of Local History,* 1997.3, p.11.
36. Lancs.R.O., 'Record of the.Court Leet of Warton, October 1607', DDTo/O/2.
37. Lancs.R.O., 'Record of the Court Leet of Warton, 19th September 1593', DDTo/O/2.
38. Lancashire Parish Register Society, Vol.73 'The Parish Registers of Warton Parish 1568 -1812', 1935, p.422,n.2.
39. J.D. Marshall (ed.), *The Autobiography of William Stout of Lancaster 1655-1752* 1967, p.43.
40. Lucas's History, p.127.
41. R.Trow-Smith, *A History of British Livestock Husbandry to 1700*, 1957, p.70.
42. Lancs.R.O., 'Record of Court Leet of Warton, October 1602', DDTo/O/2.

Chapter 5: Manor and Tenancy

1. R.G. Blackwood, 'The Lancashire Cavaliers and their Tenants', *Transactions of the Historic Society of Lancashire & Cheshire*, 117, 1966, p.31.
2. John Breay, Light in the Dales, 1996.
3. Mildred Campbell, *The English Yeoman: under Elizabeth and the early Stuarts*, 1942, pp.150-1.
4. *Ibid.*, p.152.
5. Lancaster Reference Library, 'A copy of the Custom of the Mannor of Warton', MS230.
6. David Peter, *Warton with Lindeth. A History, Part I*, 1985, p.6.

7. P.H.W.Booth, *Warton in the Middle Ages* (published by Warton Village Society), 1976, p.7.
8. Lancs.R.O., 'Warton Rental 1609', DDTo/L/3.
9. Lancaster Reference Library, 'A copy of the Custom of the Manor of Warton', MS230.
10. J.Rawlinson Ford, 'The Customary Tenant-Right of the Manor of Yealand', *Transactions of the Cumberland and Westmorland Antiquarian and Archaeological Society,* Vol.9 n.s., 1909, pp.147-160.
11. R.G. Blackwood, 'The Lancashire Cavaliers and their Tenants', *Transactions of the Historic Society of Lancashire & Cheshire*, 117, 1966, p.26.
12. *Ibid.*, pp.26-31.
13. *Ibid.*, p.26.
14. Lancs.R.O., 'Arbitration between Sir George Middleton and his Yealand tenants' (undated), DDTo/H/2.
15. Lancaster Reference Library, 'Yealand Tenantry 17th c.' (n.d.) MS.5693.
16. Lancs.R.O., 'The Award - George Middleton and his Silverdale Tenants 1671', DDTo/H/2.
17. VCH, p.181.

Chapter 6: Mills and Milling

1. R.Bennett & J.Elton, *History of Corn Milling*, 1900, Vol.I, p.214.
2. *Ibid.*, Vol.III, p.47.
3. Neil Stobbs 'Mills and Milling', *Mourholme Magazine of Local History*, 1997.1, p.3.
4. R. Bennett & J. Elton, *History of Corn Milling* , 1900, Vol.III, p.50.
5. VCH, Vol. 2, 1908, p.564n.
6. Lucas's History, p.42.
7. Lancaster Reference Library, 'A copy of the Custom of the Mannor of Warton', MS 230.
8. WMCB, March 1668.
9. Lucas's History, p.129.
10. *Ibid.*, p.42.
11. *Ibid.*, p.129.
12. *Ibid.*, p.128.
13. *Ibid.*, p.42
14. Lancs.R.O., 'Wilson and others against Towneley & wife', DDTo/l/6.
15. Lancs.R.O., 'Arbitration between Sir George Middleton and his Yealand tenants 1658', DDTo/H2.
16. Lancs.R.O., 'Lease by Dame Anne Middleton of Whitbecke milne 1676', DDTo/L/3.
17. Lancs.R.O., 'Lease by George Townely of his water corn mill (undated)', DDTo/L/6.
18. Lancs.R.O., 'Petition...concerning..White Beck Mill 1759', DDTo/L/6.
19. Lancs.R.O., 'Specifications by John Rennie of Bridges etc', QAR/5/39.
20. Lucas's History, p.114n.
21. Lucas's History, p.121.
22. James W.A.Price, *The Industrial Archaeology of the Lune Valley*, 1983, p.76.
23. Cumbria Record Office (Kendal), 'Charge to the Jury Silverdale Manor Court' WD/D/S1(4).
24. James W.A.Price, *The Industrial Archaeology of the Lune Valley*, 1983, p.91.
25. VCH, p.181
26. Neil Stobbs, 'Mills and Milling', *Mourholme Magazine of Local History,* 1997.1, p.6.

Chapter 7: Where to Live and What to Wear

1. W.G. Hoskins, 'The Re-building of Rural England', *Provincial England*, 1964, pp.131-149.
2. R.Machin, 'The Great Rebuilding, A Re-assessment', *Past and Present*, 1977, No.77, pp.35-56.
3. M.E.Garnett, 'The Great Rebuilding in South Lonsdale 1600-1730', *Transactions of the Historic Society of Lancashire and Cheshire,* Vol.137, 1983, p.73.
4. Lancashire County Council, *Warton Conservation Area*, c.1972.
5. R.W.Brunskill, *Illustrated Handbook of Vernacular Architecture*, 1971, pp.25 28.
6. Lucas's History, p.27.
7. H. Gregson, 'J.A. Fuller-Maitland', *Mourholme Magazine of Local History*, 1992.2, p.6.
8. N.Pevsner, *The Buildings of England North Lancashire*, 1969, p.267.
9. Christopher Morris (ed.), *Journeys of Celia Fiennes*, 1947, p.190.
10. Lucas's History, p.77.
11. *Ibid.*, p.27.
12. *Ibid.*, p.43.
13. *Ibid.*, p.120.

14. Georges Edelen (ed.), *The Description of England by William Harrison*, 1968, p.201.
15. R.W.Brunskill, *Illustrated Handbook of Vernacular Architecture*, 1971, p.94.
16. 'Remains Historical and Literary connected with the Palatine Counties of Lancaster and Chester', *Chetham Society*, Vol.102, (N.S), pp.29-36.
17. Public Record Office, Rental and Survey of Warton for James I, 1609, LR 2/220 (translation given to Mourholme Local History Society by Mr Paul Booth).
18. Lucas's History, p.119.
19. *Ibid.*, p.54.
20. Miss Caroline Baker, personal communication.
21. Ann H. Morley and Muriel Smalley, *Warton; the story of a North Lancashire Village*, (privately printed and published), 1976, (no page nos) Section 7.
22. English Heritage, letter.
23. National Building Records, Swindon.
24. For the use of inventories as evidence see Appendix 1.
25. R.W.Brunskill, *Vernacular Architecture of the Lake Counties; a field handbook*, 1974, p.50.
26. M.W.Barley, 'Rural Housing in England' in Joan Thirsk (ed.), *The Agrarian History of England and Wales, IV*, 1967, p.752.
27. *Ibid.*, p.727.
28. For the use of the Hearth Tax returns see Appendix 2.
29. M.W. Barley, 'Rural Housing in England' in Joan Thirsk, ed., *The Agrarian History of England and Wales, IV,*, 1967, p.727.
30. WMCB, October 1699.
31. WMCB, October 1678.
32. Lancs.R.O., 'Records of Court Leet of Warton, September 1593', DDTo/O/2.
33. Lancs.R.O., 'Appeal against fine set by Sir FrancisBindloss', n.d., DDTo/I/15.
34. J.D.Marshall, 'How often was Warton visited in the Seventeenth Century?', *Mourholme Magazine of Local History*, 1991.2, pp.3-5.
35. Elizabeth Ewing, *Everyday Dress 1650-1900*, 1984, p.24.
36. *Ibid.*, p.24.
37. *The Account Book of Sarah Fell* (quoted in Elizabeth Ewing, *Everyday Dress 1650-1900*, p.16,17.)
38. James Raine, 'Wills and Inventories from the Registry of the Archdeaconry of Richmond', *Surtees Society*, Vol.XXVI, 1853, pp.275-281.
39. Lancs. R.O., Will of Christopher Harrison, 1611.
40. John Satchell, *Kendal on Tenterhooks*, 1984, pp.53-54.

Chapter 8: Dearth, Disease and Demography

1. Edward Arnold, 'A Reconstruction' in E.A. Wrigley & R.S. Schofield (eds.), *The Population History of England 1541-1871*, 1981, p.207.
2. R.Speake, 'The Historical Demography of Warton Parish before 1801', *Transactions of the Historic Society of Lancashire & Cheshire*, Vol.122, 1970, pp.43-65.
3. W.G.Howson, 'Plague Poverty and Population in Parts of North-Western England 1580-1720', *Transactions of the Historic Society of Lancashire and Cheshire*, Vol.112, 1960, p.53.
4. For the use of Hearth Tax returns as evidence see Appendix 2.
5. R.Speake, 'The Historical Demography of Warton Parish before 1801' *Transactions of the Historic Society of Lancashire & Cheshire*, Vol.122, 1970, p.56.
6. G. Talbot Griffith, *Population Movements in the age of Malthus*, 1926, p.28.
7. R.Speake, 'The Historic Demography of Warton Parish before1801', *Transactions of the Historical Society of Lancashire & Cheshire*, Vol.122, 1970, p.55.
8. British Museum, Harleian MS 594f 105b (quoted in R. Speake, 'The Historical Demography of Warton Parish before 1801', *Transactions of the Historic Society of Lancashire & Cheshire*, Vol.122, 1970, p.52).
9. Lancaster City Council, *Census of Population 1991*, 1993, p.84.
10. R.Speake, 'The Historical Demography of Warton Parish before 1801' *Transactions of the Historic Society of Lancashire & Cheshire*, Vol.122, 1970, p.50.
11. Christopher Hill, *God's Englishman,* 1972, p.168.
12. R.G. Blackwood, 'The Lancashire Cavaliers and their Tenants', *Transactions of the Historic Society of Lancashire & Cheshire*, 117, 1966, p.31, n.43.
13. A nine year 'moving average' is usually used, that is, the average annual burial rate for the nine years of which the year in question is the centre.

14. W.G. Howson, 'Plague, Poverty and Population in parts of North-Western England 1580-1720', *Transactions of the Historic Society of Lancashire & Cheshire*, Vol.122, 1970, p.33.
15. A.H.Gale, *Epidemic Diseases*, 1959, pp.46,47.
16. Joan Thirsk & J.P.Cooper (eds.), *Seventeenth Century Economic Documents*, 1972, p.51.
17. John K. Walton, *Lancashire 1558-1939*, 1987, p.29.
18. Andrew B. Appleby, *Famine in Tudor and Stuart England*, 1978, p.126.
19. *Ibid.*, p.429.
20. *Ibid.*, pp.8,9.
21. Peter Laslett, *The World we Have Lost*, 1971, p.130.
22. J.F.D. Shrewsbury, *A History of Bubonic Plague in the British Isles,* 1971, p.175.
23. J.D. Marshall (ed.), *The Autobiography of William Stout of Lancaster 1655-1752*, 1967, p.201.
24. Richard G. Wilkinson, *Unhealthy Societies*, 1996, p.43.

Chapter 9: The Gentry and the Middling Sort

1. R.G. Blackwood, 'The Lancashire Gentry and the Great Rebellion 1640-1660', *Chetham Society,* Vol.25, 1978, p.13.
2. J.D. Raine (ed.), 'The Correspondence of Dr Matthew Hutton', *Surtees Society*, Vol.17, 1843, p.21.
3. R.G. Blackwood, 'The Lancashire Gentry and the Great Rebellion 1640-1660', *Chetham Society,* Vol.25, 1978, p.5.
4. VCH, p.171.
5. Lucas's History, p.108.
6. R.G. Blackwood, 'The Lancashire Gentry and the Great Rebellion 1640-1660', *Chetham Society,* Vol.25, 1978, p.13.
7. *Ibid.*, p.73.
8. Lucas's History, p.123.
9. *Ibid.*, p.110.
10. 'Lancashire Composition Papers', *Record Society of Lancashire and Cheshire,* Vol. 36, 1897, pp.131-8, 181-2
11. Lancs.R.O., 'Law suit between Attorney General & George Middleton, 1635', DDTo/I/15.
12. R.G. Blackwood, 'The Lancashire Gentry and the Great Rebellion 1640-1660', *Chetham Society,* Vol.25, 1978, p.141.
13. Lucas's History, p.29.
14. T. Pape, *'Warton and George Washington's Ancestors'*, 1913, p.29.
15. Lancaster Reference Library, 'A copy of the Custom of the Mannor of Warton', MS.230.
16. Lancs.R.O., 'Elen Washington not to keep an ale house 1635', QSB/1/160/20.
17. Lancs R.O., 'Ellen Washington to keep the peace 1635', QSB/1/144/8.
18. Lancs.R.O., 'Information from Lawrence Washington', QSB/1/264/15.
19. LRO, 'Threat by Leonard Washington', QSB 1/48/39 and 'Threats to John Harling' QSB 1/80/27.
20. WMCB, April 1676.
21. Lucas's History, p.93.
22. Lancs.R.O., 'Comperta Books for Kendal Deanery', ARR/15/40.
23. T. Pape, *'The Washingtons and the Manor of Warton'*, 1948.
24. VCH, p.71 n15.
25. Lancs. R.O., 'Records of Court Leet of Warton, September 1593', DDTo/O/2.
26. Keith Wrightson, *English Society 1580-1680*, 1982, p.19.
27. *Ibid.*, p.31.
28. For the use of Inventories as evidence see Appendix 1.
29. Lancs. R.O., 'Appeal against fine set by Sir Francis Bindloss', n.d., DDTo/I/15.
30. Lancs. R.O., 'Information re theft of deer 1640', QSB/1/ 228/14&16.
31. Paul Booth, 'Sir George Middleton of Leighton, a Lancashire Penruddock?', *Transactions of the Lancashire and Cheshire Antiquarian Society*, Vol.91, 1995.
32. Lancs. R.O., 'Informacions against Mr George Middleton of Leighton and others 1654', DDTo/H/4.
33. William Kent (ed), *An Encyclopaedia of London,* 1937, p.145.
34. Lucas's History, pp.32,33.

35. *Ibid.*, p.29.
36. Lancs.R.O., 'Churchwardens Presentments 1690-1714', ARR/17/43.
37. F.F.Cartwright, *A Social History of Medicine*, 1977, p.44.
38. Lancs.R.O., 'Household Account of Dame Anne Middleton, 1675', DDTo/l/14.
39. Lancs.R.O., 'Comperta Books for Kendal Deanery', ARR/17/40-76.
40. Lucas's History, p.16.
41. Lancs.R.O., 'Relief for Jennet Wallinge 1657', QSP/153/9&10.
42. Lancs.R.O., 'Maintenance for Agnes Wraston of her husband's lunatic sister 1673', QSP/397/12.
43. Lancs.R.O., 'Bridget Winder's petition for relief, 1689', QSP/809/7.
44. Lancs.R.O., 'Petition of Richard Townson 1653', QSP/81/4.

Chapter 10: Poor Husbandmen and Labourers.

1. Peter Laslett, *The World we have Lost*, 1965, p.30 (quoting Sir Thomas Smith, *The Commonwealth of England*, 1583).
2. Peter Laslett, *The World we have Lost*, 1965, p.181 (quoting James Tyrell, *Patriarcha non Monarcha*, 1681).
3. Peter Laslett, *The World we Have Lost*, 1965, p.181.
4. *Ibid*, p.182.
5. Lancs.R.O., 'Records of Court Leet of Warton, September 1593', DDTo/O/2.
6. Lancs.R.O., 'Records of Court Leet of Warton, October 1602', DDTo/O/2.
7. WMCB, April 1675.
8. John Harland (ed.), 'The House and Farm Accounts of the Shuttleworths of Gawthorpe Hall', *Chetham Society* Vols. 35,41,43& 46, 1856-8.
9. George Ornsby (ed.), 'The Household Books of Lord William Howard of Naworth Castle', *Surtees Society*, Vol. 68, 1877.
10. W.H.Chippindall(ed.), 'A Sixteenth Century Survey and Year's Accounts of Hornby Castle Lancashire', *Chetham Society*, 102 n.s., 1939.
11. Joan Thirsk, *The Rural Economy of England*, 1984, p.179; Paul Slack, *Poverty & Policy in Tudor & Stuart England*, 1988, p.47;Joan Thirsk (ed.) *The Agrarian History of England and Wales IV*,1500-1640, 1967, pp.435 & 599.
12. W.E.Tate, *The Parish Chest*, 3rd ed.1983, p.138.
13. *Ibid*, p.28.
14. H.M.S.O. (Ministry of Agriculture and Fisheries), *Manual of Nutrition 3rd edition*, 1964, Appendix A.
15. Alan Crosby, 'Oats in the Lancashire Diet, 1780-1850', *Centre for North West Regional Studies, Regional Bulletin*, N.S. No.11, 1997, p.17.
16. Lancs.R.O., 'Records of Court Leet of Warton, 1610', DDTo/O/2.
17. WMCB, March 1668.
18. WMCB, October 1691.
19. WMCB, March 1668.

Chapter 11: The Poor

1. Geoffrey W. Oxley, *Poor Relief in England and Wales 1601-1834*, 1974, p.35.
2. Sidney and Beatrice Webb, *English Local Government: The Parish and the County*, 1906, p.14.
3. Lancs.R.O., 'Records of Court Leet of Warton, October 1609', DDTo/O/2.
4. Lancs.R.O., 'Records of Court Leet of Warton, April 1612', DDTo/O/2.
5. Lancs.R.O., 'Reimbursement of Peter Robinson, Constable of Warton 1665', QSP/269/12.
6. WMCB, October 1691.
7. Lancs.R.O., 'Records of Court Leet of Warton, October 1593', DDTo/O/2.
8. Our thanks are due to Mrs K.Hodgson for information on the meaning of this name.
9. Sidney and Beatrice Webb, *English Local Government: The Parish and the County*, 1906, p.31.
10. *The Parish Registers of Warton 1568-1812*, Lancashire Parish Register Society, Vol.73, 1935, p.486.
11. Geoffrey W. Oxley, *Poor Relief in England and Wales 1601-1834*, 1974, p.64.
12. Lancs.R.O., 'Court Order for the family of John Kitson 1638', QSB/1/200/41.
13. Lancs.R.O., 'Petition of Richard Townson 1653', QSP/81/4.
14. Lancs.R.O., 'Petition of the Overseers of the Poor of Warton 1677', QSP/458/4.
15. Lancs.R.O., 'Petition of John Osliffe 1681', QSP/540/5.

16. Alan Macfarlane, *The Justice and the Mare's Ale*, 1981, Chapters 3 & 4.
17. Lucas's History, p.120.
18. Taken from 'Extracts from *Vicaria Leodiensis or the History of the Church of Leeds*' a photocopy of which is held in the archives of the Mourholme Local History Society.
19. Lucas's History, p.117.
20. *Ibid.*, p.116.
21. C.Hill, *Puritanism and Revolution*, 1962, p.227.
22. John Addy, *Sin and Society in the Seventeenth Century*, 1989, p.44.
23. Lucas's History, p.25.
24. *Ibid.*, p.25.

Chapter 12: Women and Children Last

1. Roger Thompson, *Women in Stuart England and America*, 1974, pp.31-35.
2. *A Brief history of Christ's Hospital*, 4th edition, c.1828, p.7.
3. Genesis 2.18.
4. John L.Nickalls (ed.), *The Journal of George Fox*, 1952, p.9.
5. Alice Clark, *The Working Life of Women in the 17th century*, 1919, p.91.
6. John Fitzherbert, *Booke of Husbandrie*, 1598, (Facsimile edition 1979), pp.175-178.
7. Alice Clark, *The Working Life of Women in the 17th century*, 1919, p.129.
8. Lancaster Reference Library, 'A copy of the Custom of the Mannor of Warton', MS230.
9. Lancs.R.O., 'Arbitration between Sir George Middleton and his Yealand tenants 1658', DDTo/H2.
10. Lancaster Reference Library, 'Customs within the Manor of Halton', MS168.
11. Roger Thompson, *Women in Stuart England and America*, 1974, p.163.
12. Lancaster Reference Library, 'A copy of the Custom of the Mannor of Warton', MS230.
13. Lancs.R.O., 'The Award - George Middleton and his Silverdale Tenants 1671', DDTo/H/2.
14. Lancs.R.O., 'Isabel Nicholson desires freedom from constableship', QSP/53/10.
15. Lancs.R.O., 'Petition of Thomas Lucas re constableship', QSP/564/7.
16. Lancs.R.O., 'Constableship of Agnes Waithman 1685', QSP/601/12.
17. Lancs.R.O., 'Mary Townson for throwing hot water at constable 1635', QSB/1/160/12.
18. Lancs.R.O., 'Informacions against Mr George Middleton of Leighton and others 1654', DDTo/H/4.
19. *Ibid.*
20. Lancs.R.O., 'Comperta Papers for the Deanery of Kendal (1723)', ARR/15/40-76.
21. Lancs.R.O., 'Bastard child of Anne Fisher 1658', QSP/161/3.
22. John Findlater, 'Illegitimacy in the seventeenth century in Warton parish', *Mourholme Magazine of Local History*, 1996.3, p.13.
23. J.D.Marshall 'Out of Wedlock: Perceptions of a Cumbrian Social Problem in the Victorian Context', *Northern History,* Vol XXI, 1995, p.203.
24. E.A.Wrigley & R.Schofield, 'Infant and Child Mortality in England in the late Tudor and early Stuart period', in C.Webster (ed), *Health, Medicine and Mortality in the Sixteenth Century*, 1979, p.61.
25. Lloyd de Mause (ed), *The History of Childhood*, 1972, p.1.
26. Richard Parkinson (ed.), 'The Life of Adam Martindale written by himself', *Chetham Society*, Vol. 4, 1845, p.206.
27. A.V.Neale & Hugh R.E.Wallis (eds),*The Boke of Chyldren by Thomas Phaire, 1553*, 1955, p.31.
28. Peter Laslett (ed), *Bastardy and its Comparative History*, 1980, p.187.
29. Keith Wrightson, *English Society 1580-1680*, 1982, p.109.
30. Margaret Spufford, 'First steps in literacy:the reading andwriting experiences of the humblest seventeenth century spiritual autobiographers', *Social History*, Vol.4, 1979, p.414.
31. Peter Laslett, *The World we have lost*, 1965, p.3.
32. J.D. Marshall, *The Autobiography of William Stout of Lancaster 1655-1752,* 1967, p.70.
33. Lancs.R.O., 'Petition for Leonard Houseman 1661', QSP/221/11.
34. Lancs.R.O., 'Warrant for arrest of Thomas and George Hubberstie 1634', QSB/1/140/18.
35. Lucas's History, pp.35-37.
36. Lancs.R.O., 'Records of Court Leet of Warton, October 1602', DDTo/O/2.
37. Lucas's History, p.78.

Chapter 13: Four Acres and a Cow

1. Joan Thirsk, 'Industries in the Countryside' in F.J.Fisher, (ed.), *The Economic History of Tudor and Stuart England*, pp.70-88.
2. James W.A.Price, *The Industrial Archaeology of the Lune Valley*, 1983, p.90.
3. For the use of inventories as evidence see Appendix 1.
4. For the Hearth Tax see Appendix 2.

5. Joan Thirsk (ed.), *The Agrarian History of England and Wales,* Vol.IV, 1967, p.397.
6. Lancs.R.O., 'Tithe Book of Warton Parish (Wool and Lamb) 1631', DDTo/H/4.
7. Cumbria R.O., 'View of the Moiety of the Manner of Silverdale 1563', WDD/D/D/Acc.950/33.
8. WMCB, March 1668.
9. Joan Thirsk (ed.), *The Agrarian History of England and Wales,* Vol.IV, 1967, p.402.
10. Cumbria R.O., 'View of the Moiety of the Manner of Silverdale 1563', WDD/D/D/Acc.950/33.
11. N.M.Postan, *The Medieval Economy and Society*, Vol.1 of the Penguin Economic History of Britan, 1972, pp.143-146.
12. *Ibid.,* p.149.

Chapter 14: Making Ends Meet

1. Quoted in W.T.McIntire, 'The Port of Milnthorpe',*Transactions of the Cumberland And Westmorland Antiquarian and Archaeological Society*, Vol.36 n.s, 1936, pp.34-35.
2. Helen Hamilton, 'The last Silverdale Fisherman', *Keer to Kent*, No.30, 1996, pp.8-9.
3. Lucas's History, p.45.
4. Peter Cherry, *On Morecambe Bay,* 1986, (privately published) p.78.
5. Lucas's History, p.30.
6. *Ibid.*, p.46.
7. Lancs.R.O., 'Household Account of Dame Anne Middleton, 1675', DDTo/I/14.
8. Lucas's History, p.139.
9. Robert Taylor, 'The Coastal Salt Industry of Amounderness', *Transactions of the Archaeological and Antiquarian Society of Lancashire and Cheshire*, vol.78, 1975, pp.20-21.
10. J.D. Marshall, T*he Autobiography of William Stout of Lancaster 1655-1752*, 1967, p.34.
11. Robert Ashmead and David Peter, 'Warton Crag Mines', *Mourholme Magazine of Local History,* Vol II.1 1983, p.8.
12. A cord: a variable measure of wood, usually a pile 8ft x 4ft x 4ft. *Oxford English Dictionary.*
13. B.G. Awty and C.B. Phillips, 'The Cumbrian Bloomery Forge in the Seventeenth Century', *Newcomen Society Transactions*, Vol.51, 1979-80,pp.25-40.
14. Lancs.R.O., 'Sale of Wood at Leighton', DDTo/L/16-28.
15. Lancs.R.O., 'Household Account of Dame Anne Middleton, 1675', DDTo/I/14.
16. Lucas's History, p.64.
17. *Ibid.,* p.64.
18. SMCB, p.120, (c.1690).
19. Lancs.R.O., 'Records of Court Leet of Warton, April 1613', DDTo/O/2.
20. WMCB, March 1668.
21. Andrew White, 'Early Shipbuilding in Warton Parish',*Contrebis*, vol XVII, 1991-2, pp.14-21.
22. J.D. Marshall, *The Autobiography of William Stout of Lancaster 1655-1752*, 1967, pp. 282-286.
23. Lancs.R.O., 'Records of Court Leet of Warton, April 1608', DDTo/O/2.
24. Lancs.R.O., 'Household Account of Dame Anne Middleton, 1675', DDTo/I/14.
25. WMCB, October 1690.
26. WMCB, March 1668.
27. WMCB, October 1797.
28. Lancs.R.O., 'Records of Court Leet of Warton, October 1612', DDTo/O/2.
29. Charles Singer and E.J. Holmyard (eds.), *A History of technology*, Vol.2, 1956, p.154.
30. WMCB, November 1720.
31. Lancs.R.O., 'Household Account of Dame Anne Middleton, 1675', DDTo/I/14.
32. Lucas's History, p.127.
33. B.G.Awty and C.B.Phillips, 'The Cumbrian Bloomery Forge in the Seventeenth Century', *Newcomen Society Transactions*, Vol.51, 1979-80,p.27.
34. Lancs.R.O., 'Records of Court Leet of Warton, October 1613', DDTo/O/2.
35. WMCB, April 1669.
36. John Jenkinson, 'Silverdale Pottery', *Mourholme Magazine of Local History,* 1996.2, pp.12-15.
37. B.J.N. Edwards, 'Late Medieval Pottery Kilns at Silverdale', *Contrebis* 2 No.2, 1974, p.41-43.
38. Lancs, R.O., 'Records of Court Leet of Warton. May 1610', DDTo/0/2.
39. Lancs.R.O., 'Records of Court Leet of Warton, October 1602', DDTo/O/2.
40. Lancs.R.O., 'Household Account of Dame Anne Middleton, 1675', DDTo/I/14.
41. The total of adult males over the 100 year period is estimated as 2.5 times the population at any given year. This allows for a 40 year mature working life.
42. This total includes occupations deduced from the contents of inventories, but not specified in the document.

Chapter 15: Faith and Religion, Reformation to Restoration.

1. J.Bossy, *The English Catholic Community 1570-1850*, 1975, p.92.
2. Christopher Haigh, *Reformation and Resistance in Tudor Lancashire*, 1975, p.290.
3. J.Bossy, *The English Catholic Community 1570-1850*, 1975, p.187.
4. Dan Sailor, *The County Hanging Town*, n.d., pp.9-14.
5. Lucas's History, p.13.
6. VCH, p.159 n.62.
7. J.D. Raine (ed), 'The Correspondence of Dr Matthew Hutton', *Surtees Society*, Vol.17, 1843, p.182.
8. Lancs.R.O., 'Copy of the certification of Thomas Middleton 1605', DDTo/O/2.
9. Lucas's History, p.72.

Chapter 16: Faith and Religion, The Post-Restoration Years

1. VCH, p.178, n.30.
2. Lucas's History, p.19.
3. John L.Nickalls (ed), T*he Journal of George Fox*, 1952, p.458.
4. J.C.Dickinson, *Land of Cartmel*,1980, p.79.
5. Lancs.R.O., 'Comperta Books for Kendal Deanery 1665-1740', ARR/15/40-76.
6. J.Bossy, *The English Catholic Community 1570-1850*, 1975, p.251.
7. Joseph Gillow, 'Historical notes on Leighton Hall and Yealand Registers', *Catholic Record Society Publications*, Vol.XX, 1916, pp.35-37.
8. *Ibid.,* p.34.
9. F.J. Vaughan, 'Bishop Leyburne and his Confirmation Register of 1687', *Northern Catholic History,* No.12, 1980, pp.14-18.
10. 'Sherlock, Richard', *Compact Edition of the Dictionary of National Biography,* 1975, Vol.2, p.1913.
11. 'Lancashire and Cheshire Church Surveys', *Record Society of Lancashire and Cheshire*, Vol.1, 1878, pp.121-122.
12. Lucas's History, p.113.
13. *Ibid.,* p.112.
14. Lancs.R.O., 'Comperta Book for Kendal Deanery 1718', ARR/15/40-76.
15. Lancs.R.O., Quarter Session Records, QSP 592/24-30; QSP 724/11.
16. Lancs.R.O., Quarter Session Records, QDV/4/20d.
17. Lancashire Parish Register Society, Vol.73 '*The Parish Registers of Warton Parish* 1568-1812', 1935, p.490.
18. John L.Nickalls (ed), *The Journal of George Fox*, 1952, p.104.
19. Joseph Besse, *A Collection of the Sufferings of the People called Quakers*, 1753 edition.
20. John L. Nickalls (ed), *The Journal of George Fox*, 1952, p.132.
21. Minutes of Yealand Preparative Meeting, 1652.
22. Nicholas Morgan, *Lancashire Quakers and the Establishment 1760-1830,* 1993, p.36.
23. *Ibid.,* p.37.
24. WMCB, March 1668.
25. WMCB, October 1672.
26. Nicholas Morgan, *Lancashire Quakers and the Establishment 1760-1830*, 1993, p.37.
27. Elfrida Vipont, *The Highway*, 1957, p.134.
28. Elfrida Vipont, *The Story of Quakerism*, 1954, p.54.
29. 'Declaration to Charles II, 1660', *Quaker Faith and Practice,* 1994, (no page numbers), entry 24.04.
30. VCH, p.159,n.71.
31. Lucas's History, p.25.
32. Lancs.R.O., 'Church Wardens Presentments', ARR/17/43.
33. Lucas's History, p.15.
34. *Ibid.,* pp.112-117.
35. John Addy, *Sin and Society in the Seventeenth Century*, 1989, p.44.
36. Jonathan Lumby, *The Lancashire Witch Craze*, 1995.
37. Lancs.R.O., 'Records of Court Leet of Warton, September 1593', DDTo/O/2.

Chapter 17: Silverdale Chapel

1. VCH, p.181 n.20,21.
2. Rev. F.R. Raines, 'Notitia Cestentriensis', *Chetham Society*, Vol. 22, 1850, p.557.

3. 'Plundered Ministers Accounts, Pt.1', *Lancashire and Cheshire Record Society* Vol.28, 1893, p.231.
4. Lucas's History, p.50.
5. P.E.H. Hair, 'The chapel in the English Landscape', *The Local Historian,* Vol.21 No 1,1991, pp.4-15.
6. Lucas's History, p.50.
7. Lancs.R.O., 'Dispute between the Vicar of Warton & the Inhabitants of Silverdale 1686-1695', DRCh/37 Bundle 122.
8. Lucas's History, p.50.
9. *Ibid.*
10. VCH, p.182 n.31.

Chapter 18: Warton's Church and Warton's Festivities

1. Lucas's History, p.31.
2. *Ibid.*, p.11.
3. *Ibid.*, p.12.
4. *Ibid.*, p.18,19
5. *Ibid.*, p.13.
6. *Ibid.*, p.21.
7. *Ibid.*, pp.22,23.
8. *Ibid.*, p.10.
9. *Ibid.*, pp.10,11.
10. *Ibid.*, pp.23-25.
11. *Ibid.*, p.24.
12. J.D. Marshall, 'A Funereal Topic', *Mourholme Magazine of Local History*, 1990.1, pp.3-4.
13. J.D. Marshall, *The Autobiography of William Stout of Lancaster 1655-1752,* 1967, p.107.
14. Lucas's History, p.25.
15. *Ibid.,* p.24.
16. *Ibid.,* p.40.
17. *Ibid.,* p.126.
18. *Ibid.,* p.25.
19. Lancs.R.O., 'Records of the Court Leet of Warton, October 1602', DDTo/1/14.
20. Lancs.R.O., 'Records of the Court Leet of Warton, September 1593', DDTo/0/2.
21. Lancs.R.O., 'Household Account of Dame Anne Middleton, 1675', DDTo/I/14.

Chapter 19: Making One's Mark

1. See Appendix 4, 'Matthew Hutton'.
2. Lucas's History, p.149. [Translation from the Latin, John Blundell, Oxford 1991.]
3. Keith Wrightson, *English Society 1580-1680*, 1982, p.184.
4. Lancs.R.O., Untitled (contains minutes of the Governors of Archbishop Hutton's School from 1832), PR3332/Acc.5192.
5. John Addy, *Sin and Society in the Seventeenth Century,* 1989, p.35.
6. J.D. Raine (ed), 'The Correspondence of Dr Matthew Hutton', *Surtees Society*, Vol.17., 1843, p.263.
7. *Ibid.,* p.34.
8. Lucas's History, p.32.
9. David Cressy, *Education in Tudor and Stuart England*, 1975, p.66.
10. Lancs.R.O., Untitled (contains minutes of the meetings of the governors of Archbishop Hutton's School from 1832), PR3332 Acc.5192.
11. J.D. Marshall, *The Autobiography of William Stout of Lancaster 1655-1752*, 1967, p.72.
12. David Cressy, *Education in Tudor and Stuart England*, 1975, p.65.
13. J.D. Marshall, *The Autobiography of William Stout of Lancaster 1655-1752*, 1967, p.74.
14. Lancs.R.O., 'Warton Parish Bundle', DRCh/37/138.
15. Lucas's History, p.35.
16. *Ibid.*, p.36.
17. J.D. Marshall, *The Autobiography of William Stout of Lancaster 1655-1752*, 1967, p.72.
18. *Ibid.*, p.70.
19. Lancs.R.O., 'School Log Book, Archbishop Hutton's School', PR 3332 acc.5308.
20. Lancs.R.O., Untitled (contains minutes of the meetings of the governors of Archbishop Hutton's School from 1832), PR3332/Acc.5192.
21. Lancs.R.O., 'Dispute between the Vicar of Warton & the Inhabitants of Silverdale 1686-1695', DRCh/37 Bundle 122.
22. R.D.Houston, 'The development of literacy, Northern England 1640-1759', *Economic History Review,*2nd series, 35, 1982, p.206.
23. Keith Wrightson, *English Society 1580-1680*, 1982, p.194.
24. *Ibid.*, p.197.
25. Raine, James, 'Wills & Inventories from the registry of the Archdeaconry of Richmond', *Surtees Society,* Vol.XXVI,1853, pp.275-81.

26. Lancs.R.O., Will of Christopher Harrison, 1611.
27. Emmeline Garnett, *The Dated Buildings of South Lonsdale*, 1994, p.181.
28. Lancs.R.O., Will of Richard Jackson, 1680.
29. Lancs.R.O., 'Household Account of Dame Anne Middleton, 1675', DDTo/I/14.
30. Lucas's History, p.32.

Appendices

1. J.D. Marshall, 'Agrarian Wealth and Social Structure in pre-industrial Cumbria', *The Economic History Review*, 2nd series, Vol.XXXIII, No.4 1980, p.507.
2. C.M.L.Bouch and G.P.Jones, *The Lake Counties 1500-1830*, 1961, p.142.
3. J.D. Raine (ed), 'The Correspondence of Dr Matthew Hutton', *Surtees Society,* Vol.17, 1843, (hereafter quoted as 'The Correspondence'); T.D.Whitaker, *An History of Richmondshire*, Vol.II, 1823; *The Dictionary of National Biography*, 1975; J.Rawlinson Ford and J.A.Fuller-Maitland, *John Lucas's History of Warton Parish* (compiled 1710-1740), 1931.
4. Peter Lake, 'Matthew Hutton - a Puritan Bishop?',*History,* Vol.64, No.211, 1979, pp.182-204.
5. The Correspondence, pp.8,9; Thomas Fuller, *Church History of Britain* (ed.James Nichols 1842), Book 10, Section 2. Para. 42/3, Lucas's History, p.106.
6. The Correspondence, p.11.
7. *Ibid.*, pp. 9,10.
8. Lucas's History, p.106.
9. Owen Chadwick, *The Reformation*, 1972, p.125.
10. The Correspondence, p.xviii.
11. *Ibid.,* Letter I, 7th June 1565, p.53.
12. Peter Lake, 'Matthew Hutton - a Puritan Bishop', *History,* Vol.64, No.211, 1979, p.184.
13. The Correspondence, p.105.
14. Historical Manuscript Commission, Fourteenth Report, Appendix Part IV, 'The Manuscripts of Lord Kenyon', London, HMSO, 1894, p.7.
15. The Correspondence, Letter LXXXV, 16th August 1598, p.143.
16. Patrick Collinson, *Archbishop Grindal 1519-1585*, 1979, p.302.
17. *Ibid.*, p.200.
18. The Correspondence, p.xx.
19. Patrick Collinson, *Archbishop Grindal 1519-1585,* 1979, p.285.
20. The Correspondence, Letter VI, 12th August 1577, p.58.
21. Sir John Harrington, *Briefe View of the State of the Church of England*, in The Correspondence, pp.28-30.
22. The Correspondence, Letter LXXXIX, 27th August 1599, p.147.
23. T.D.Whitaker, *An History of Richmondshire*, Vol.II, 1823, p.315.
24. *Ibid.*

INDEX

INHABITANTS OF WARTON PARISH MENTIONED IN THE TEXT*

BORWICK

Addison,	Jenet	1603	82
	James	1637	148
Bacchus,	Richard	1600	81
Bindloss,	Christopher}		
	Francis}	(see main Index)	
	Robert}		
Bower,	William	1600	81
Chorley,	Thomas	1698	68
Cockerham,	John	1611	77
Cockerham,	John	1611	150
Drinkhall,	Elizabeth	1638	81
Graveson,	Leonard	1600	81
Godsalve,	Alice	1607	80
Mansergh,	Thomas	c 1701	124
	William	1699	147
	John	1699	147
Pleasington,	John	1633	40
Sander,	William	1676	79
Sherlock,	Richard	(see main index)	
Thornton,	William	1600	81
Townson,	George	1638	103
Williamson,	William	1600	52,81
Wilson,	James	1627	151

CARNFORTH

Bainbridge,	Peter	1683	146
Hadwen,	Agnes	1620	77
	Margret	1632	78
	Alice	1683	129
	Anthony	1630	146
Hodgson,	Robert	1614	53
Lucas,	Richard	1651	129
Lucas,	John	(see main index)	
Mason,	Richard	1675	149
	Isabel	1683	129
Nicholson,	Isabel	1651	129
	John	1696	147
	Thomas	1696	147
		1641	149
Waineman,	William	1677	123
Waithman,	James	1613	150
	Jarvice	1613	150

LINDETH

Waithman,	John	1607	52
	William	c 1668	165-166

Dawson,	John	1653	79
Greenwood,	Thomas	1626	78
Hadwen,	John	1677	47
Harris,	John	1718	187
Helme,	Richard	1593	174
Hest,	Thomas	(see main index)	
Houseman,	Thomas	1635	150
Howsman,	Anthony	1602	134
Hynd,	John	1669	124
Ingleton,	Robert	1614	81
Jackson,	Richarde	1593	49
	Ellen	1616	110
	James	1718	187
Jackson,	Francis	(see main index)	
Johnson,	John	1593	184
Kenie,	Elizabeth (L)	1644	131
	John (L)	1644	131
	William (L)	1644	131
Kitson,	Thomas	1638	69
		1649	101
	Margret	c 1590	101
	John	1638	121
Lamberson,	Robert	c 1670	105
Lawrence,	John	1681	123
Lawson,	Thomas	(see main index)	
Lucas,	John	1676	146
Lynsey,	Thomas	(see main index)	
Nicholson,	Elizabeth	1675	110
Owborne,	William	(see main index)	
Rippon,	John	1677	123
Sander,	Robert	1616	110,150
Smorthwaite,	James	(see main index)	
Swainson,	Elizabeth	1632	146
Tailor,	Robert	1577	105
Waithman,	Robert	1609	120
Walker,	Richard	(see main index)	
Walling,	Jennet	1632	110
		1632	106
Ward,	Thomas	1698	43
	Agnes	1611	131
Washington,	John	c 1590	101
	Leonard	c 1629	101
	Elen	1635	101
	Lawrence	1642	101
	Thomazin	1642	101
	Alice	1642	101
	Anne	1631	101
	Catherine	c 1670	102
Wilson,	John	1692	147
Winder,	Bridget	1698	106
Wraston,	Agnes	1673	106

* Individuals with the same surname have been listed together, but this cannot be taken to mean that they are related. Where there are two page references for the same name the implication is that they refer to the same individual, but this cannot be taken for granted.